At the Root
of This Longing

"In the spirit of *Women Who Run With the Wolves* and *Reviving Ophelia,* this book has the potential to change lives."
—*Publishers Weekly*

"[An] eloquent meditation on spirituality. When Flinders convinces us that spirituality and feminism are part of the same truth . . . the book takes on unbelievable power. Give yourself time to absorb the many complexities of *At the Root of This Longing.* Then await the profoundly life-altering conclusions you take away."
—Patricia Holt, *San Francisco Chronicle*

"Carol Lee Flinders provides the rationale, the means, and the inspiration to create a balanced, essential life—one which responds to the urgings for a strong social voice that matters and a contemplative solitude that lasts. She is the perfect witness and a wonderful writer."
—Clarissa Pinkola Estés, Ph.D., author of *Women Who Run With the Wolves, The Gift of Story,* and *The Faithful Gardener*

"Imagine that you're enjoying that rarest of pleasures—a leisurely visit in the late afternoon with a dear friend, a visit where together you explore the subtle, hard-to-penetrate questions that you never before have put into words. Questions about what it means to be a woman on a spiritual path, about the path itself, about yourself as a woman. You feel yourself relax more deeply than you have in a long time. You sigh and put your feet up. And you smile with relief and gratitude that, finally, you have found your way to such a good, honest, engaged discussion.

"This is how I felt reading Flinders's book. Grateful. And full, and wanting to send copies to all my friends."
—Sherry Ruth Anderson, Ph.D., coauthor of *The Feminine Face of God*

"Moving, warm, and very wise . . . tackles an issue central to women right now. Flinders sorts out the tangled strands of our longings and reweaves them into a vivid and glorious pattern. These are really difficult questions, delightfully and profoundly resolved."
—Margaret Miles, dean and vice president for academic affairs, Graduate Theological Union and author of *Seeing and Believing* and *Reading for Life*

"From cover to cover, this work both evokes and challenges popular images of power-filled, feminine beings. The multi-hued voices at the root of Flinders's reflections are deeply nourishing."
—Rachel Bagby, J.D., vocal artist, activist, and author

"Absorbingly written and very revealing . . . many women for whom patriarchal religion remains central will be touched and intrigued by Flinders's intellectual struggle."
—*Booklist*

"*At the Root of This Longing* is a passionate and personal memoir, as well as a guide for the perplexed."
—*Parabola*

At the Root
of This Longing

At the Root
of This Longing

*Reconciling a Spiritual Hunger
and a Feminist Thirst*

CAROL LEE FLINDERS

HarperSanFrancisco
A Division of HarperCollins*Publishers*

HarperSanFrancisco and the author, in association with The Basic Foundation, a not-for-profit organization whose primary mission is reforestation, will facilitate the planting of two trees for every one tree used in the manufacture of this book.

A TREE CLAUSE BOOK

HarperCollins Web Site: http://www.harpercollins.com
HarperCollins®, ✿ ®, HarperSanFrancisco™, and A TREE CLAUSE BOOK® are trademarks of HarperCollins Publishers Inc.

Book design by Martha Blegen

FIRST HARPERCOLLINS PAPERBACK EDITION PUBLISHED IN 1999

Library of Congress Cataloging-in-Publication Data
Flinders, Carol.
At the root of this longing : reconciling a spiritual hunger and a feminist thirst / Carol Lee Flinders. —1st ed.
Includes bibliographical references and index.
ISBN 0-06-251314-1 (cloth)
ISBN 0-06-251315-X (pbk.)
1. Flinders, Carol. 2. Women—United States—Biography.
3. Women—Religious life—United States—Case studies. 4. Feminist spirituality—United States. I. Title.
HQ1413.F56A3   1998
303.42'092—dc21   97-18358

04 05 06 07 ✦/RRDH 10 9 8

In Loving Memory of Suzanne Lipsett
1943–1996

Contents

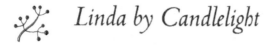 *Linda by Candlelight*

Every night, just after sunset, the woman would sit cross-legged on the ugly shag rug, light a candle, and place it on a saucer in front of her. She would watch for a moment and observe how the candle-light pushed back the shadows in the room and held them at bay. Gently, then, she would close her eyes, sit up straight, and begin to recite to herself, slowly, attentively, a daisy chain of short prayers.

> *Let nothing disturb thee,*
> *Let nothing affright thee.*
> *Everything is changing.*
> *God alone never changes . . .*

When she had come to the end of Saint Teresa's "Book-mark Prayer," she would move on—perhaps to a prayer of Saint Catherine of Siena:

. . . and the soul is closed in God,
and God in the soul,
as the sea in the fish
and the fish in the sea.

If her mind began to wander, she would bring it back, over and over, and she would continue in this way for a full hour. Every night, no matter what, she would light the candle and call down the spirit of one light-filled being after another, summoning them into her own deep darkness and grief.

My friend Linda was in her early forties when she hit that place you pray you'll only ever read about—sliding into it, the way you do in a nightmare, mute and in slow motion. Depression enveloped her, so black and unrelieved that it blotted out everything that had carried her from one day to the next. She left her marriage—left the single-handed fight she'd been waging to preserve it—and in effect left her two teenaged children, too. ("It wasn't just that I had no money," she told me, "I had nothing inside. Nothing for them, nothing for myself.") The salary from her part-time teaching job barely paid the rent on a grim little studio apartment. By day she could work: her students were a distraction, one gets through. Nights, things tended to bottom out. Late one sleepless night, though, she picked up a book that a previous tenant had left in a closet and found the one thing she *could* do. It was a brief, plainspoken introduction to the practice of meditation—a form of meditation that involved the use of inspirational passages.

"I was so desperately unhappy," she told me, "and that was my lifeline. I would place myself at the feet of each of them in turn—Teresa, Clare, both Catherines—and beg them to give me strength."

In time—and it took a good long time—strength came, and light . . . full-time work and reunion with her children. The marriage could not be retrieved, but the bitterness that had surrounded its dissolution has all but gone. She meditates mornings now as well as evenings, and it's no longer a desperate stratagem. Footsteps, rather, on a path that's firm underfoot.

The traditional use devout Catholics have made of women like Saint Teresa or Saint Clare has been to ask them to intercede on their behalf. God, in this view of things, is something like an overextended CEO with bad mood swings: unreasonable to think he'd concern himself directly with our difficult children, our more difficult marriages, our worries about money and health and neighborhood violence.

As old ways of thinking about God slip away, though, ideas about intercession have altered, too. When Linda invoked her favorite saints, intercession was the farthest thing from her mind. Her appeal was direct and visceral: "Be here for me now—yes, *you*—and stay the night, and walk me through my days." She had studied their lives and their words, had felt her way toward their humanity, and knew that none of them was a stranger to long, dark nights.

Through meditation, Linda was able to come to grips, by slow degrees, with the demons of her own mind. Each time a wave of fear or anger or despair arose, she would pull her attention gently back and place it instead on the words of the prayer, and as the very capacity to make that choice grew stronger, she began to feel safer. But by using those particular prayers, she was also reaching out toward what tradition calls the company of saints, a concept that is as universal as sanctity itself. "I take refuge in the Buddha," says the age-old monastic vow of Buddhism. "I take refuge in the dharma (the law). I take refuge in the sangam (the brotherhood and sisterhood of seekers)."

Deep in our collective memory is the understanding that when a Teresa or a Clare comes along, everyone benefits. Grace wells up, and everybody's thirst is quenched: Clare's contemporaries called her "a clear stream of God's bounty." Linda was not, in fact, a Catholic; she's only a Christian in the broadest sense of the word. But she knew without question that the very extremity of her plight—her terrible thirst—was sufficient claim.

I suspect that it's probably always been in this spirit, both trusting and fierce, that women have invoked their saints—as best friends, and in ways that hark back to the magical, lighting a candle and calling them down into the circle of their need. This is why I have placed Linda's story here at the beginning. I mean her to be present throughout, like a faint watermark on every page, the simple fact of her seated alone and resolute before her candle. She is Everywoman—every one of us who has felt the firm, implacable pull that Mechthild of Magdeburg called "the inward tug of God" and who has done our best to answer it.

On the face of things, my own story bears little resemblance to Linda's. On the face of things, as my forties gave way to my fifties, there was barely a ripple. I had reached my own kind of impasse, though, and if nobody else was aware of it yet, they would have been shortly: things had begun to crumble fast along the edges. That they stopped crumbling—that, like Linda, I found strength, after all, and light for my journey—had everything to do with the fact that I, too, had put together a "company of saints" who would prove allies and helpmeets in a struggle I hadn't even known lay ahead.

The seeds of that struggle lay in the distant past. I was twenty-three when I first took up the practice of meditation with a spiritual teacher. The women's movement was just getting under way, and I was certainly tuned in to its first stirrings. But the grief I'd been feeling around the experience of being a woman in this culture wasn't easy to isolate from the grief the Buddha said comes of entering the human context in the first place. Probably it made sense to address the bedrock problems—fear, greed, anger—and figure the others would get taken care of along the way.

And in fact, choosing the particular teacher I did (in Berkeley during the late sixties you really did have your pick) was certainly not a betrayal of my nascent feminism. Eknath Easwaran had been a professor of English from Kerala State in India; he came from one of the few matrilineal communities in the world. In his family, descent is traced through the mother. His own spiritual teacher was his mother's mother. When he read the works of various mystics and commented on them with regard to meditation, he was as likely to read Teresa of Avila or India's Mirabai as he was Meister Eckhart or Shankara. Never did he convey by so much as a raised eyebrow or a smile at the wrong places anything that would suggest women were not fully the equal of men—spiritually, intellectually, or creatively. Through Easwaran I gained access to the worlds of Sri Ramakrishna, India's greatest modern saint and a devotee of the Divine Mother, and Mahatma Gandhi, who credited his wife, Kasturba, with teaching him the transformative power of nonviolence.

No, I would have to say that on the balance my sense of what it means to be a woman has been immensely enhanced by my having chosen the path and teacher I did. I would also have to say that given the sheer bitterness of gender warfare this past several decades, I feel that I could have done much worse than to sit out the entire period in a northern California meditation community. It's not a bad moment in history to be surfacing—surfacing, that is, as a feminist.

Because, of course, my affinity for the women's movement didn't vanish at all, it only went underground. When it reappeared years later, it was focused and impassioned as it had never been the first time around. This time I didn't have the option of brushing it to one side as I had before, and that was awkward, because it wasn't at all clear how I was going to integrate my feminism into my spiritual practice.

Other women my age have written about the struggles they've had when their emerging feminism brought them into conflict with the religious traditions they'd lived in all their lives. My difficulties have been different, in part because I don't belong to a formal religion at all, let alone one that smacks of patriarchy. I've never had to deal with misogynist liturgy, and nobody in my community has ever set up lines of authority that routinely exclude women just because they are women. It took some doing to actually locate the sources of my difficulties. When I finally did, I was taken aback to find that they had to do with the very fundamentals of religiosity.

I've had to ask myself whether my own experience is too out of the ordinary to have much bearing on the struggles other women face in reconciling their feminism with their spiritual paths and practices. I've come to believe that, on the contrary, since I've had to get so far beneath the surface of things even to figure out where my own feminism and spirituality were "rubbing," I've ended up thinking from a place where the differences among our religious practices don't count for much. Beyond the question of how offensively patriarchal a particular religion might be is a much more basic one: how deeply have I allowed negative readings of "woman" to penetrate my own thinking and to undercut the feelings of personal sovereignty that *any* sort of religious commitment requires—and once I've determined that, what can I do about it?

Initially, I just wanted to figure out whether spirituality and feminism were compatible. But as I forced myself to be more and more specific about what I meant by *spirituality* and what I meant by *feminism,* I discovered, somewhat to my astonishment, that they were not *merely* compatible at all. Eventually, I would have to conclude that for me, at least, they are mutually necessary: for the aims of either to be fully realized, both would have to be accommodated.

To travel from that first position to the second has been a long and arduous journey. I couldn't have completed it—insofar as it is complete—were it not for the circle of helpmeets I built up over the years that culminated in the publication of a book about women mystics called *Enduring Grace.* The women I wrote about there are all from the European Catholic tradition. There are others in my circle who are not, and of course there are some men, too: men like Saint Francis of Assisi and Mahatma Gandhi, who as they journeyed Godward left gender in the dust. But it was crucial that most of my companions were women for a reason I really only understood when I read Gerda Lerner, a living helpmeet whose histories of patriarchy and the rise of feminist consciousness have helped me tremendously. It's the First Law of Lerner that "women's history is essential to women's emancipation." In other words, when a woman is about to break away from cultural norms for women—to build a house, run for president, break a horse—learning that even one other woman has done it successfully brings that act into the realm of possibility after all; it has, indeed, what economists call a multiplier effect on the likelihood that she'll actually do it. I'll never forget what it did for me at eleven years of age to read the biography of Marie Curie. Up until then nothing in my life had given me any reason to imagine a woman might carry out scientific research. My only firsthand knowledge of *any*

women who worked outside the home were my schoolteach-
ers. Madame Curie's story was a direct hit. For months I went
around telling everyone I was going to be a molecular physicist.
By the same token, much later, once I came to know something
about Clare of Assisi and Catherine of Genoa, I saw in them a
brand new rendering of "woman." The specifics eluded me, but
I knew that in some very profound way these women had resolved exactly the sort of conflict I was looking at. They'd resisted what was to be resisted and embraced what was to be
embraced. They would be my mentors, my touchstones. I installed them in my imaginative life much as Hindus install the
image of a deity in a temple.

For a variety of reasons, Julian of Norwich presides over the
first half of this book. Her place is taken in the second half by a
figure who may not ever have existed, a princess who figures
centrally in the Indian epic Mahabharata. The matchless Draupadi
is one of those characters whose story has been told so much, and
whose story means so much to the people who hear it, that she is
for them a living presence. She has become so for me.

The division of the whole into these two parts is my conces-
sion to the layered quality life can sometimes have. . . . Beginnings, middles, ends, and elaborate digressions were threatening
to undo me until I realized I was going to have to tell one whole
strand of the story in a separate narrative. In other words, the
second half of the book covers roughly the same period of time
that the first one does and simply shifts the focus from one set of
events and inquiries to another. It seems reasonable to have done
this: at any given moment a great many things can be happening
at once whose connections become clear only much later.

BOOK ONE

Julian's Visions

Three days and three nights she lay ill, and on the fourth night she received the last rites from the village priest. For three more days she lived, though, and at last all sensation stopped, first in the lower part of her body and then above. Her head fell to one side, breathing was all but impossible, and she could feel the life force slipping out of her.

Abruptly, then, it was over. The pain, the loss of sensation, every trace of illness was gone, and only now did she remember that she'd asked for this to happen—exactly this. She'd wanted to think her life was ending, because once she had felt death and tasted it, she'd reasoned, she would turn her thoughts more resolutely to what lay beyond. She'd even specified the year . . . her thirtieth.

But she'd asked for something else as well, and she had to wonder now whether that, too, was at hand. Her eyes hadn't moved from the crucifix her curate had set before her hours earlier, and now she saw that from under the crown of thorns blood was trickling, "hot and copious, a living stream" and she knew that Christ's very self was there with her. Even before she'd imagined the other she'd wanted this: to know firsthand what it was to be present at the Passion.

Reality was all that she'd asked for. Of Holy Writ she'd had her fill, and thunderous sermons and God in a consecrated host. Instead, she wanted God against her skin and vibrant in her ear and plain before her eyes, and so vehemently did she ask this that she received it. She came to know God's love by touch that day, as "warm clothing that wraps and enfolds us"; she heard God's voice tender as a mother's and saw God's own countenance, "that could melt our hearts for love and break them in two for joy," and everything she thought she'd known about the wrath of God and the punishment of sinners was from that day on inconceivable.

Her revelations continued for twenty-four extraordinary hours, rounded off with a bravura turn by the Fiend himself, a living gargoyle with a spotty red face and misshapen paws who all but throttled her until she remembered that the devil can stand anything but ridicule and laughed him out of the picture.

CHAPTER I

Synchronicities

A few years ago, when I'd made the last revisions and double-checked the last footnotes of a substantial writing project, I relaxed into a kind of fallow spell. The timing was right, because my fiftieth birthday was bearing down on me, and a measure of anxiety seemed to be congealing around that fact—much more than I'd anticipated (one does brace oneself for this one) because I had every reason to be content with where things stood. Marriage, son, health, work, friends: everything was fine. I couldn't account for the flutters I was feeling somewhere around my solar plexus.

Later on, I would learn that many women experience something very like what I did that summer and fall. Some speak about it in terms of cleaning house, an almost reckless desire to simplify and streamline. For one friend knitting is more to the point: wanting to go back and pick up stitches that may have been dropped along the way. To me it felt like hitting a blank place on the map—as if I'd come up over a rise and found myself looking out across a vast inland ocean nobody had told me was there. The flutters were real, but so was a certain exhilaration.

It's taken me some time to be comfortable using the term *synchronicity,* Jung's term for the curious way in which ordinary, external reality can suddenly click into alignment with one's inner, archetypal world. When I first heard of the phenomenon I thought I was being asked to believe synchronicities are planted in front of us by an unseen hand like clues in a cosmic scavenger hunt. This was way too anthropomorphic for my taste. But gradually I came to understand that these events, or recognitions, have to do with something mystics have always tried to convey: that the knowledge and the truth and clarity we are seeking isn't "out there" at all, but deep inside. Certain insights *want* to break out into daylight, but we hold them down, fearing the kind of change that might take place if we knew them experientially and all at once. Down through time, we've evolved different methods by which they can emerge, in small, manageable doses. We throw the I Ching, we deal out tarot cards, we analyze our dreams, and through these fissures in ordinary logic we can in effect nudge ourselves along—Self talking to self in a heavily coded language.

Perceptions of synchronicity work, I believe, in about the same way. When a message wants to move from the unconscious to the conscious level, we experience a kind of turbulence first, the flutters that signal disequilibrium. Finally, though, something in us manages to paint it across the very landscape, where we can't help but read it, and we draw from that reading the courage to strike out into the wilderness and make up our new maps as we go along. This was exactly what happened to me now. A beguiling little bit of synchronicity gave me the gentle shove I needed—and put me in touch with someone ideally suited to keep me company.

I had been on good terms with Julian of Norwich for more than half my life. She was the subject of my doctoral dissertation and, more recently, one of the subjects of the book I'd just written about women mystics. I'd reread her *Revelations* at regular intervals, as much for their long, lovely, incantatory rhythms as for as their utterly original content. I imagined she must have looked like Vanessa Redgrave or Emma Thompson—enormously kind and serene, a composite of the best women friends I've ever had. I had never consciously invoked Julian, but her anchorhold, dimly lit, with a fireplace at one end and a cat, was in my mind's eye a real place, and a safe place. . . .

Even though I'd written about Julian twice, I'd never given any thought to how old she'd been when she wrote her famous *Sixteen Revelations of Divine Love*. Now that fifty was not just a stray bit of biographical data, though, but a state of mind—and body—that I knew intimately, I wondered for the first time what Julian's experience had been. The version of the *Revelations* that she wrote when she was fifty is actually a rewrite. A much shorter version was composed when she was thirty, soon after the experience it describes. Did Julian's decision to recast her story have anything to do with the flood tide of raw, creative energy I was just beginning to experience myself—along with sleepless nights, intense anxiety states, and rooms that seemed always to be overheated? What an astonishing thought: that a fourteenth-century anchorite could have had a body as well as a soul, and a woman's body at that, hormones coursing through it, wreaking their own kind of regular havoc just as they were in mine.

It intrigued me to reflect that when I'd written about Julian in *Enduring Grace,* I'd been almost as old as Julian herself was when she wrote her fuller rendering of the *Revelations,* but there was more. When I'd written about Julian the first time, I realized, in my dissertation, I'd been thirty, the same age she was when she wrote her first draft of the *Revelations.* Better still, I remembered that I'd actually filed the dissertation in the spring of 1973, exactly six hundred years after the actual showings.

As coincidences go, this was all pretty tame stuff. But long exposure to medieval visionary writings gets one into the habit of treating even small "wrinkles in time" with respect, for throughout the Middle Ages, long before the term *synchronicity* was coined, the visible world was understood to be crisscrossed with "the footprints of God."

Julian's revelations had come in rapid succession, and only once, but one of the most important, a cryptic little tableau involving a devoted servant and a benign master, did not yield its meaning until she had pored over it diligently for nearly twenty years, in keeping with "an inward instruction" to attend to every detail, no matter how ambiguous or mysterious.[1] She was to *work with* this particular little tableau as tenaciously as a Buddhist practitioner might work with a *koan*. I was already in an exceedingly impressionable frame of mind: it seemed appropriate now to figure I, too, had received something midway between a gift and an assignment. That was certainly how it felt.

Unfinished Business

And Julian seemed to be right in the middle of it. The small parallel I had discovered between her life and mine prompted me to ask, in the first place, whether I had experienced anything like Julian had in my own thirty-first year. And of course I had not. No life-threatening illness and no visions. Nonetheless, the year in question had displayed, with respect to my life overall, a comparable luster. A few years earlier, during the late sixties, at the culmination of another even more profound period of disequilibrium, I had found my way to a spiritual teacher, Eknath Easwaran, and had met the man I would marry. In 1970, forty-five of us had moved to a dairy farm in the northern California countryside and established our spiritual community there. It had taken a staggering amount of work to settle in—renovating half a dozen all-but-abandoned structures, planting a vegetable garden, bringing electric lines, plumbing, and sewage disposal systems up to county codes—but by 1973 the worst was over. Each morning we'd walk out of our cottages and trailers and geodesic domes (it really *was* the seventies) into breathtaking loveliness. What with wild iris, flowering plum, and heirloom apple trees, white egrets stalking the meadow ponds, and swallow-tailed kites hovering overhead, my own cup was full to overflowing. Even now, when I pick up the dissertation I wrote during these years, I find that something of the wonder and great good happiness of that time can be felt between the lines.

The subject of my thesis was a comparison of the Short and Long Texts of the *Revelations*. The critical difference between the two had to do with Julian's insistence in the Short Text that there was no contradiction between her visionary experience and what she had been taught as a Christian. In the Long Text, written twenty years after the showings, she acknowledges that there really had been a problem after all. For while the revelations were unfolding, she had come to see that God is love—all love. What we experience as sin and punishment are merely errors, which are committed most often out of excessive zeal, and consequences, which instruct us. In other words, nothing in her visions substantiated the orthodox teaching that God is wrathful or that he punishes us for our sins. Julian struggled throughout the Long Text to reconcile these two clearly different perspectives on God, sin, and punishment, and it is this struggle that generates most of the material she added to the Short Text. "And between these two oppositions," she wrote, "my reason was greatly afflicted by my blindness. . . . I cried within me with all my might, beseeching God for help. . . ." (Long Text, Chapter 50).

Reflecting on Julian's situation now, I asked myself once again whether there might have been something analogous to it in my own. During my own twenty-year interim between writing the dissertation and composing the chapter on Julian in *Enduring Grace,* had I, too, found reason to reconsider anything? Had there been concealed in the perfect balance and joy of my own thirty-first year an unacknowledged conflict—a piece of unfinished business that I would have to deal with over time, as Julian had? One of those dropped stitches?

And of course there had been. As I allowed myself to name it, I knew that the time for resolving it had come. I knew, for that matter, that I had been trying to resolve it over the years, though only in bits and pieces, and half consciously, never quite allowing the conflict to declare itself.

The conflict lay between my spiritual path and my feminism, and there was no way in the world I could go on pretending it wasn't there.

~

There was one moment, sometime in the early 1970s, when my dilemma had emerged almost clearly enough for me to have put it into words. It was during an informal question-and-answer session with my teacher. Since only a few people were present, I felt able to ask what was for me, then, an awkward question. Haltingly, I explained to him that it was very difficult to grow up a woman in this culture, because the popular image of woman has so much to do with Eve and her characterization as the archetypal temptress, source of sin and all the suffering in the world. It was tacitly understood, I told him, that to be a woman was to be devious, frivolous, sensual, and intellectually deficient. As a medievalist, I had had to read volumes of ostensibly religious literature that was permeated with hatred of women. As a contemporary woman, I could feel the lingering effects of all that hatred—not merely in literature or theology, but in the very structures of daily life. When I thought about it at all, anger would arise that felt outright explosive. I trailed off, inchoate.

Easwaran smiled, and very kindly, but he did not answer, and I was, for the time being, crushed. Was it such a stupid question?

Over time, though, I saw his response—his *non*response—in a different light. I learned that the Compassionate Buddha had employed the Noble Silence all the time, and that it wasn't so much a put-down as a refusal to talk about something that didn't pertain directly to the Eightfold Path. When you've got an hour with the best financial consultant in the business, you don't ask her how to balance a checkbook. Spiritual teachers like practical questions, not speculative ones. If I had asked something like "How should I deal with my anger?" or "How can I learn not to be swayed by external pressures?" I'd probably have gotten an answer. But in fact I hadn't been so much asking as complaining—reflecting, really, on a situation I was only just beginning to grasp.

Interestingly enough, though, just a couple of years ago I was present one afternoon when Easwaran was talking about the Buddha, and he paused to explain what *he* believed the purpose of the Noble Silence to be. "It meant that there was no reason for the Buddha himself to answer that particular question. 'I'll give you the tools,' it meant, 'but it's up to you to work it out.'"

This was much better. A silence on the part of one's teacher was not necessarily a comment on the merit of the question but rather on the inappropriateness of expecting the teacher to answer it for you. It was my own culture I'd been complaining about, after all, and my own place within it. The teacher's responsibility stops, in such cases, with providing "the tools"—the disciplines, the perspectives, the personal example. These take a long time to absorb. How to use them, and which tasks to apply them to once I had them in hand—those would be my decisions.

As I recalled this episode now, the feelings I'd been struggling with of late made more and more sense. The maps I'd relied on for years *were* out of date, and I really was entering a kind of wilderness. But it was high time I did. A relatively tough assignment was falling due, but it was one I had tacitly accepted. It had the feel of one of those "sorting" chores that the protagonists of myths and fairy tales have to carry out—Psyche, for instance, charged with reducing a small mountain of seeds, thoroughly mixed, to separate piles of rice, corn, wheat, barley, and oats. Only in place of seeds, it seemed it was my own innermost impulses I needed to sort out. On the one hand, there was this stubbornly recurrent itch that had made ordinary life impossible: a thirst, a tug, a rooted incapacity to commit to anything that didn't taste and smell of God. By a crude shorthand, my spirituality. And on the other hand, just as stubborn and problematic, my feminism.

The journey I felt myself beginning now was only a journey in the figurative sense. Like Julian (I consoled myself), I would be traveling sitting still. Not for her the pilgrimage to Canterbury, and not for me the wild river expedition in Borneo or the camel ride across the Kalahari with which so many of my contemporaries were greeting their crone years. This was an interior journey, and I would begin it by revisiting the period when I was writing my dissertation—the formative years, really, of my spiritual practice and perceptions.

CHAPTER 2

"To Burn a Little and Spill a Little": The Early Years

I had barely glanced at the dissertation in the twenty years since I'd completed it, and it was a shock to begin reading it now and find how vividly it brought that whole period to mind.

I'd lived, then, in two distinct worlds. Long weekends, quarter breaks, and summers were a blur of construction and ditchdigging and gardening in the country, all dirt and sunlight and sore muscles. Midweek, back at the university to teach or use the library, I often felt as alien as if I'd been dropped there from another planet.

Now, as I read, the breathless, awestruck feeling of those days washed over me again. A particular phrase would bring to mind quite unaccountably the ravelly old Fair Isle sweater I wore most mornings when I wrote: even in late spring the tiny trailer under the eucalyptus where my husband and I lived was cool until the afternoon; by the time the sun streamed in the windows I'd be somewhere else, chopping vegetables for dinner, running a drill press, cutting down thistles, doing whatever I was doing with my best semblance of undivided attention.

Recalling the quiet, almost unvarying rhythm of those days, I've thought about how much spiritual communities everywhere resemble one another—scholarship in the morning, manual labor in the afternoon, mental prayer at dawn and twilight—and I've realized that in preparing to write the thesis I was practicing what the Catholic monastic tradition calls *lectio divina.* Literally translated, that's simply spiritual reading, but it implies a real pondering. We become absorbed, and in that state we absorb. We become permeable, so that the teachings in question can engage much more of us than the intellect alone.

It is essential that they do this. When you first take up a spiritual practice, it is understood that you won't have assimilated it fully. You may have adopted its tenets in a provisional way, as working hypotheses, but more than that you really cannot do until you've lived with them for a considerable period of time. It's the difference between a honeymoon and a marriage.

Reading my way through Julian's *Revelations,* taking notes for the thesis, I discovered that her teachings were deeply harmonious with those that informed the spiritual practice I had undertaken. Julian made it abundantly clear, for example, as Easwaran always has, that one really can experience God in this very life "by many secret touchings of sweet spiritual sights and feelings, measured out to us as our simplicity may bear it"(LT 43). At the same time, her insistence on downplaying the importance of supernatural phenomena ("I am not good because of the revelations, but only if I love God better") (LT 9) also matched Easwaran's to the letter ("God reveals Himself in action. If you want to judge your progress in meditation, ask yourself: Are you more loving? Is your judgment sounder? Do you have more energy? Can your mind remain calm under provocation?").[1] It was a joy to feel my scholarly and spiritual lives flowing together.

To talk substantively about my spiritual practice, I must say something about my teacher. Easwaran is fundamentally a teacher of meditation. Everything he's done in this country for the past thirty-five years has been with the intention of bringing meditation and the disciplines that support it out of the monastic settings where they were developed and making them available to people in every walk of life and every religion. Though he grew up in an orthodox Hindu family, he doesn't think of himself as a Hindu teacher. He mistrusts restrictive orthodoxies with a passion that has only grown over time. Like Gandhi, he believes that all faiths have validity and that none is perfect: each has taken shape in a particular time and place and can't be any wiser or truer than its context permits. His alignment has never been with one particular religion, but with the mystics of all religions—the women and men who tell us God can be experienced firsthand.

The task he set before our community—and everything else was secondary—was to bring the process of thinking under our conscious control. Through meditation and the repetition of a holy name, or *mantram,* he maintained, one can learn to direct attention at will. If you couldn't do this, then you could not expect to live in harmony with other people or serve life in any substantial way or accomplish any of the other things that *all* religions ask their adherents to do.

I cannot describe my spiritual practice as Buddhist, therefore, or as Hindu or Catholic or Sufi, though I feel that in a sense it is all of these. I meditate as best I can on Native American prayers and Taoist verses, on passages drawn from the Bible or the Upanishads, on passionate love songs composed for the

One Beloved by a Spanish monk or an Indian princess-turned-minstrel. And I trust that this daily exertion of will and heart will bring me along to wherever I am meant to go at the pace that is right for me. That feeling I've spoken about earlier, of being somehow *under assignment*—though in the most benign imaginable way—has never left me since I met this quiet man from Kerala in a small chapel upstairs from the Associated Student offices on the Berkeley campus.

Easwaran discouraged severe ascetic practices, but he taught us to honor the deeper purpose of those practices, which is to unify desires completely into the kind of laserlike intensity one sees in the life of a Teresa of Avila or a Mahatma Gandhi. We were to take our desires seriously—even small hankerings, for a cigarette or a blueberry Danish—and understand what enormous power they contain.

There was no dogma, and no coercion, but a lot of talk about choices. In every moment—in every *instant,* he showed us—we are choosing, and those choices all have consequences.

Keep your eyes open.

Get conscious.

Know where you're headed.

He moved among us all day, checking the progress of our renovation efforts and admiring openly the range of skills these ordinary American students had brought with them or had picked up readily. Everything we were doing provided similes he would use in his evening classes. The undoing of deeply entrenched habits can be daunting work, but when those tendencies were likened to gophers evading the garden cat, the whole business took on a comic aspect: "They pop up here, then over there, you have to become as alert as they are. Learn to think like a gopher!"

Even a pot of scorched oatmeal could be turned into an object lesson: "My granny used to say, if you don't burn a little, and you don't spill a little, you'll never learn to cook: don't stay away from the kitchen, and don't run away from life, just because you're afraid you'll make mistakes.

"Of course," he would murmur bemusedly, "if you're still burning and spilling when you're thirty or forty or fifty, there may be cause for concern."

May Quietness Descend

Everything in our days built toward those evening classes. Loopy with fatigue, reeking of Tiger Balm liniment, we would sit in close-packed concentric half-circles, some of us on the floor, the rest on chairs and old pews left over from a time when the meditation hall had been a chapel for the novitiates of the tiny Catholic monastic order from whom we'd bought the place. We ourselves were not, of course, members of a monastic order, but we had certainly taken a step in that direction. While there was no real onus placed on marriage (quite a few weddings took place our first two years on the land, including my own), it was understood that the longer you could hold off entering a one-to-one relationship the better it would be for your meditation and the community as a whole. So one sensed a certain subtle undercurrent in the room those evenings that no amount of hard labor ever quite doused—though nothing excessive, and nothing you wouldn't expect to find in a crowd of bright, healthy twentysomethings who knew their way around Berkeley and gave a lot of thought to holy celibacy.

We sat up straight, cross-legged, and between verses of one ancient scripture or another, Easwaran would tell us stories—marvelous stories, drawn from the life of every saint and seer in the book. The scene was in itself the oldest story of all, for it reinvoked the sacred circle of times past: the Buddha in the deer park, Saint Teresa at the convent of Saint Joseph, Gandhi at his twilight prayer meeting. The teacher looks about and assesses the temper and the mood of the gathering, and when he speaks, or she speaks, the stories told and the words chosen and the images evoked are precisely attuned to these particular souls, *right now*, tonight. Gentle teasing soothes ragged nerves. Deep, loosening-up laughter happens, and unembarrassed tears—all in response to stories that came to form a tacit backdrop to the life we shared. Stories like this one, so widely extant in the Hindu tradition that nobody can remember who told it first.

A disciple comes to his teacher distraught. "When can I see God? I've been trying so hard, for so many years, and I seem to have got ten nowhere!"

The teacher smiles sympathetically, stands, and tightens his wearing cloth around himself for the short walk to the Ganges, beckoning the student to follow him. He walks on out into the water, waist high, and when the student is alongside he tells him to duck down so that his head is well underwater. When he does, the teacher seizes him by the hair and holds him under. A full minute passes, and finally the aspirant bursts upward, gasping and coughing.

"Why on earth did you do that to me?"

"When your head was underwater," the teacher asks, "what were you thinking about?"

"Air," the student said honestly. "All I could think about was how badly I wanted to breathe."

"When you are thinking about God in that way—nothing but God, day and night—with that same desperate desire, then I promise you, nothing will be in the way, and you will see God."

Stories like this were deeply affecting, but if anybody looked as if she still hadn't gotten the point, there were always more. Like the one about Saint Thérèse of Lisieux and one of her novitiates——her own sister, in fact, who asked her one day why she wasn't making the kind of progress in her prayer she felt she should be. Honoring the Great Silence of Carmelite life, Thérèse lifted her sister's hand gravely and wordlessly and, with the fine-tipped pen she used for sketching, wrote on her fingernail, "Too many desires."

The purpose of all the stories, and the laughter and the tears they invoked, was to move us gently away from ordinary distractions and turn us inward. At the end of the talk, the lights would be dimmed and we would begin to meditate. Word by sacred word we would recite to ourselves invocations from the Upanishads: "Let quietness descend upon my limbs, my speech, my breath, my eyes, my ears. . . ." Or verses like clear running water from the Dhammapada of the Buddha; or the simple, steadying lines from Teresa's Bookmark Prayer: "Let nothing disturb thee, let nothing affright thee. . . . *Who has God lacks nothing*." When the mind wandered, you brought it back——gently, firmly——to the words of the passage.

It's like a process of grafting, this form of meditation. Mysteriously, the words become part of you, persuading you way below the level of everyday comings and goings that, indeed, God is real and that if you can let go of everything that is *not* God, you can know that reality firsthand.

All Shall Be Well, and All Manner of Thing Shall Be Well . . .

And of course that was exactly what Julian said had happened to her. She had seen God, and she'd never gotten over it. So it was quite a short walk of the imagination from those evening classes in our meditation hall to Julian's anchorhold the next morning. I cherished those early hours poring over her *Revelations* in silence. I've realized since then that she was, in a sense, my own personal point of entry into the contemplative tradition: someone who spoke the same language my ancestors had and, even more than that, a woman. Because of her, the whole impossibly ambitious undertaking seemed just a bit more possible.

Julian is truly a mysterious figure, probably best known today for the haunting promise she made in the *Revelations* and that T. S. Eliot would incorporate in *Four Quartets:* "All shall be well, and all shall be well, and all manner of thing shall be well. . . ." She lived for part of her lifetime in an anchoritic cell adjoining Saint Julian parish church in Norwich, and most likely she took her name from the church itself. As an anchorite, she would have been formally enclosed there in a somber ceremony modeled after a Christian burial service: From that day forth, she was to understand, she was dead to ordinary concerns and attachments. (Her neighbors, we gather, were supposed to get the same message. The *Ancrene Riwle,* a kind of handbook for the anchoritic life, inveighs against gossiping at the window and also against giving reading lessons to the village girls.)

From the scant information Julian gives us about herself, we can place her birth date around December 1342. We don't know whether she was already enclosed on May 13, 1373, but we do know that it was the pivotal day of her life. Beginning early that morning, she relates, while it was still dark, she experienced over a twenty-four-hour period a vivid series of what she called "showings." God *revealed* divine truths to her in sixteen distinct episodes. In one she saw Christ on the cross and in another saw his mother as a young girl—saw, not with ordinary eyesight, but with "spiritual vision." In still another she saw the whole of creation, reduced to the size of a hazelnut. Not all of her showings strike us as actual visions—some sound more abstract, like teachings, or precepts—but for her these, too, were visions because she apprehended them "with the eye of mine understanding." She experienced them not as ideas, in other words, but firsthand. For her, the revelations constituted a sacred text that belonged to all humanity: she was only the trustee.

All but unknown for centuries, Julian and her work are phenomenally well received today. There are several reasons for this, but one is that certain of her teachings fit contemporary sensibilities like a glove. One of these is her declaration that at no time during her visions did she see any evidence that God is wrathful or that he punishes us for our sins. By thrusting aside the image of an angry, punitive God, Julian brought into question beliefs that were fundamental to conventional Christian thought. But she also opened the way for an even more original teaching. Struggling for some way to describe adequately Jesus' loving care for humanity—his immense tenderness, and the intimacy of his attentions—she announced finally, working herself into a perfect thicket of conflicting pronouns, that Jesus is truly our Mother.

"Our saviour is our true Mother," she exults, "in whom we are endlessly born and out of whom we shall never come" (LT 57).

Today it is hard to grasp how radically Julian was departing from ordinary church teachings. She was not the first to speak of Jesus as Mother, but she was, as far as we know, the first woman to do so. Augustine, Bernard of Clairvaux, and Anselm of Canterbury had all touched upon the theme, but nobody else had explored or celebrated it as fully as she did. With Julian, moreover, it was not a matter of theology at all—at least, not in the narrow sense of the word. She didn't reason her way to the conclusion that motherliness was as much an attribute of God as majesty, she experienced it.

> For the almighty truth of the Trinity is our Father, for he made us and keeps us in him. And the deep wisdom of the Trinity is our Mother, in whom we are enclosed. And the high goodness of the trinity is our Lord, and in him we are enclosed, and he in us. (LT 54)

The fact is, I made relatively little of this material in my dissertation. I did see that Julian's discovery of God's maternality was in line with other changes she'd made in her account of the showings—changes that seemed to distance her teachings in a variety of ways from narrowly monastic views of spiritual progress. She reflects, for example, that before the visions she had sought physical suffering as a penance but that since then, over time, she had discovered that "life itself is a penance." I saw how consistent with one another were the changes that she was making, but I didn't really identify them as "feminine." I made no attempt in the thesis to relate anything about Julian to the emerging women's movement, and I'm not sure I even saw any connections.

That might seem strange, because by the early seventies the movement was certainly heating up. But feminism was still in its early and most reactive stages. The more nuanced and thoughtful work that would have made those connections clearer hadn't started to appear yet. And, again, feminism was, to my mind, a political phenomenon, and I didn't think political activism was likely to do that much for women.

The members of my community were anything but reclusive or apolitical by temperament. Collectively, we had a long history of engagement. Three individuals had been arrested at

Sproul Hall during the free speech movement, and our eldest member, Mary D., had been a Quaker and vigorous antiwar activist for twenty years. Three men were performing alternate service as conscientious objectors, and one woman had just finished a stint working for the Welfare Rights Organization in New York City. Life in Berkeley had awakened even the most sluggish among us to social injustice in all its permutations. But we were in the pristine moments of an undertaking we believed went to the root of all forms of injustice. If figures like Teresa of Avila and Mahatma Gandhi were any indication, a life based on prayer and meditation could culminate in a real freedom from conventional attitudes toward gender and the mental straitjacketing that comes with those attitudes. And I thought I had some idea how that life works: as you meditate, your sense of who you are—and who everyone else is, for that matter—is less and less tied up with externals. Not only does gender stop mattering so much, so does race and age and how much you weigh. . . .

Life in my immediate vicinity was inconceivably rich at the time, and nourishing. Needs I hadn't even known I had were being met. It wasn't that I was deaf to the voices of Germaine Greer, Kate Millet, Gloria Steinem, and the like; they just seemed to be coming from very, very far away.

CHAPTER 3

"Be Like the Banyan Tree": Harder Than It Sounds

Twenty years passed, and the tenor of life in our community remained much the same. There were, of course, adjustments. After the initial flurry, which we came to think of as our frontier period, we realized that the siege of plumbing and plowing and painting that had seemed both onerous and endless was only an overture. The real work, the inner work, was much harder, and we'd barely begun it, and it could go on indefinitely. We didn't live by a formal Rule or any other inherited structures, and there were times when some of us half envied the Benedictines their full-blown liturgical calendar with its appointed days for bearing down and lightening up and the certainty threaded all through it that you could regularly put last month's failures behind you, and even the whole year's, and begin afresh, newborn as the infant Jesus himself.

But in fact, something similar did evolve for us that was subtler and unspoken, tied very much to the place itself and our
own history there. We'd moved to the land in the dead of winter, and it was so wildly overgrown that our first spring was a
running revelation of antique lilac and rose bushes we didn't
know were there until they bloomed. Mornings, we would eat
breakfast together on the wide porch of the Victorian farm-
house in an incredulous half-daze, enclosed in a curtain of wisteria blossoms three or four feet long that ran the length of the
house, translucent, so the sun poured through in a pale purple-
white haze, the murmur of the bees so hypnotic we hardly
spoke. It was as if beauty itself were standing guarantor to the
whole venture. Something of that feeling returns each spring
with the wisteria.

The seasons turned and turned back upon themselves.
Morning and evening the meditation hall filled and emptied;
springtime to summer, and summer to fall, the garden went
through its changes and we learned to eat by its rules: green
beans and zucchini in the summer, and kale all winter long. We
put a six-color press in what had been a milking parlor and set
up a bindery next-door, and just about every year after that a
new book was edited, printed, and bound.

A rhythmic baseline did emerge, in other words, and at last
like our Benedictine counterparts we, too, began to experience
time in its cyclic mode. Within its rounds, most of the things that
happen to people anywhere happened to us. Marriages were
contracted and some dissolved; there was illness, and there were
close brushes with mortality. Some people left, others moved in.
We had babies (in modest number—holy celibacy retained much
of its attraction), and we schooled them. Without making a terrific fuss about it, we all poured energy that under other circumstances would have gone into building careers into building up

the Blue Mountain Center itself and its publishing arm, Nilgiri Press. A couple of well-used Volkswagen vans served many in an elaborate system of carpooling; we shopped at secondhand clothing stores and took turns preparing meals—vegetarian, of course, whole grain and hearty. There was so colossally much to do, and to learn *how* to do, that for years we basically didn't look up.

Meanwhile, of course, news filtered in continuously of ethnic wars, famines, violently suppressed revolutions, proliferating nuclear weapons. . . . And, closer to home, a mounting obsession with high living that culminated in the Wall Street scandals of the late eighties.

We studied Gandhi closely throughout those early years, which meant that even though we lived at a remove from the worst things that were going on, we didn't have the luxury of thinking we weren't involved. Gandhi always brings you back to yourself—the beam in your own eye, the discrepancy between your own actions and the ideals you profess. He insists that you look beyond the headlines for the root causes of each new horror, and always the trail leads back to forces in consciousness, like envy and fear and the lust for power, and always you have to recognize those same forces in yourself.

Mornings, that first year or two, I worked on my thesis; afternoons, if I wasn't helping with dinner, I would be cutting thistles in the meadow or helping to fill in some of the huge erosion ditches that overgrazing had carved into our hillsides. Later, while I was waiting for a teaching position to turn up within reasonable commuting distance, I agreed to help put together a vegetarian cookbook. And I suppose that if I were to have to identify the period when feminism began to reassert itself in my thoughts and work, it would be this one.

Laurel's Kitchen proved to be the right book at the right time. Its solid success helped vindicate our leap of faith. Perhaps you really could begin to change the world from inside a spiritual stronghold, and clearly you didn't have to be perfect—didn't have to be a Gandhi or a Mother Teresa—to do it. "Be like the banyan tree," Easwaran would tell us. "The individual leaves are very small, but together they give such dense shade that even the hottest midday sunlight cannot break through, and many people can find shelter beneath it."

Coauthoring *Laurel's Kitchen* gave me something I hadn't sought, something that I'd told myself didn't interest me and that I probably feared might undercut my commitment to meditation itself—a professional identity. A year or two after the book itself was published, a Denver food editor called and asked me to write a weekly column. Outlandish, I thought. Good publicity for the book, someone else murmured. I'll do it for two months, I said. Two months stretched to a year, and then another, and soon twenty-three papers were carrying the column. When my son was born late in 1979, I realized that writing the column would allow me to work at home. I could savor the magical years of his infancy. By the time I finally got around to quitting, in the fall of 1989, he was a lanky ten-year-old, longer by now on wisecracks than out-and-out magic. As a food writer, meanwhile, I'd picked up an air of authority somewhere along the line that no amount of graduate work had been able to give me.

Maybe the difference was that I'd been cooking since I was a child, and I *knew* whether a recipe was good or not. It wasn't a matter of weighing one critic's opinion over another, I just knew. I made pronouncements, I took stands, and I didn't wobble. I informed my readers that despite what enthusiasts were saying, raw tofu is not, by most of us, digestible. I warned them that elephant garlic is an inferior product and that fava beans might poison them (assuming they have the genetic predisposition, rare but not to be trifled with). I bullied them into baking their own bread and growing their own spinach, and more.

During the last months, I got so shrill I was annoying even myself, and it was clearly time to move on. Still, it had been twelve years well spent, and I knew it. Having to write about things that were concrete, and in language any reader could follow, was a great antidote to the obscurantism of graduate school. Having to do it every week, without fail, was terrific discipline.

By the time I'd researched everything I wanted to write about in the columns and books (two editions of the cookbook itself plus a breadbook), my intellectual and political landscape had changed dramatically. I had learned about the growing crisis in the world's seed supply, for example: that sturdy native strains thousands of years old are being crowded out by hybrid varieties that don't reproduce themselves and require costly inputs like fertilizers and pesticides. In all kinds of ways I had come to understand more clearly the relationship between third world poverty and first world consumption patterns and to see that colonialism hadn't gone away at all, only "morphed" into a form of oppression far more malign for its being so very faceless. Little by little, without leaving my home, I'd forged a whole new set of connections with the larger world. And more than that, while I'd never thought of myself as "silenced," I realized at some point during those years that I'd begun to break through layers of inhibition I hadn't known were there. I'd begun to find my voice.

My timing, of course, could have been better. There our community members were, leaves on a banyan tree, each more happily anonymous than the next . . . and me with my own by-line, *loving* it.

To the casual eye *Laurel's Kitchen* was a joyous paean to the home-centered life and the woman-centered home. But my ambivalence was right there in plain sight. The book's introductory narrative depicted a friendship between two very different young women. One was Laurel, who embodied with borderline comic exaggeration the Berkeley "earth mother," politics well left of center, dispensing kitchen wisdom with one hand and oatmeal cookies with the other. Laurel was of course real, and absolutely wonderful. She still is. And I needed her there to give voice to the book's basic philosophy. But I knew that many women readers would find it hard to identify (I certainly did) with someone who was so competent, so enthusiastic, and so single-mindedly nurturant. She needed a foil—someone who hung back and hesitated and worked out her own compromises. Hence the second character, who was me. Sort of.

Rhetorically, the structure was inspired, because it let a great many important things get discussed easily and naturally. But it served my own needs as well, to write in two tracks, because I was feeling, in my heart of hearts, conflicted. Earth mother or virgin huntress. Homemaker or scholar. Feed the world or find myself. On the one hand . . . on the other . . .

A Common-Enough Divide

I struggled to represent my feelings on all of this accurately as I wrote away on kitchens and co-ops, because so much of what Betty Friedan had written in *The Feminine Mystique* (about "the problem that has no name") had rung absolutely true to me. I had watched my mother and her friends and had seen the frustration and pain Friedan described. At the same time, though, it didn't seem to me that their restlessness had as much to do with boredom as it did with the galling awareness that the work they did in the home *and that they knew to be valuable* was held in such low esteem by the culture at large. It seemed wrong to me to confuse the liberation of women with the same abhorrence of manual labor that was pitting rich against poor all over the world. Even the few years I'd spent living in community had proved to me that the work people do in a home taking care of one another *can* have value, beauty, and dignity. I had grown up a farm kid and had seen men and women work together regularly—*having* to work together to make it from one year to the next. My father cooked when it was called for, and my mother helped with the planting when that was called for, and my brother and I picked what had to be picked and bought our school clothes with our earnings, and nobody felt particularly demeaned. Tired, yes, and grubby, but not demeaned.

Once again, it was Gandhi who helped me sort it all out. For him, hand labor, or "bread labor," was fundamental to non-violence—as much a privilege as a responsibility—and with respect to that work, he bent gender stereotypes deliberately, almost to the breaking point. He taught himself how to cook and use the spinning wheel. He learned nursing skills and used them, and he even learned to run a sewing machine so that he could make sari blouses for his wife, Kasturba. Long after he had sworn off stimulants of any kind, he would make tea for her in the morning. His letters to loved followers working in villages far from his ashram sound like notes from a fussy aunt: "How is your digestion? You might try adding a few grapes to your diet. . . ."

Initially, that is, I don't think I framed my vacillations over nurturance and womanhood in terms of feminism. The closest I came to doing so was when I was wavering over whether to include in the introduction to *Laurel's Kitchen* a glimpse of South

Indian village life that our teacher had placed before us often, drawn from his own boyhood:

> Every evening, as the sun set, one of the women of our fam-
> ily would light an oil lamp, and as she carried it out to the
> veranda, everyone would look up in quiet delight to see her
> soft black eyes and warm brown skin glowing above the
> polished brass lamp. The beauty of this simple ritual made
> unforgettable the words that Granny used to repeat time
> and time again: "Be a lamp in your home, my daughters—
> be a lamp to everyone around you."

I knew very well that images of this sort were under severe scrutiny by feminist critics. I knew how double-edged and dangerous to women the "angel in the house" motif was that poet Coventry Patmore had made so popular in Victorian life and thought. I knew it had required women to stay in their houses and be angels precisely so that men could raise hell everywhere else; that it imposed a superhuman purity on women that was in some way supposed to offset the incorrigible naughtiness of their empire-building male counterparts; that by defining women as caregivers to the exclusion of all else, it barred them from becoming proficient in any other area of life and blinded them to the terrible iniquities of the colonial policies that had built and overfurnished the houses they maintained. I knew some of the appalling effects this kind of arrangement can have on women's life, and I knew enough about other cultures, including India's, to know that this pattern of cruelly unfair expectations is not limited to British or American family structures.

I knew all of that, and I thought hard about the decision. But finally I did include this cameo glimpse of Kerala womanhood,[1] because . . . I think because I knew that if I had tried to explain my reservations to the Kerala women in question (and in fact I had met at least half a dozen of them), they would have shaken their heads in disbelief and laughed and laughed and laughed. I didn't know exactly what it was, but I was pretty certain these women had hold of something that was still eluding Western feminist analysis.

Years later, I would learn that there was a name for the ambivalence I kept feeling during the *Laurel's Kitchen* years. Feminist theorist Ann Snitow calls it "the common divide"—a tension between needs that pull us in two different directions at once. On the one hand, one feels moved *as a feminist* to celebrate the beauties and strengths of women's culture, so long and grievously ignored, and to identify oneself *as* woman and *with* other women. On the other hand, most of us have also felt—again, *as feminists*—another kind of need as well: this one can pull us sharply *away* from other women, or at least from being "woman identified," because women have been so relentlessly defined— as nurturant, patient, and compassionate, for example—that we simply aren't taken seriously by a male-centered culture that reveres boldness, individual achievement, and the ability to subordinate others. Indeed, from this second perspective, feminine culture can look like a culture of limitations—of closed horizons and thwarted impulses. Worse, it can *feel* like that, insofar as women have managed to internalize many of those negative stereotypes.

I'd experienced the "common divide" long before I got around to dramatizing it in Laurel's Kitchen. I remembered how unsettled I had been my last quarter at Stanford the spring of 1965, when senior panic broke out and suddenly my talented, able, wonderful girlfriends could think of nothing but attaching themselves to a guy. As their student identities began to slip away, and they had to imagine themselves for the first time outside the university setting, they simply folded. They had no positive ways to think about themselves as women beyond the most traditional. Carnaby Street fashions were coming into vogue that spring, and the dark floral print fabrics, the puffed sleeves, the empire waistlines and narrow, short skirts worn over pale stockings underscored what the Beatles and Stones were telling us in a thousand different ways: we were there to please.

Fortunately, there had been other voices in the air that spring, and some of the most alluring were right across San Francisco Bay from us. Alone, come June, I had headed for Berkeley, not much less timorous than the various friends for whom I'd just been a bridesmaid, but drawn as if by an invisible cord to the very epicenter of the student revolution and the antiwar movement . . . to a clerical job on the campus and my first apartment, and with my first paycheck, comfortable clothing, and enrollment in a judo class.

A Son is Born . . . And a Feminist

My own wedding would not take place for another six years, and by the time it did, so rich were those years, I was in no real danger of defining myself solely as "wife." After all, I had made the much more definitive decision—to join a meditation teacher and community—absolutely on my own. Finding voice as a writer after that, and discovering in myself a certain creative stamina I hadn't known was there, had strengthened in subtle ways my feelings of "self." So, for that matter, had meditation. It just seemed more and more as if there were someone *in here* now, looking out, moving along, making real choices instead of just bobbing along with the current. Becoming a mother in 1979 consolidated all of these changes, though in some ways it left me even more confused. Inhabited for nine months by another self, I was unsure for a long while after my son's birth whether I was once again a single self in one body or one self in two bodies. Having a child proved to be as radically transformative as anything I had ever experienced. It changed the girl I had been forever, jostling the abstractions of the Berkeley graduate student, mocking gently the heavenward pinings of the spiritual initiate, and linking me by main force to the earth and whatever was going to become of it.

And if nothing else in my life experience had made me consciously and explicitly a feminist, having a son most certainly would have. To watch a boy you love move unsuspectingly from childhood into adolescence—flesh of your flesh, bone of your bone!—and then come up against the unbelievably arid and limiting version of manhood that this culture offers is to see at once the full extent of male privilege and its terrible, terrible cost. From the bleachers of Little League games, from the sidelines of soccer matches, I've watched, mesmerized, as little boys practice guy-ness. As the mother of a good athlete—even, on occasion, a rather splendid one—I've had a ringside seat on what our culture does to bring a boy across the threshold of what it dares to call manhood. Over the course of a season I've seen some boys *get it* and seen, then, how obsessively the others watch them—the lordly bearing, the quietly masterful gesture—knowing they must get it, too, for *it* will precede them into classrooms, fraternities, boardrooms, and bars, and it will be worth far more there than talent, hard work, or honesty. I have heard more than one disgruntled coach, groping for the most stinging reprimand he could lay hands on, say, "You guys played this game like a bunch of girls."

And whenever I heard that, it made me very, very angry.

The anger that grew steadily in me over those years didn't have much directly to do with my own experiences as a woman. I had my scars—who didn't? But they were faint and small compared to those of other girls and women I knew. I'd never been a teenager desperate for a safe abortion or a single mother supporting her family on minimum wage, never been a woman of color or elderly. I'd been fortunate in my upbringing and blessed in my marriage. I hadn't been trying to make my mark in any professional arena, and the men in my community didn't make me feel particularly oppressed. So when my anger flared up, it was usually over something I'd seen "out there": when I saw a little girl dressed like a streetwalker—or for that matter a streetwalker dressed like a little girl—or read an interview with a member of a Spur Posse; when I met a woman friend downtown who couldn't buy groceries because her estranged husband had withheld child support; or when I heard that an overzealous San Francisco policeman trying to break up a United Farmworkers' rally had broken Dolores Huerta's ribs instead, I would see red. Twenty-five years' meditation notwithstanding, I would lose it.

As a student of Gandhi, I knew better than to focus my anger on the individuals who were directly or even indirectly to blame. "Hate the sin," he always said, "but not the sinner." This particular sin seemed so pervasive, though—this systematic demeaning of women and girls—that it seemed for most people to represent "normal." How might one even begin to get at it?

In what I see now as an indirect response to the deeply ingrained misogyny I was seeing more and more clearly, I began to pull together for myself a body of evidence, and imagery, to support my belief in feminine strength and dignity. My initial intention was nothing more ambitious than to strengthen my own nerve and faith. The feminists of the nineteenth century fascinated me, and I wrote a long essay on Jane Addams for a book on peacemakers that never got published. I wrote about my own grandmother for the introduction to the second edition of *Laurel's Kitchen*. I studied the lives of Olive Schreiner, Dorothy Day, Mother Teresa, and Eleanor Roosevelt. I've mentioned *lectio divina;* now, it seemed, I was drawn to the intense practice of *lectio femina,* and before long, for a serious spiritual aspirant, I was wandering rather far afield.

I rationalized my infatuation with M. F. K. Fisher ("After all, I'm a food writer") and then with Alice Walker and Toni Morrison ("I need to keep my ear for good prose"), but each marvelous writer led me to another, and finally I stopped trying to explain myself and began pulling books in hand over fist, reading not just for myself at all, but on behalf of the young girl I had been once, who would have given anything for these narratives of feminine courage and creativity and, yes, unabashed feminine sensuality—a girl who might well have found the courage to speak and write her own truths much sooner if she'd had them.

Because of the commitment I'd made to meditation and to the center's work, it wasn't easy to justify the stacks of paperbacks that were growing around my bed. It was like finding myself wandering around in a Kathmandu bazaar when I was supposed to be climbing K2. And yet, I don't think there was a way in the world I could have done otherwise, for I was intuitively certain, somehow, that I was still on track. There was so much truth here—not *ultimate* truth, mind you, not the stuff of visions and revelations, but ordinary honesty, uncensored accounts of feminine experience. The authors all seemed to be talking to one another, building on one another's testimony. Alice Walker said it so well, that each of us has a small part of the whole story. That whole, immense story, much too long withheld, seemed to be unfolding itself now with the force of a monsoon.

And before long I realized that there was a piece of the story that was mine to tell. It had to do with women like Teresa of Avila and Clare of Assisi. For years I'd been reading everything I could about them on account of their gift for contemplative prayer, but now, taking their womanhood into account as I never had before, I began to think of them as the real foremothers of contemporary feminism, too.

I'm not sure I'd have come to that conclusion if I hadn't fallen so much under the spell of Mahatma Gandhi. When Gandhi was asked what sort of God he believed in, he used to say that for him, truth is God. In Sanskrit the word for truth is *satya,* which means "that which is" but also "the highest good." Gandhi introduced the term *satyagraha* to describe his program of nonviolent political action. It would be used with reference to a whole way of life or to a specific act of resistance: one can carry out a satyagraha against a particular governmental policy or an individual. Gandhi himself used to say he had carried out his first satyagraha against himself, and he claimed to have learned the technique from the women in his life, especially his wife, Kasturba.

Satyagraha entails a fierce clinging to the fundamental truth, which is, Gandhi explained, that we are all one. Any attempt of one individual *or* race *or* class *or* gender to oppress another, said Gandhi, is a violation of that unity. This was why, for him, religion and politics were inseparable, and it was also why the full emancipation of India's women was central to his nonviolent revolution, as strategy and aim, means and end. Once I began to grasp what he meant by satyagraha, it seemed to me a perfect description of what the great women mystics of the West had been up to. They'd held revealed truth tight and followed wherever it led.

What finally consolidated my feminism, then, once and for all, was the experience of entering that grand story Alice Walker speaks about—of taking it in, first, and then realizing that I was responsible for part of it, too. As I fought through the pious nonsense that accumulates around someone like Clare of Assisi or Catherine of Siena and tried to discern the woman at the core, the same thing happened to me that has happened to many other women who've set out initially to recover lost and silenced feminine voices. Too constrained or timid or plain bewildered to speak for ourselves, unready, perhaps, to open certain doors in our own consciousness, we take the part of another someone who's been silenced, for example, by much harsher and more overt forces than we have—and break *her* silence. It might be our mother or grandmother, a woman of our own ethnic background or religious tradition, or one who has undergone a significant experience that we have, too, like illness, divorce, conversion, or exile. We choose our alter egos carefully and practice ventriloquism under the guise of scholarship or journalism, and eventually, often before we realize what's happening, we've begun to exercise our own voices.

So there it was. Somewhere in the dense green canopy of shade that was my home and spiritual family, there was this one small leaf twitching about and calling an unconscionable amount of attention to itself. And once again, it was me.

Julian, Once Again

Julian of Norwich was of course among my "ladies," and if anyone had wanted to measure just how far my feminism had evolved in twenty years they'd have had only to compare my current reading of her *Revelations* with the one contained in my dissertation. I was amazed to see now how much of her had eluded me that first time. Her breathtakingly serene trust in the visions, for instance—in her own *experience*, that is, as opposed to what she had been taught as a Christian—seemed to me deeply consistent with the great value contemporary feminism sees in claiming one's own experience. Julian actually said she regarded the showings as a more reliable source of spiritual understanding than holy scripture. She had grown up in a setting that told her what to believe—told her, for example, that God was a harsh taskmaster, though no harsher than we deserved. She'd set out on a journey to the very center of herself and had learned when she got there that, on the contrary, God was all love, and basically we were, too. On the basis of what she knew firsthand, confident to the point of gaiety, she had proceeded to dismantle the whole orthodox reading of sin and its consequences.

There was all of that *blood*, too: blood flowing like raindrops off of an eaves, drops as round as scales on a herring—so much blood, Julian remarks, that one would think the room would be soaked. And yet it isn't depicted as grisly or repugnant at all. "The bleeding continued until I had seen and understood many things. Nevertheless, the beauty and the vivacity persisted, beautiful and vivid without diminution"(LT 7). For Julian, I realized this time, the blood and water flowing from Christ's side would not have been tokens of defeat, as they might well have for a male author—but rather concrete signs of his endlessly nurturant love. The pierced body of Christ crucified was for her a birthing body, and therefore a triumphant one. Like our best contemporary women writers, Julian was unafraid to "write the body," and when I saw this now, I treasured her all the more.

My feminist eye, trained now by writers like Carol Gilligan *(In a Different Voice)* and Mary Belenky and her colleagues

(Women's Ways of Knowing), saw also that Julian was constitutionally unable to tolerate the divisive, oppositional modes of thought that characterize traditional, male-centered scholarship and theology. She writes lyrically of the "fusion" in love of Creator and creature, but she doesn't stop there. *None* of the sharp distinctions traditionally made between sin and repentance, past and future, joy and sorrow, body and spirit—between male and female, for that matter, or love and knowledge or "high" diction and "low"—survived the powerful drive for unity, for what she calls "one-ing," that characterized her discourse.

In that same vein, I understood now as I hadn't before how very fortunate we are that Julian appears never to have learned Latin, the language of formal scholarship—of "universals" and abstractions as opposed to local, vernacular realities. The Middle English in which she wrote was the language of intimacy rather than formal distance. Its very warmth matched the intensity of her desire to communicate, and its melodic softness made it the perfect medium for conveying a doctrine that was all hope, all joyous certainty.

CHAPTER 4

First You Have to Admit There's a Problem

By the late 1980s there was no question but that feminism had put down deep roots in my life. The invisible protective walls of ashram life hadn't kept it out; or maybe I'd brought the seeds along with me, in the hem of a coat or the tread of a shoe. In any case, there it was, leafed out and sturdy, if yet unclassified. It was a little like finding a three-foot-tall cannabis bush in the backyard. . . . How long before my neighbors noticed, and how would they feel about it when they did?

I had a pretty good idea. "Feminism just puts up walls!" I'd heard one of them say at the other end of the dinner table. "Even the *word's* divisive." And nobody had rushed in to object.

It is a premise of the life I share with my community, and the method of meditation we practice, that whenever you give your attention to something—an idea, a word, an emotion, an image—you in turn strengthen its hold on your thoughts. Concentrate on a prayer or a holy name as you fall asleep, and it'll be there for you when you wake up disoriented at 3 A.M. Worry about losing your job or gaining weight, and *that'll* be waiting for you instead. Correspondingly, when you pay a great deal of attention to the differences among people, that very preoccupation can exacerbate differences and make common ground seem impossible. One of our strengths as a community has been a willingness to make light of the things that separated us, like age, sex, or taste in music, and focus instead on the shared yearnings that had brought us together in the first place. As students of a teacher whose own teacher had been a woman, moreover, who reminded us continuously that the Self is neither male nor female, and who had placed women in leadership roles all along, we had enjoyed an enviable sanctuary from the more acrimonious gender battles raging elsewhere in the culture. Without that sense of safety, and trust, and mutual respect, we could never have accomplished what we did.

No, from the first stirrings of this inquiry it seemed clear that it really wasn't about the members of my community. I might have wished some of them had more enlightened views on feminism. I might even have wanted to shake one or two and say, "Feminism doesn't put up walls or create divisions. Feminists are only trying to get everyone to see the walls that are already there!" But when you live with several dozen other people for as long as we've been together, you're accommodating one another all the time. Heaven only knows, in other words, how many times my friends may have wanted to shake *me* and tell me something I really needed to hear, then taken a good look at me and refrained for the time being.

Life in an intentional community is like being inside one of those rotating cylinders full of water that rock collectors use to polish their rough treasures. Little by little, over the years, a lot of the roughest edges get smoothed away. Maybe we even begin to shine a bit. And without anyone's having to invoke words like *sexism* or *patriarchy,* the right sort of adjustments do keep getting made. When we first organized the kitchen schedule, for example, nobody questioned the appropriateness of assigning eight or nine hours a week to each of the women, while the men put in only three or four. The men were presumed to be working full-time or carrying out Manly Tasks at home: maintaining the water system, taking out compost, cutting firewood. . . . Years later, though, we reconvened and agreed unanimously that since lots of women were working full-time, and since nurturant work is a privilege nobody should be denied, it made more sense to just add up all the necessary hours, including the Manly Tasks, and divide by the number of able bodies. Now everybody puts in five to six hours a week in the kitchen or garden, regardless of gender or employment circumstances.

Finally, and more fundamental, the whole basis of our common life was a shared determination to go beyond "othering," though we've never called it that, preferring certain admittedly old-fashioned expressions like "inflated self will." When people are making a sincere effort to outgrow egocentricity, and they're practicing spiritual disciplines in a systematic way, they will eventually get to the place in their hearts where they've been drawing lines and building walls on top of them, and they'll see that they simply can't get any further until they take down the walls and erase the lines. There's no established time frame for all this, and it can certainly take a while, but a setting where individuals are working at it offers poor growing conditions for sexism, racism, and the like. Just knowing that the men around you are *trying* not to regard women as sexual objects makes life immensely more comfortable.

Finally, as one of Easwaran's students, I felt myself privileged, on account of his granny, to have been drawn into a certain mysterious kind of female lineage. I was grateful beyond measure for that and wouldn't for the world have wanted to jeopardize it. Nor did I want to bring turmoil into my meditation.

But all was not well—not at all well.

A metaphor occurred to me then, and it still seems accurate: when you strain a muscle, and it hurts, the natural response is to put a heating pad over it. Any trained caregiver will tell you to use ice instead, though, not only to reduce inflammation, but also because the receptors that carry "pain" and "cold" messages to the brain travel on the same neural pathways. In order to tell you it's cold, your back has to *stop* telling you about the pain it's also feeling. When the injury is mild and temporary, cold packs can suffice; if the pain keeps coming back, though, more aggressive measures are called for.

Similarly, my feminism and my spirituality have always been closely connected, laying claims on me at the same level. I'd taken up meditation out of a driving and, yes, *aching* need for self-knowledge and meaning. My feminism had arisen out of that same well of feelings, and in many regards the life I'd chosen had satisfied it. Part of me, though—the part that never lost awareness of the attitudes that demean women and girls so universally and systematically—was like a muscle that was sore from continual strain and misuse. It was hot to the touch. If after all these years it was still flaring up, then surely it was time I attended to it.

Closer to Clarity

It was also like one of those times when you realize your two best friends can't stand each other, and instead of leaving it at that, you keep inviting them to dinner parties, hoping they'll see how much they have in common—only to realize finally that they don't see any such thing and that the whole business matters much more to you than to either of them . . . that *you're* the one who has to account for being "of two minds." I was sure that feminism and spirituality ("real" feminism and "real" spirituality, meaning, of course, my own versions of each) were compatible. At least that. But I was a long way from understanding how these two strong tugs in myself could be aligned—how I could start filling in that blank space on the map.

One thing that helped me begin sorting things out was that my relationship to my own spiritual path had shifted just a bit. Easwaran's books were widely available now, and people were coming from all over to retreats, wanting to meet him and learn how to meditate. This meant that in addition to being his students, many of us were having to function as teaching assistants, too. We led workshops or gave background talks on the meditative tradition; even eating lunch with guests was a real responsibility, and in order to do it as well as we could, we tried continuously to put ourselves in the position of someone hearing it all for the first time. When I did that with respect to the women retreatants, doors began to open. I started hearing certain refrains that were really intriguing.

The best way to get to the bottom of something is to teach it. Better even than writing about it, because teaching places you in front of living, breathing students who are either getting it or not getting it and who are generally incapable of pretending they are if they aren't. So it was more than just fortunate that about this time the opportunity also came along for me to teach again at Berkeley. While I was still in graduate school I'd developed a course on the literature of mysticism for the comparative literature department, and the professor who'd been teaching it since then was on sabbatical. Would the department chair mind if I slanted the course somewhat this time and emphasized the works of women mystics? No, the chair didn't mind it all. She rather liked the idea. . . .

The two situations were very different, of course. Most of the Berkeley students were much younger, and their interest was understandably more academic, while the retreatants' relationship to the subject was engaged and practical. The two groups resembled each other closely in one respect, though, and that was a pronounced skittishness with regard to "gender talk." Whenever I was speaking to an all-female class or workshop, there was no problem. But whenever even one man was present, women who'd been voluble and relaxed would all but clam up. A few might be outspoken, almost as if they'd been appointed to the role, but the rest sat still as mice. This shocked me at first, particularly when I saw it happening on the campus, because in my years away I had assumed that student discourse was moving along apace with the books everyone appeared to be reading and the films one knew they were seeing. But as I watched and listened, I saw that no matter what you knew these young women actually thought about relationships between the sexes or the status of women in the culture, they were elaborately careful not to trouble or offend the men in the room.

The dynamic certainly varied from one class to the next. The young men who'd enrolled in my very first "reentry" class at Berkeley were impressive in their openness to feminist perspectives. But even there I became more and more aware of a silent policing that nobody ever remarked upon. All a male student had to do if the discussion was veering in a direction that made him uncomfortable—say we were trying to decide whether the fasting of medieval women saints might have had anything to do with anorexia—was to shift slightly in his chair or turn his head to one side quizzically or open his eyes wide in comic exasperation. Immediately, everything would freeze, and the process was so subliminal I don't believe the student in question even knew what he'd accomplished.

When I was teaching meditation workshops, on the other hand, where the students in question were typically middle-aged folks, many of them couples, there was not as much obvious reason for the gender-related issues to come up. Again, though, I was struck by how rapidly the barometric pressure in the room dropped when it became apparent, for example, that when a husband and wife both worked outside the home, as most of them did, it was the wife who generally had a harder time imagining how she was going to fit even half an hour's meditation time into her day.

To "teach mysticism"—whether it is applied or theoretical—is to present a whole way of looking at human existence that departs radically from anything you might call normal. The basic assumptions about almost everything really are different—assumptions about what life is *for* and what use we are to one another; how we regard our own desires and one another's. Anyone who sets out to make sense of all this to contemporary audiences learns to anticipate resistance. In fact, much of what you are trying to do in that situation is to elicit doubts and misgivings actively so that meaningful conversations can take place.

It was in the course of this kind of deliberate rousting out of students' reservations that I saw something I hadn't seen before. Watching my women students closely, *listening* as a good teacher must, I began to see that women have their own quite specific areas of resistance to the idea of a structured, systematic meditative practice. And this seemed to me very interesting.

One can understand right away the sort of anxiety contemporary women feel with regard to particular religious traditions. They've heard about the prayer orthodox Jewish men offer up in synagogue, "Blessed art thou, O Lord, who hast not made me a woman." They know that traditional Buddhism maintains that you have to be born a man to attain enlightenment. Not many know that in Catholicism nuns are categorized as laity, but most of them have one or two other stories about Christianity's treatment of women that are at least as off-putting. In Islam, Hinduism, the Church of Jesus Christ of Latter Day Saints, and most other faiths, it's the same story. Every religion comes into being in a particular historical context, and misogyny is so pervasive in human history that religious institutions and liturgy can't help having been infected by it.

But religion itself wasn't the subject of these classes. On the contrary, what I was trying to do was to help my students discern, examine, and even try on the golden thread that runs through *most* religions. I wanted them to learn about the whole range of techniques and lifeways, preserved often as esoteric teachings, that are known to deepen interior prayer. Though these teachings can appear to be embedded in orthodox religious doctrine, I maintained, they are universal, and they can in fact be lifted up out of orthodoxy and practiced to good effect outside the religious medium in which they've been preserved.

Why, then, given the scrupulous care I was taking to separate the unfortunate excrescences of orthodox religion from what seemed to me the authentic core teachings, did gender seem still to be so problematic?

There was so much reticence around issues of gender that I could only feel my way along, and admittedly I'll probably never know with absolute certainty which concerns were initially just mine and which were my students'. But when I began to structure class discussions around what I *thought* their concerns were, the sheer passion of those discussions confirmed my guesses over and over—especially when I was able to break the class down into smaller groups, most of which were made up entirely of women. After each meeting I'd find myself making note of everything that had been said, who'd said it, and even how loud she'd said it. I was doing something I hadn't done for years, not since I'd been a graduate student poring over Dante and Chaucer. As if I were reading a text—a medieval allegory, where meaning darted about elusively, just below the surface—I was looking for *motifs*.

CHAPTER 5

Four Tracks into a Wilderness: Revelations of a Sort

The classes in mystical literature that I was teaching at Berkeley were, of course, cross-cultural, so I organized many of my lectures around themes or preoccupations that appear as commonly in Hindu or Buddhist sacred texts as they do in the works of John of the Cross or the Sufi mystic Ansari of Herat. We looked at the universal appeal of certain symbols that seemed almost more than symbols—like fire or the ascent of a mountain or rivers rushing to the sea—and we noted the various ways in which the student-teacher relationship is characterized in Hinduism, Buddhism, Judaism, Christianity, and Sufism. In the process I came to see that certain of the most fundamental concerns of mysticism look very different when seen from a feminist perspective. As I thought more deeply about these areas of apparent conflict, mulling them over as I drove to and from Berkeley or walked our dog in the hills back home or trimmed broccoli into long spears for dinner, I realized that the conversation that had been trying to take place in my own mind between my two cherished value systems was at last taking on weight and substance. Its terms had been defined.

I was able to admit now that what I'd been treating as a pedagogic difficulty (How can I help these *other* seekers get past the roadblocks feminism has put in *their* way?) was very much my own. This was a huge step, because it meant I was allowing certain things to come into question that I'd thought were beyond question. The group sense of my community has always been that there is a time when doubt should be given full rein: when you're first taking up a spiritual practice. During that time, take nothing at face value. Ask all your questions. Work the soil, *then* you can plant the seeds. And I thought I'd done that. Only now it seemed that in certain ways I was twenty-four all over again, or even sixteen! I felt seriously unsettled and bristling with a whole new kind of question, and all of this weighed heavily on my sense of who I was as an aspirant. Everything felt clouded and heavy.

At the same time, I really did take courage from the example of Julian's apparent working assumption, that if two things really were true, then somehow or another you should be able to reconcile them. Eventually, I would conclude that I had done absolutely the right thing in deciding to bring my spiritual commitment and my feminism into open and unconstrained dialogue. My grasp of both would be deepened immeasurably, and it continues to be. During those first scary months, though, I felt sometimes as if I were picking up two raw ends of electric cable and drawing them very tentatively toward each other. In one hand I held everything I'd gleaned from my teacher and my practice. In the other was everything I knew as a woman living in a male-centered culture. Would sparks fly? Would a tremendous current leap out between them? Or would it flow through me instead, and if it did, would I survive?

I did survive, of course, and began rather swiftly to get a clearer sense of exactly where the critical stress points were along the interface between feminism and spirituality. Four seem to me to be particularly salient.

1. Silence

Be still, then, and know that I am God.

—PSALMS 46:9

Years ago, when our son was about seven and wanted nothing more in the world than to get a firsthand look at the foxes we knew lived in the forest that marks our property line (we'd heard them barking and seen them at a distance), I overheard my husband telling him how he could get his wish. Late in the afternoon, he said, but well before sundown, he should enter the clearing where we'd found their scat, seat himself behind a bush, and wait without moving or making a sound. At first everything would be quiet, because the animals and birds would have seen him come. But then, if he sat still—and it would probably take half an hour, maybe more—they'd forget about him and start moving about and making their own noises, and if he were very lucky, and *very* still, Br'er Fox and his family could well put in an appearance.

In truth, I don't remember whether it worked—Br'er Fox got so bold later that summer, establishing his family in our very woodpile, that we became quite sanguine about his movements. I do remember realizing, though, as I listened to Tim, that he was giving our son his first spiritual instruction:

"Sit *very* still, wait as long as it takes . . ."

In the presence of the sacred, and even while we're waiting for it, we fall silent. The early Christian monastic tradition is rooted in the teachings of men and women who left the clamor of the cities and sought out the absolute stillness of the Egyptian desert to pray and fast, and it is in keeping with the teachings of the desert mothers and fathers that daily life in a Carmelite convent is still characterized by the "Grand Silence." Most other forms of Christian monasticism are less austere, but there probably isn't a contemplative tradition anywhere that doesn't ask its adherents to govern speech to a considerable degree. Hindu teachers, for instance, maintain that excessive speech dissipates *prana,* which is their term for both "breath" and "vitality." When we are silent, they tell us, *prana* collects, like water in a catchpool, and meditation deepens in the process.

As a young woman learning to meditate in the late 1960s, I don't recall objecting to any of this except insofar as it was *hard.* Hard remembering to ask myself, for example, as my teacher suggested, whether the remark I was about to make could pass through what Islamic tradition calls "the three gates": *Is it true? Is it kind? Is it necessary?* I hadn't even begun to recognize yet how many gates already governed my speech simply because I was a woman: *Is it amiable? Is it accommodating? Is it*—for I had academic degrees to live down—*ever so slightly ditzy?* [1]

When I tried to hear these teachings as a young woman might today, of course, it all had quite a different ring. Silence is easily as central a concern in contemporary feminism as it is in mystical traditions, but for what would appear to be exactly opposite reasons.

"Down the corridors of my preteen years," journalist Ann Taylor Fleming recalls, "the word I remember hearing the most was 'hush' or some variation on it, a quashing chorus of 'shhs' that inevitably greeted one of my characteristically high-decibel riffs on the world and served to intensify my feeling of choking." [2]

Down the corridors of *all* time, feminist scholarship has shown us, that same quashing chorus has silenced women, excluding us so effectively from all avenues of discourse that ultimately it not only impaired our capacity to speak at all—to say what we mean, without fear of consequence and in language that does not subvert our intentions—but even lessened the ease with which we imagined what we *might* say if we thought we could. The emergence of second-wave feminism in the early 1970s had everything to do with what was happening to women in consciousness-raising groups of one kind or another. "We wanted to speak," one writer recalls, "we constructed occasions to speak, we heard ourselves quavering out difficult sentences, we waited to hear a supportive response." [3] The responses *were*, of course, largely supportive, because the women who made up the groups were for the most part white, middle class, and reasonably well educated. As a truly revolutionary activity, consciousness raising clearly had its limitations. Nonetheless, the experience did affect many women in ways that proved irreversible. For it wasn't just that they spoke, it was that they found the courage to say things that women just didn't say: truths that ran counter to the culture's accepted version of femininity.

The need to find voice is at the core of feminist concerns today—not merely at the literal level, but in the fullest sense. So sensitized are women today to the issues of silence and voice that we find new meaning in old texts. Indeed, a passage appears toward the end of the *Revelations*, for example, in which Julian describes a terrifying experience that took place in a dream she had just before the very last of her showings. The devil appeared:

> He grinned at me with a vicious look, showing me white
> teeth so big that it all seemed the uglier to me. His body and
> his hands were misshapen, but he held me by the throat
> with his paws, and wanted to stop my breath and kill me,
> but he could not. (LT 67)

Riveting as I found this description to be when I first read it, its wider implications were lost on me. Writing today, when more than two decades of feminist scholarship have made us all more deeply attuned to such meanings, scholar Ritamary Bradley is able to connect it—accurately, I believe—with Julian's entirely justifiable fear of being silenced about her visions. For Julian to act as a teacher, Bradley reminds us, and speak out about her showings, would have meant courting death at the stake.[4] Indeed, in the earlier Short Text she had insisted "God forbid that you should say or assume that I am a teacher; for I am a woman, weak, ignorant, and frail" (ST 6).[5]

Julian's apparent fears of being silenced would be felt with particular force by contemporary Catholic women engaged in the struggle for ordination of women and greater inclusion of women at every level. But recent developments in that struggle make it seem relevant to the rest of us as well. Many of the women who have been advocating opening the priesthood to women are having second thoughts. They've seen what happens to women who've become attorneys, professors, doctors, and officers in the military: that it's one thing to enter these highly competitive and traditionally hierarchical fields, and quite another to function freely and effectively within them. Rather than pressing for the ordination of women, therefore, these church activists are advocating a long hard look at the very idea of the priesthood and the hierarchical model of things it presumes. One of the subtler aspects of the debate over "voice" and "silence" is that there is an immense difference between having permission to speak and enjoying the hope that someone might actually listen to you.

2. Self-Naughting

Doing our own will is usually what harms us.

—TERESA OF AVILA, *Interior Castle* (3,2,12[6])

*There comes a time when an individual becomes irresistible
and his action becomes all-pervasive in its effects.
This comes when he reduces himself to zero.*

—MAHATMA GANDHI,
CITED IN EKNATH EASWARAN, *Gandhi the Man*

Among India's numberless representations of divinity, none is more visually arresting than the magnificent figure of Shiva, Lord of the Universe, *dancing*. Spectacularly fit and graceful, he has an extra pair of arms that allows him to make the traditional gestures of protection and invitation while at the same time holding a conch shell and a mace. A cobra, wrapped loosely around his waist, swirls outward as he dances. He stands on one foot, in a pose that conveys incredible balance and strength and joy, and as your eye travels around the circle of fire that frames his figure and comes to that single foot, you realize it is planted directly upon a tiny human figure, writhing and grimacing.

Horrified, we ask—Is it a baby? A dwarf? A demon?

No, we are told, it is the ego:"self" in its smallest and tightest construction. Its Sanskrit name is *ahamkara,* and that literally means "the 'I'-maker," the part of each of us that goes about stamping things "mine" and making interminable speeches about "me" and "what I need." Egos are the one sacrificial offering Shiva is said to want, and his ecstatic dance represents the bliss and the freedom the human being is supposed to experience who manages to make that sacrifice.

Every culture treasures stories of women and men who have managed to trample ego underfoot. Miracles blossom on all sides as these individuals go through their day; light gathers around their heads, and fragrance clings to their garments. It's hard not to fall in love with them, hard not to at least *want* to believe in them. And yet, when we look at the way they got there—the terrible austerity and the almost ruthless handling of their own ordinary human inclinations—I'm not sure their stories play that well today. Not among women. For we are wary of selflessness.

At the meditation retreats and workshops I've helped lead over the past ten years, I've had to tell people all kinds of things they didn't want to hear. No, you can't expect to meditate effectively after a heavy meal. Yes, you have to do it every day, and ideally at the same time every day. No, you can't do it while you're driving, and no, background music isn't helpful.

Those are all relatively easy. The ante rises sharply with the introduction of a supporting discipline my own teacher calls with a certain ingenuousness "putting other people first," which is really a velvet-gloved rendering of the practice medieval monastics called "self-naughting" or "vanquishing self-will." For contemporary seekers, self-naughting has about as much appeal as straw bedding and unleavened barley bread. Regrettably, though, it can't be brushed aside as one of those medieval excrescences. It is perhaps the bedrock spiritual discipline. Its relationship to meditation has nothing to do with morality. Reduction of self-will has a direct and uncannily powerful impact on meditation itself—a connection that really has to be experienced to be understood—because of the enormous amount of vitality used up in protecting one's self-interest on every front from one moment to the next. As soon as that pre-occupation drops off even a little bit, the mind calms down, and the capacity for focused attention extends considerably.

Obviously, we hasten to explain, one doesn't try to "become zero" overnight. You begin by identifying those areas in your life where you are most accustomed to having your own way. Are you usually the one who decides what movie you and your partner will see? Is it your palate that generally determines the dinner menu? How about those little unspoken arrangements and scheduling patterns—how many are set up at your particular convenience? Once you have spotted the places where you are especially protective of your own interests, you can begin to challenge yourself: You watch the film your partner wants to and figure out how you can enjoy it, too. You notice that the young woman next-door is ill and could really use some help with her three-year-old. You spend an evening a week helping out at a homeless shelter. *Gradually,* we emphasize, egocentricity diminishes and meditation deepens.

We are always careful, too, to recognize that putting other people first doesn't mean becoming a doormat. You have to tell your child no several times a day, and even in dealings with adults, allowing someone to exploit you or harm you is a dis-service to them as well as to you.

Once we've made these provisos, and it's clear we're not pitching some kind of mindless self-abnegation, things usually relax. Or at least they appear to. I'm no longer surprised, though, when one woman or another will come forward after these workshops and explain privately that she really had not been able to see herself in our characterization of rampant self-will, riding roughshod over the needs of neighbors and family, shortchanging friends and colleagues to enlarge her own options. On the contrary, she is already acquiescing to the needs or desires of people around her to the point where she feels sometimes like a rag doll: the person whose needs are there expressly to be overlooked . . . the angel in the house. Deciding that she wanted to meditate, and would come to this retreat to learn how, had felt to her like a healthy and long-overdue step toward nurturing her *own* sweet self, thank you.

Feminist writers have long expressed their misgivings about selflessness as a normative expectation of women. It was with heavy irony that the French philosopher Luce Irigaray observed, "The path of renunciation described by certain mystics is women's daily lot."[7] But the whole concept of selflessness came under fire, all across popular culture, with the codependency movement of the mideighties. It was then that many wives, daughters, mothers, and sisters learned for the first time (as did more than a few husbands, sons, fathers, and brothers) how effectively we sometimes connive with the weakness of others, tiptoeing around their substance abuse, bedding them down and taking them to work, ignoring their cruelties: needing so badly to be needed, needing to see ourselves and even define ourselves as loving caretakers that we perpetuate their condition by never even allowing it to be named. The movement has had its excesses. For a while, it looked as if nothing even resembling familial nurturance was going to survive the purge, and it was a relief when countervailing voices were raised. But the movement against codependency taught contemporary women to make some crucial distinctions. Between living by a socially constructed model of virtue, for example, and living by one's own lights; between settling for relationships that are nearly ready-made—"off the rack," so to speak—and enduring long stretches of *no* relationships while they sit tight and wait for the quirkier, riskier sort that springs from real affinities and shared passions; between yielding to compulsive drives in our relationships, whether external or internal, and making genuinely free choices that take their own needs as well as everybody else's into account.

The profile of the definitively codependent personality is the stuff of television sitcoms today. Many are coming to see the connection between a need to nurture that is out of control, and a sense of self that is profoundly underdeveloped. We understand now that people at the far end of the codependency scale are selfless all right: they quite *literally* have no self—no sense of worth or personal history. Surely, women insist today, this couldn't be what spiritual teachers ask of us.

And I don't believe for a minute that it is. But I know, too, that there are a great many women feeling their way into one meditative practice or another for whom this has not been made crystal clear—who have tried with considerable difficulty to articulate to fellow seekers or mentors the misgivings they have about "self" and selflessness and were met with blank looks or worse. I'm increasingly of the opinion that the best help Western women can get in this area is from other Western women who've struggled with these issues themselves and begun to get a handle on them. Fortunately, a good number of them are writing and talking about their own experience. Women like the Venerable Thubten Chodron, a Buddhist nun who used to be Cherry Greene from Los Angeles, who speaks volumes when she reflects, "Sometimes it's difficult to figure out what is Buddhism and what is culture." She recalls how hard she tried to be meek and quiet like nuns she'd met from Tibet until she realized finally, "Hold on, something isn't working. This isn't me." [8] Or like Anne C. Klein, Buddhist scholar and practitioner, who observes with real subtlety:

The loving self, the self that is loved, are nowhere denied in Buddhist traditions. That such a self can be permanent, unconditioned, autonomous, or causeless is vigorously denied. The middle way is finding a path, a way of being, that encompasses both these perspectives.[9]

3. Redirecting Desires

Cut down the whole forest of selfish desires, not just one tree only. Cut down the whole forest, and you will be on your way to liberation. If there is any trace of lust in your mind, you are bound to life like a suckling calf to its mother. Pull out every selfish desire as you would an autumn lotus with your hand.

—THE COMPASSIONATE BUDDHA,
FROM THE DHAMMAPADA, TRANS. EKNATH EASWARAN

I've heard mysticism called the science of desire, and it seems apt. Every mystical tradition I know emphasizes restraint of the senses as a means of deepening prayer or meditation. Some stress the value of fasting for sharpening attention; others like to tell us how little sleep we really *need* compared with the amount that we simply enjoy. Clothing is another area where we're told that personal tastes can run riot at the expense of mental equilibrium, and interior decorating is still another. Sex, though, heads the list.

It's rarely understood, but prudishness has nothing to do with the mystic's perspective on sexuality. There's nothing *wrong* with sex, we're told, it just doesn't go far enough. No earthly lover can reach the real depth of our need, because our deepest need is for what is permanent. "How can I rest anywhere, O God," asked St. Augustine, "when I am made to rest in thee?"

Even the most intensely fulfilling erotic pleasure passes, leaving us in a kind of dead zone, waiting for the next flutter of desire to stir us into movement again.

To make the sort of interior pilgrimage Teresa of Avila lays out in *Interior Castle,* she makes it abundantly clear, we must be heart-whole. As long as I still believe in sex as a source of lasting happiness—or power or food or even long weekends in the mountains or *anything* finite—then no matter how much I want the mysterious something else that mystics speak of, I can't walk toward it because my consciousness is divided. Pulled in two directions at once, I am paralyzed. This is why Gandhi said that no one can carry out nonviolent civil disobedience who cannot say no to himself or herself. A *satyagrahi* must be without fear. Anyone who is powerfully attached to sensual satisfactions—of any kind—is also powerfully attached to the body itself and therefore bound to preserve it.

And once again, I recalled that as a young woman I had embraced this "science of desire" unreservedly. I never felt that my teacher was foisting some kind of warmed-over asceticism on us at all; on the contrary, he was offering us powerful tools for getting some control over our lives, and the tools *worked.* I'd wanted to stop smoking for a couple of years but hadn't been able to. Within weeks after I'd begun to meditate, it proved almost effortless to stop: every time the urge would come up I'd go for a brisk walk repeating a mantra. The rhythm of my footsteps took on the rhythm of the mantra—just as he'd said it would—and gradually my breathing would get deeper and slower, and at that point, mysteriously, the desire-nexus would break. The same technique worked with the bakery I had to pass walking to campus in the morning: I could actually *pass* it now.

The effect on meditation was palpable. The mind really was just that much steadier. And this was a profoundly liberating discovery. "Taste lies in the mind," Gandhi used to say. The likes and dislikes we imagine all but define us are not bone deep, they are merely conditioned responses of the mind. Through meditation we can undo that sort of conditioning, and each time we do, we in turn free up the very capacity to attend. Again, the concept of *prana* is relevant. In every powerful compulsive urge a great deal of vitality is tied up—life force. Breath. *Prana*. And of course nowhere in human consciousness is more of the life force tied up than in the very desire through which life perpetuates itself.

In a culture that is as riveted on sexuality as ours, loosening up those knots can be immensely difficult. One obvious place to start is to avoid wildly sensate films and books, music—anything that makes you more intensely body conscious. And this is exactly where we begin to run into problems. A recent magazine cover, and my own ambivalent response to it, comes immediately to mind.

The cover photo was a partial view in black and white of a woman's face, her mouth and one eye, mostly, both half closed in an expression it would be evasive to describe as anything but orgasmic. Superimposed on the photo were the words *Hot* (in orange), *Unscripted* (bright pink), and *SEX* (bright orange and very large) and in smaller (pink) letters: "How Women Are Redefining Sensuality & Pleasure." As magazine covers go, it wasn't any more explicit or suggestive than most. It wouldn't have stood out on the shelf at the supermarket. Only this wasn't one of those supermarket periodicals, it was *Ms.,* and I was dismayed. Scanning the table of contents, finding the usual rich mix of topics and personalities, I couldn't help wondering why instead of this decidedly sensational composition I couldn't have had a beautiful photograph of Rosa Parks to look at all month instead or professor of law Lani Guinier or the young woman who got wolves back into Yellowstone Park—or even one of her wolves.

And yet I knew that the editors of *Ms.* were absolutely on target in urging women to take charge of their own sexuality—lipstick lettering and all. The frank and freewheeling debate on sex that is going on right now within feminism can be disconcerting to many of us for one reason or another, but that it must take place is beyond question. "Sexuality is to feminism," says Catharine A. MacKinnon, "what work is to marxism: that which is most one's own, yet most taken away." [10]

The dominant theme in feminist conversations about women and desire is the observation that because of cultural constructs of "woman," women are commonly estranged from their own desires—from *all* their desires. Think about what is implied when a woman is labeled ambitious or competitive, and what the same epithets suggest about a man; think about the social stigma a woman incurs, as opposed to a man, for weighing 10 or 15 percent more than her ideal body weight or for using drugs or drinking too much or holding forth at a dinner party until the other guests are restless. Women have very powerful reasons for curbing *most* of their desires—reasons that have nothing in the world to do with morality or health or courtesy or, above all, with spiritual practice, but rather with the simple fear of ridicule ("She's really *hard*." "She's a pig." "She's a real lush.") and ostracism. The gender gap is, of course, far, far wider where sexuality is concerned.

Contemporary women are well aware of this imbalance and its unfairness and, whether they declare themselves feminists or not, are rejecting it. In film—even in very conventional movies —this spirit of resistance translates into the near-obligatory inclusion of episodes in which young women get drunk or eat themselves into a stupor, swear inventively, or "moon" their boyfriends; where elderly women smoke marijuana, middle-aged women gather to watch a male stripper . . . and life goes on. In less conventional films, female desire is explored in greater depth, in conjunction with the development of female subjectivity. In films like *The Piano* or *Like Water for Chocolate, Angel at My Table, Camille Claudel, Shirley Valentine*, and *Carrington*, female protagonists come to terms with their own desires and move, simultaneously, to a greatly enhanced sense of self, even at the risk of life, limb, and sanity. The sexuality at issue isn't sexuality in the most narrowly defined sense but rather a broader erotic impulse that is linked with creativity of one kind or another—musical, literary, artistic, even culinary.

I could *almost* see where these two perspectives on desire might converge. And it seemed to me that for a contemporary woman seeker who feels the accuracy of both, they really must converge. If I am to become a full-fledged scientist of desire—this seems to me the real crux—and if I'm to carry out my own original research, I have to take my turn at working with the stuff of desire "hands on" and uninhibitedly. All the theoretical background in the world is no substitute for time in the laboratory, and that's exactly what girls and women are discouraged from having.

The authors of *Mother Daughter Revolution* relate a conversation between the dean of a prominent Ivy League school and an alumna regarding the fact that the school had no women Rhodes scholars. There were plenty of girls who had the grades, the dean explained, as well as the athletic talent and the record of social responsibility required for this very prestigious graduate fellowship. But when the interviewers asked them what they wanted the scholarship *for*, the girls simply didn't know what to say.

> Wanting had no place in their lives. These were champion "good" girls who had done everything right; they were accustomed to doing well and jumping through hoops.

Although successful, they were disconnected from the desire that sprang from the "yes!" within them.[11]

There is a wonderful moment in M. F. K. Fisher's memoir *The Gastronomical Me* when just such a young woman is blessed with the right kind of adult mentoring and gets a good hard shove toward the desire that springs from a "yes!" within. She is traveling with her uncle from Los Angeles to Chicago on a train during the era when dining cars were fine eating establishments. Painfully shy and self-conscious, she finds it is all she can do, come dinnertime, to glance at the menu and murmur that "anything" will do. Patiently, over days, her uncle coaxes and coaches her along until she begins to place her order consciously and with a certain enthusiasm. When they reach Chicago, though, they are joined by his nearly grown-up son, and her fragile confidence collapses. Uncle Evans takes them out for supper, and once again when the menu comes Mary Frances's eyes drop and she whispers that really anything will do. But she looks up, and her uncle's eyes catch hers, and something clicks.

> I knew that it was a very important time in my life. I looked at my menu, really looked with all my brain, for the first time. "Just a minute, please," I said, very calmly. I stayed quite cool, like a surgeon when he begins an operation, or maybe a chess player opening a tournament. Finally I said to Uncle Evans, without batting an eye, "I'd like iced consommé, please, and then sweet breads *sous cloche* and a watercress salad . . . and I'll order the rest later."
>
> I remember that he sat back in his chair a little, and I knew that he was proud of me and very fond of me. I was too.

Teresa of Avila was only a couple of years older than this when she stopped by *her* uncle's house on her way to her sister's farm, where she was to recover from an illness that was really more of a nervous breakdown she'd undergone a year or so into her novitiate as a Carmelite nun. Nobody really knew what was wrong with her, but her uncle looked at the pale, thin young woman with the great dark eyes and gave her a book—told her she could take it with her, thought it might help. The book was a treatise on contemplative prayer by a Spanish Franciscan, and it probably saved Teresa's life, because it equipped her to begin the journey inward that her whole being required and that life in a crowded, worldly convent had made all but impossible.

The two stories have for a long time been connected for me because in both of them a young woman's capacity to desire and choose is taken seriously—by an uncle!—in a small exchange that proves to be formative.

In other words, I think we do have to acknowledge the relevance of some modest version of ascetic practices to meditative spirituality. To busy myself night and day deciding what I like and what I don't like makes me a hostage of circumstance and fills my mind with anxiety. But if I've never been encouraged to think of myself as someone capable of making choices in the simplest matters—what tastes good to me, how I like my room to look, what kind of people I want to be around—there is a certain kind of fire and light that will quite possibly never ignite in my life. I won't know how to *reach out* for what matters most or even, possibly, to recognize it when it comes—when it whispers to me, from the depths of my own being.

The whole tangle of questions around desire would remain puzzling for me, and I suppose they still are. But just opening it out for examination was a great relief: I could feel a certain pressure beginning to ease up already.

4. Enclosure

*It seems I'm saying something foolish. For if this castle
is the soul, clearly one doesn't have to enter it since it
is within oneself. How foolish it would seem were
we to tell someone to enter a room he is already in.
But you must understand that there is a great
difference in the ways one may be
inside the castle.*

—TERESA OF AVILA, *Interior Castle* (1,1,5)

Julian had her anchorhold, Catherine of Genoa a closet in
the hospital she oversaw; Teresa of Avila made it her life's work
to see that Carmelite convents would be genuinely enclosed and
that each nun should have her own cell. Julian of Norwich all
but "wraps" her reader in the language of enclosure. "For as the
body is clad in cloth, and the flesh in the skin, and the bones in
the flesh, and the heart in the trunk, so are we, soul and body,
clad and enclosed in the goodness of God" (LT 186).

The literature of mysticism is shot through with images of
enclosure. Of walled gardens, interior castles, cocoons, and beehives. There is no great mystery here. Meditation is synonymous
with turning inward, and it requires that we withdraw attention
from everything around us. It is all but impossible to do this if
we have reason to feel self-conscious or vulnerable or apprehensive. There is something less obvious, too, about what used to be
called "vibrations." A place where people have prayed just *feels*
like a place where people have prayed, and as you walk into it
that simple fact falls gently around you like a soft cape. It con-
duces to deep prayer or meditation.

For twenty-five years I have been "enclosed" with forty-
some others, coming and going by day but returning each night

to a cluster of buildings surrounded by trees and hills . . . enclosed in a deeper sense, too, by the commitment we share to a specific set of disciplines and a willingness to forego some of the pleasures of contemporary life that run counter to those disciplines. In our early years, we had next to no idea what was going on "outside" for weeks at a time—not so much because of our rural setting, though that certainly helped, but because we were too engrossed in what we were doing to notice. And this seemed fine to me. "A sapling must be fenced about carefully," goes a Hindu proverb, "if it is to grow into a sturdy tree."

Now I had to wonder, though. Suppose I were twenty-something right now and just beginning to meditate. Would I adapt so effortlessly to being "fenced about"?

Today, when Western women commit themselves to a spiritual practice, they are almost never entering a literal enclosure —rarely a Carmelite cell and never, to my knowledge, an anchorhold—though somewhere in the Himalayas there probably shivers this very moment a Vassar graduate who has her cave, her deerskin, and her Shaivite mantram. They might well be joining a community, though, or a convent, or even simply the circle of a particular teacher. They might only have decided to *confine* themselves, that is, weary of the spiritual smorgasbord, to one set of teachings—to one path. Even this step, though, can set off loud interior alarms.

"Ours has been a history of confinement," writes essayist Nancy Mairs, "in the childbed, in the crinoline, in the kitchen, even (if all other safe harbors fail) in the asylum. . . . But most have needed no turn of an iron key, no leather thong. We've known where we belong."[12]

In their physical bodies and in the realm of archetypes as well, women have long been seen as "that which encloses." They are the vessels, deemed sacred in the best of times, that hold both life and the mysteries whereby life goes on replicating itself. To poets everywhere, women are "walled gardens" of delight and fecundity. But that very imagery seems typically to mean that someone else is going to have to maintain the walls in question. For the qualities that identify a woman as both sexually desirable and maternal—tenderness, softness, a yielding sweetness—seem also to have implied that she will not "have it in her" to keep her surrounding walls in good repair. It is as if, from the male point of view, we were boneless—as if we could at any moment *spill out* of enclosure if the walls are anything but high and strong. *Peter, Peter, Pumpkin Eater . . .* Wherever gender is highly polarized, as it is in most traditional cultures, one runs into this dilemma: the very strength of purpose and sense of her own worth that would permit a woman to guard her own chastity are felt to be incompatible with what are regarded as core feminine qualities. Strength and vigilance are all his, softness and pliancy all hers. She must be enclosed, and he must have the only key.

I had just become aware of the complexity of this particular motif—at how intensely contradictory women's responses are to the thought of enclosure—when a friend, Turkish by birth, published a pictorial history of the harem. Alev Croutier's grandmother and great aunt had been brought up in a harem and were among the last women to have lived in harems: the institution was abolished in 1909. For Alev, exploring the history of harems meant in a sense exploring her own—her connection, through the mother-line, with women who'd spent their entire lives behind walls.

The harem, she explains, was a domestic arrangement that originated in twelfth-century Istanbul and prevailed in Muslim households throughout the Ottoman Empire until the twentieth century. It has long gripped the Western imagination, though, becoming, through our poets, painters, storytellers, and couturiers, she maintains, "a unique archetype of the collective unconscious."

> The word *harem,* derived from the Arabic *haram,* means "unlawful," "protected," or "forbidden." The sacred area around Mecca and Medina is haram, closed to all but the Faithful. *Harem* refers to the separate, protected part of a household where women, children, and servants live in maximum seclusion and privacy. Harem also applies to the women themselves and can allude to a wife. Finally, *harem* is "House of Happiness," . . . acceptance of the master's exclusive rights of sexual foraging, a place where women are separate and cloistered, sacrosanct from all but the one man who rules their lives.[13]

Fascinating, I thought, to watch the meanings slide into one another. The fact that the same word was used to demarcate both the Islamic holy of holies and the domestic inner sanctum is arresting, because it suggests that the individual household is a replica of Islam itself—its microcosm—and that the duty of defending the household is thus little short of a holy charge. The head of the household was, accordingly, the guardian, or steward, of the individuals who lived under his care—not merely of their physical well-being but of their moral and religious status as well.

The distinction, of course, between stewardship and ownership has always been problematic, and the emotional logic behind *harem* arises out of this very muddle. When a man sees his home as an embattled kingdom and himself as the warrior responsible for its defense, the ancient logic of warfare would seem to entitle him to those "exclusive rights to sexual foraging" mentioned above. Furthermore, it is a universal rule of war that when a city is under siege the ordinary rights of its inhabitants are routinely suspended—curtailed by curfew, blackout, and censorship. Since the harem was conceived as a fortress under *perpetual* threat—from sensuality itself as much as from particular assailants—ordinary rights were never conferred to begin with. Subjectivity itself, on the part of its inhabitants, was unimaginable, indeed, treasonous.

Wherever embattled male heroism is the central narrative, I realized, it tends to override all other kinds of narrative and all other possible "subjects." Recognizing that the institution of harem is grounded in social and religious conditions that no longer obtain, I kept feeling, as I learned more about the institution, that in certain very important ways it still bears on us heavily—way beyond its effects on our art, literature, music, and clothing. To my knowledge, no public figure in the Western world today claims that the harem is a useful model. And yet, rooted as it is in the murky world of collective fantasy, the institution persists, ghostlike, in tacit agreements as to "how things ought to be." Harems exist now only in fairy tales, but harem logic is alive and well.

I thought, for example, of the friend who called the police because her husband had struck her repeatedly. They came to the house, but they wouldn't come inside, and that puzzled her until she realized that they were honoring the very threshold as bounding another man's private space and identifying her, because she was inside that space, as "his" also.

I thought, too, about how curious it is that in a society where women presumably have full freedom to come and go, we are in fact constrained almost as effectively by the threat of direct criminal violence—in the streets, the parks, the workplace—as women are elsewhere by social or religious decree backed up by institutional violence.

I thought, and this is to me particular chilling, of the reply of a Roman Catholic bishop in my own part of northern California when he was asked about charges of child molestation running back twenty years against one of his own priests. Admitting that he'd been aware Father X had brought young boys to stay overnight with him on many occasions, he said he'd never felt it appropriate to say anything because "a priest's apartment is his castle."

The enclosure of women is a custom feminists have had no choice but to challenge—everywhere, in all its forms, including the figurative enclosure that results when women are barred from education and participation in the free exchange of ideas. Bella Abzug was only putting a new spin on an old feminist metaphor when she closed her address to the Fourth International Women's Conference at Beijing with the words "Our call is to scale the Great Wall around women everywhere."

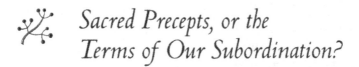

CHAPTER 6

Sacred Precepts, or the
Terms of Our Subordination?

Once I had identified these four "windows" into
the dissonance I'd been feeling between feminism and meditative spiritual practice, some disturbing implications suggested
themselves.

To summarize . . .

No two spiritual teachers lay out identical paths for their
students, and some will even adapt their teachings to the needs
of particular students. Yet certain precepts would seem to be
constants in meditative practices, however broadly or narrowly
they might be interpreted.

- Be silent. Curb speech, but still the mind as well,
  particularly thoughts of "I" and "my." "He who speaks
  does not know," says the Tao. "He who knows does not
  speak."

- Put yourself last, or, in the words of Thomas à Kempis, "Seek always the lowest place, and to be [sic] inferior to everyone." Unseat the ego.

- Resist and rechannel your desires. Disidentify yourself with your body and senses. Learn, indeed, that your body does not belong to you.

- Enclose yourself. Turn inward, and move into a protective "container." Disentangle yourself from as much external and public activity as you can.

It had never occurred to me before, but now I realized that however ancient and universal these disciplines may be, they are not gender neutral at all. Formulated for the most part within monastic contexts, they cancel the basic freedoms—to say what one wants, go where one likes, enjoy whatever pleasures one can afford, and most of all, to *be* somebody—that have normally defined male privilege. That is, men in any given social class have always possessed these liberties to a far greater degree than women of the same class. To the extent that he embraced these disciplines, therefore, a man entering the religious life would have experienced a dramatic and painful reversal of status: hopefully, an all-out assault on ego. Yet no one around him would have been in any doubt that he had undertaken that reversal voluntarily. The assault was understood to be self-administered.

Women, on the other hand, have not been in a position to renounce these privileges voluntarily *because they never had them in the first place.* Quite the opposite. If you knew nothing about mystical literature, you might think these precepts had been excerpted from a book of counsel for young brides in just about any ancient and/or traditional culture we know. They sound remarkably like the mandates young girls have always received as they approach womanhood and that, in veiled forms or under tacit threats, they still receive. They are the terms of our subordination, and each of them has been repudiated, directly and literally, by contemporary feminists, who urge women instead:

- Find your voice; tell your story, make yourself heard at the highest levels of every institution that affects your life.

- Know who you are. Establish your authentic identity or selfhood. Identify your needs and learn how to meet them.

- Reclaim your body, and its desires, from all who would objectify and demean it, whether it is the fashion industry, pornographers, or even the medical establishment. Recognize the hatred of the female body that pervades contemporary culture, and oppose it.

- Move about freely and fearlessly. Take back the streets. Take back the night and the day.

It had proven relatively simple after all, to locate the places where feminism seemed to be colliding headlong with spirituality, but the outcome of doing so was, for me, revolutionary. I felt as if I were looking at two distinct cultures, with two sets of values, for whom the same word could well have had two different meanings. Clearly, the various forms of impasse I'd identified weren't just "my problem" at all. They had to be affecting women in great numbers. The implications were many and far-reaching, and I'm still unfolding them. . . .

In the first place, it was obvious now why a woman who has embraced the basic tenets of feminism might have a difficult time imposing spiritual disciplines upon herself: As a feminist, she is in a very real sense already on a path: a path that asks courage of her and self-awareness and the willingness to walk alone. The instructions she receives upon taking up a spiritual practice, then, would seem to point her back in precisely the direction she's coming from, and not in a vague way, either. Point by point, they echo the mandates she's been working hardest to put behind her. She might well grasp the connection drawn in the Bhagavad Gita, for example, between restraint of desires and deepening meditation. But if she's spent years resisting the temptation to eat brownies so that she wouldn't gain weight, then several more years eating them after all as a declaration of independence from the tyranny of fashion magazines, it's confusing, at the very least, to find herself renouncing them once again, this time for the sake of her meditation. What if she slips and starts to gloat over the pounds she's begun to shed—what will *that* do for her meditation?

And suppose, I thought further, that it isn't even about brownies? Suppose it's about getting an advanced degree or writing a book or having a baby or breaking off a friendship or starting up a new one? Or going to Paris? Or Tibet? What if it has to do with her sexual orientation and whether her parents, her boss, or even her spiritual teacher can handle knowing about it? Hard to imagine that her feminist instincts and her spiritual yearnings are likely to see any of these decisions in exactly the same light. How is she supposed to sort it all out? Sticking with a program of spiritual disciplines is difficult under the best of circumstances, but when the voices in your head are carrying on like a radio talk show, it can be almost impossible.

Worse still, what about the woman who has never seriously questioned the conditions laid out for her as a woman? She's endowed with charm, grace, a mild temperament—she's someone for whom compliance is no real strain and who has always been amply rewarded for it. Or maybe she's simply *afraid* to raise questions. In either case, she has governed her behavior carefully, lest she be found "abrasive," "assertive," "pushy," or "ambitious."

She has been "feminine," rather, and habitually attentive to the needs of others. When a woman of this disposition thinks about taking up spiritual disciplines and learns how much importance is attached to silence and self-naughting, restraint of desires and enclosure, does she conclude—like the character in Molière who realizes he has been speaking prose all his life—that she has been a spiritual aspirant all her life?

If she does, if she happily goes on doing what she's been doing with just a slight shift in reference point, and if nothing in her raises a disquieting question—about authenticity and courage and self-awareness (about Paris, for pity's sake, and Tibet!)—she may be setting herself up for just as rocky a ride as her feminist counterpart. Because the awkward thing about meditation is that it functions as a mirror, whether you want it to or not. The mind's contents become disconcertingly visible—like butter, says the Indian tradition, being churned out of buttermilk. It may take a few years, but somewhere down the line every troubling perception this woman has refused to admit is likely to plant itself firmly before her and demand its due, and if it does, the practice she's slapped together out of what was already on hand is unlikely to hold up under the strain.

Deeply committed feminists, I now saw, could well have a difficult time embracing spiritual disciplines, but so, for other reasons, could women who have kept feminism at a distance. Both kinds of individuals would find it hard to embrace a meditative practice with anything like the tenacity and passion that are called for, it seemed to me, because both are in a crucial sense divided—to borrow Emily Dickinson's phrase—"where the meanings are."

Even as I was coming to this understanding I found myself thinking back across the past twenty years with new and painful comprehension. For the two scenarios I've just described weren't hypothetical to me at all. I felt I'd watched each of them lived out on several occasions. When somebody takes up a spiritual practice and then drops it, or comes into the circle of a particular teacher and then leaves, it's wiser not to tie oneself into too many knots wishing it had been otherwise. Everybody has her own itinerary and her own timetable. But I couldn't help wondering whether some of the friends I still missed might not have been able to work through the conflicts that had sent them packing if we'd been able to talk about them openly and honestly—if the language had been available that would have *allowed* us to talk. I wondered, because finding even some of the language I'd been groping for was already alleviating my own feelings of confusion and dissonance.

By bringing to light the very different meanings that feminism and spirituality seem to attach to enclosure, silence, self-naughting, and restraint of desire, I'd moved much closer to understanding my own difficulties reconciling the two commitments. I had felt these contrary pulls but hadn't been able to see them, and as a result they'd been much more troubling than were these two brief but explicit laundry lists. To get the clarity I needed, I had drawn, of course, overly simplified pictures of both feminism and meditative spirituality. But there was real practical value in doing so. Take the supposition, for example, that feminism advocates voice while mystics are all for silence. If I thought a little harder, as I was moved to do, because I wasn't really happy with all this polarizing, I began to remember some very interesting things that contemporary feminists say about the role attentive listening can play in women's psychological development.[1] By the same token, I had to recognize that the long silence of a mystic-in-the-making usually gets broken eventually in prophetic utterance or call for reform or inspired teaching. Thinking about both these "wrinkles" in my own assumptions led me in turn to reflect how often I'd seen expressed in both contexts the sense that "for everything there is a season." That, in the words of Carol Gilligan, for example, "speaking and listening are a form of psychic breathing." [2]

And at this point I began thinking about the mysterious rhythm of *all* things and to wonder whether the powerful rhythms built into women's biological lives may not predispose us to perceive more readily than do men the ebb and flow of virtually everything in life and to move with it, so that ultimately we don't so much ask *whether* to speak or be silent, but *when*. And this in turn led me to recall that elusive quality medieval Christian writers called *discretio* and the Indian tradition calls *viveka*. Discernment. It's about being able to see into the heart of things in the moment and make the best choice accordingly, and those who talk about it say it really comes only with depth in meditation. Clare of Assisi spoke of the special role within her convents of *discreti*—women whose judgment was deemed *by the community* to be particularly sound. How interesting, then, to take the next step and wonder which women contemporary feminists might recognize as *discreti*, and why.

The dialectic process that I'd set up, then, without thinking of it as such, led me from the very outset into a clearer grasp of both of my most cherished commitments and, even more than that, to the places where they actually illuminate one another. Chief among these, I saw right away, is the issue of "choice" itself. Enclosure, silence, self-naughting, and restructuring of desire are proven avenues, say advocates of meditative spirituality, to resources that remain untapped in most of us. Well they might be, feminists are quick to reply, but unless a woman can choose them freely, knowing that she *could* come and go as she likes, say what she wishes, and be *somebody*, then her apparent embrace of those renunciations is relatively meaningless and surely can't be expected to bear fruit. And it seemed to me that this was what was troubling so many of the women I'd worked with—that they felt mistrustful of themselves, amateurish, as makers of choices.

What would have to happen, I wondered now, before women could feel themselves able to make the sort of choice that spiritual practice requires, from one moment to the next, authentically and, therefore, effectively? I had come to certain conclusions that made that question urgent. I'd finally begun to understand why feminism and spiritual disciplines strike so many women as an either/or proposition. But at the same time, I'd begun to see something else that made the integration of those two commitments imperative. It struck me in the form of a hypothesis: *What if* the structures that have kept women silent and disempowered for so long are too deeply embedded in human consciousness—in yours, mine, everyone's—to be touched by anything resembling ordinary political activism or even mass education?

Gandhi believed that British imperialism was not just a political arrangement at all but rather a set of deeply held beliefs about what constitutes a human being—about which of us "count"—and because the Indians themselves had internalized those beliefs, Gandhi saw that no merely political approach could even begin to challenge it. Nothing short of satyagraha would be effective: "soul force" alone would work because it goes to the deepest level, transforming the individual who wields it in thought, word, and deed—transforming her, in fact, *first,* before it works in those against whom it is being used.

The satyagrahi is only as effective as she is fearless, and she is fearless insofar as she values the service of truth even more than life itself. But satyagraha can be employed, Gandhi insisted, only by individuals who have passed through the crucible of spiritual discipline and thereby "made themselves zero" through numberless acts of self-discipline. The reason is obvious enough. If I am unable to eat anything but the food I'm accustomed to, incapable of having my desires thwarted in ordinary ways, then clearly I'm far away from the sort of self-mastery that would let me meet violence with nonviolence. We work up to that capacity in little, little ways, Gandhi insisted, undertaking voluntary silence, for example, from time to time and training ourselves to eat the simplest foods, accepting certain kinds of de facto enclosure, like performance of "village uplift" in some remote part of the country, or even imprisonment. (Gandhi treated his own times in prison as opportunities for consolidating his spiritual resources. He rarely spoke, and he headed the letters he sent from Yervada Prison "Yervada Mandir"; a *mandir* is a temple.)

Choice, obviously—the capacity to make choices in reasonable freedom—is the crucial issue. It's the ability of a satyagrahi to choose freely that makes her who she is. She isn't acting under compulsions of any kind. Not fear, not greed, not anger— not even anger at social injustice. She's trained herself, over years, not to give way to compulsions, internal or external, and in the process she has dismantled every last thought of herself as weak or inferior.

Suppose, then, that a feminist takes up meditation and the allied disciplines in the spirit of satyagraha, intending to become wise enough and strong enough to challenge sexism effectively. She is alarmed, though, to discover that some of those disciplines *feel* exactly like a very familiar set of practices that have long constituted her subordination, even her degradation. How can she be sure she is electing them freely, for her own reasons, and not merely acquiescing to those old deeply internalized mandates ("Be quiet. Stay inside. Don't be *forward*.") and the attached rewards ("There now. What a nice girl. We'll take care of you.")? Where is all this heading? Will she lose her fierceness

—her "edge" and passion for social justice? Submission to these disciplines can make her free, they tell her, but submission feels so much like . . . *submission*.

It's a terrible dilemma. When you're choosing something as important as a spiritual path, you want to do it with an unclouded mind. But that clouded mind is the very reason you're having to consider such a desperate measure. How can it be trusted? "You can't get a job without a union card," goes the old teaser, "but you can't get a union card until you have a job."

In theory, it looks hopeless. In practice, though, I believe it is not. Thinking back on my own first months of meditating, I can identify three reasons why it felt right to proceed: three distinct reasons to trust myself and what I was getting myself into.

In the first place, I had started modestly, with the most minute choices imaginable. Not whether to buy another pack of cigarettes or a Danish pastry, and not even whether to get out of bed early enough to meditate before the streets got too noisy. All of these were down the road a ways; all of them would require a will that had undergone a certain amount of strengthening.

No, the initial step was just to close my eyes one afternoon and feel what it was like to keep my attention on the words of the Twenty-third Psalm for thirty minutes. The only actual choice I was making was to bring my mind back whenever it wandered. All this meant was that for those few moments I was refraining from doing something that everything in my background had conditioned me to do: I was resisting the mind's desire to travel wherever it wanted. Such a small thing—but everything else has depended upon it, because it taught me that there was an "I" that could stand outside the flow of thoughts and hold a course of its own.

Meditation *works*. It was that simple. It makes a difference. Making that discovery on even a very small scale seemed ample reason to trust the direction in which I was moving. And yet even that very simple act was a leap of faith I wouldn't have taken if someone hadn't jollied me into it in the most engaging way imaginable. "Don't take my word for it," Easwaran shrugged, smiling and offhand. "Give it a try: you've nothing to lose." Meeting him when I did, feeling the mysterious lurch in the heart that signals real connection, and sensing absolutely nothing coming from him that felt manipulative or insistent was the second ground for trust.

As meditation deepens and becomes more difficult, the teacher really can lift one almost effortlessly across some of the worst stretches. This is why Indian teachers speak of "guru's grace." But they warn us, too, that to go far on the spiritual path you must have "the grace of your own mind," and that this can be even harder to come by. It seems to me that the grace of our own minds is exactly what's been taken away from women, by dint of our collective history. When women take up spiritual disciplines, we find ourselves having to face down and walk through memories passed through the mother-line: of silences forced upon us and enclosures we couldn't leave, of selfhood withheld as a matter of course and desires flung in our teeth . . . memories stored not so much in the conscious mind as in our bones and even our muscles . . . memories that tell us over and over how weak we are, how unimportant.

I've come to realize that there was in my own early months of meditation something that offset and dispelled this dark weight. Indirectly, but very powerfully, it constituted the third ground for trust—in my own judgment, in my teacher, and in the disciplines he taught. It was made visible in a life-sized portrait of Easwaran's grandmother that hung for years behind his chair every evening when he spoke, and it issued out of every reference he made to her and his mother and the matrilineal tradition from which they'd sprung. It is through the women, he has always maintained, that India's spiritual values have been transmitted from one generation to the next. The reverence for women that permeated Easwaran's ancestral home permeates the life of the community he founded here as well, and down the years it has steadily refuted everything Western culture has told us about what it means to be woman.

Once I'd seen exactly how important my exposure to Granny was—particularly in those fragile early months—I began to wonder whether something analogous has to take place for any Western woman who would integrate her feminism with a spiritual practice. Someone in her life, or at least, very powerfully, in her imaginative life, must give her reason to rejoice that she is a woman.

The analogy I'd struck between Gandhi's followers and the contemporary women's movement seemed to me well worth pursuing. Whenever I've brought this up with others, though, a very pointed question arises: Who, for women, are the British? Who is the *enemy?* Feminism's opponents are quick to leap in with what they suppose to be the answer: men. It's *men* women see as the enemy and the oppressor. Which, of course, is nonsense, but it's nonsense that persists. Gandhi didn't see the British as the enemy, and feminists don't see men as the enemy, either. The enemy, rather, is the theory and practice of male superiority. The role that racism played in the British *raj* is played by sexism in the lives of women and girls.

Racism was at the heart of India's grief, but it was racism tricked out in institutional trappings, legitimized by all kinds of constitutions and decrees—backed up by such a long pedigree that it seemed always to have been there, synonymous with civilization itself. Is it reasonable to imagine that women—all women, everywhere—are standing before something comparable, as immense, long-standing, oppressive, and as *concrete* as British imperial rule was to Gandhi's India? And second, if such a thought is reasonable, are there historical grounds for supposing that "soul force" in one form or another might constitute effective resistance to it? The work of contemporary feminist historians provides ample reason for answering both questions in the affirmative.

I've been careful not to use the word *patriarchy* until now: I certainly never used it prior to the point in my life I've been describing. The term had always seemed so provocative: discussions polarized swiftly and angrily whenever it was introduced. Finally, though, I concluded that there may really be no way to get an accurate understanding of those "mother-line memories" and what they are doing to us—and more than that, how we can uproot them—without looking at their historical origins.

It had been a huge step forward for me to find that I could now spell out in fairly unambiguous terms exactly why my feminism and my spiritual practice seemed to keep scraping across one another. But no sooner had I taken that step than I realized that I couldn't have accomplished it if I hadn't been working from a premise that's become available really only in the past ten or fifteen years—the understanding that however idiosyncratic the personal history is of every woman and every girl, that personal history has been shaped in all kinds of ways by the inherited collective history of *all* women. If I'd been pressed to say something about women's history in, say, 1975, I could have sketched out only a *non*history—an omission, understood to be valid, given that women's real function in life is to assist and support, invisibly and inaudibly. Over the past couple of decades, though, feminist scholars had been hard at work constructing "a usable past"[3] for women—an account of the development of Western culture, that is, that explains the apparent absence of women without legitimizing it and in the process equips us to imagine the sort of culture that might have been and still could be.

For years now—indirectly, by a kind of osmosis—I had been absorbing this notion of a "usable past." But I'd never examined the relevant scholarship directly and never thought about what kind of light it might shed on my own experience. Deciding to look into the history of patriarchy would turn out to be pivotal for resolving the tensions I felt between feminism and spirituality. It showed me that contrary to what I'd believed, patriarchy is not arguably "natural" at all, and not even particularly ancient, compared with the far more woman-friendly cultures it has all but displaced. And it showed me that a great many individuals have worked hard, and still do, to make it *appear* to be both natural and as old as time. It took a while for me to grasp how perilously imbalanced our culture is (one grows up believing that "male centered" is normal; for all my feminist inclinations there was still so much I hadn't brought into question). But once I grasped that imbalance, I saw how fundamentally incompatible it is with anything I would recognize as authentic spirituality. How could anyone harbor contempt for women or for "the feminine" in oneself or others and pretend to aspire toward unitive consciousness or universal love?

My son's high school biology class required each student to keep something alive, in the laboratory, over the whole school year—a lizard, a turtle, ideally a community of life forms, like a terrarium or an aquarium. My son kept fish, and in the process I learned that there are drops you have to put into a fish tank to neutralize toxic chemicals. If you don't, given what's in the water these days, the fish can't breathe, and they die. That image kept occurring to me now, as I found myself being drawn to a rather startling hypothesis. Far from feminism being incompatible with spirituality, could it be that male-centered cultures aren't even *safe* for spiritual aspirants, let alone whole communities, until something like feminism comes into the picture?

I believe one can make little sense of the four areas of conflict I've outlined—voice or silence, freedom or enclosure, and so forth—without understanding the specific developments in the collective history of women that made them so problematic in the first place So I'll be discussing those developments now. But, more than that, I want to convey something of the process by which I found my way into that collective history, because in an odd way it proved to be an exceedingly interactive one.

Initially, I went into one of those twilight zones that are so alluring to anyone with a scholarly bent: your critical faculties are all but suspended for the moment, you're just *taking it all in,* and, yes, it does feel a bit like ordinary greed. But before long something else started happening. Almost effortlessly, like someone piecing together one of those patchwork dresses that were popular in the late sixties, I had begun to construct my own rendering of a "usable past"—a frame of reference that made my personal history comprehensible. A garment that fit. Specifically, I had begun to spot fascinating connections between what I could surmise of prepatriarchal spirituality, the Christian mystical tradition, and contemporary feminism. To figure out what those connections really were, and what they meant, I needed, in turn, to get a much clearer understanding of the values and motifs associated with the sacred feminine. The effort to do this was rewarded many times over in the discovery of one motif in particular that I think lets us begin to settle the apparent feud between feminism and meditative spirituality—settle it, in fact, in the manner of a Shakespearean comedy: with a wedding.

I saw now that no historian can hand anyone her "usable past." Each of us must compose her own, and a working knowledge of women's history is our common starting point. The process will be different for every woman who undertakes it—as different as our backgrounds, gifts, passions, and needs make us from one another. The resources available for such an undertaking are multiplying every day now, as more and more women set down what they know, and I hope every woman will *want* to undertake it.

In the next four chapters, I've tried to replicate the process by which my own version of a usable past took shape. I hope that here and there, between the lines, the reader will be able to sense something of the great joy I felt as I watched the pieces come together into a coherent whole. The four polarities I've mentioned repeatedly—voice versus silence, and so forth—have been indispensable. Taken together, they form a kind of leitmotif throughout these chapters. I've made no attempt to give them equal time, however. In a particular context, one or two may be more pertinent than the others, because, useful as it has been to treat these problems separately, I believe they really are, at bottom, four aspects of *one* problem. Tug on one, the other three come quickly into view. . . .

CHAPTER 7

Stone by Stone: Laying Down the Law of the Fathers

Remember the Fathers of Our Country? I'm thinking of the portraits of George Washington and Abraham Lincoln that used to hang in all elementary school classrooms. Without thinking about why, I used to project femaleness onto Abe. George was hopeless, but Abe was supposed to have wept over slavery, so he became, for me, "the soft one." Because really, I must have been reasoning, What kind of a country needs two Fathers and no Mother?

I Guess Because They're Bigger

Very few women like to discuss patriarchy, I've found, or even give much credence to the concept. Their reluctance makes sense. Refusing to give whatever-it-is a name or see its connections with the past allows us to minimize it and believe that with patience and good cheer it might just resolve itself. Besides, anybody who does start looking at the conditions under which women have lived down through time and, worse, wants to talk about them, is likely to be charged with portraying women as victims, lowering general morale, and undercutting the strides women are presumably making toward full parity.

I had probably felt all of that, and I knew the official scholarly objections: that the word *patriarchy* really applies only to the Greek and Roman systems of law that gave the father absolute economic and legal power over his wife and children . . . that modern Western systems of law operate differently: we live in a democracy . . . that only in movies about the Mafia does "The Father" hold absolute authority. But the acute sensitivity I'd observed among the women I'd been working with to the threat of being enclosed, silenced, or treated as objects suggested to me that they didn't necessarily view themselves as "equals under the law" at all. I understood the contention that the word *patriarchy* has no contemporary application now that Western women have been granted civil rights, but I found much more compelling the argument that since the top administrative posts in virtually all our institutions are held by men, we live in a world that is patriarchal by default, if not by decree. And it was evident that this de facto patriarchy was deeply inimical to women's attempts to take up spiritual disciplines.

When I did begin looking at the history of patriarchy, I was struck immediately by the fact that it is in many ways a source of very good news for women.

In the first place, looking squarely at patriarchy teaches us that somewhere back there, for reasons that aren't even particularly mysterious, the oppression of women *began*. Our status in society shifted, and shifted dramatically. It probably shouldn't have startled me so much to take this in, but it did. I realized that my unexamined assumption had been something like, "Well, this is how it is, and I'm sure it's always been like this because . . . they're bigger than we are."

I knew better, of course, and had for a long time. *The Godfather* may have sold millions of copies during the early 1970s, but out here in the counterculture, anthropologist Colin Turnbull's beautiful study of life among the Congo Pygmies, *The Forest People,* had had its own modest success. Its portrayal of intimate daily interactions among a people whose way of life was essentially Neolithic allowed one to start forming educated guesses as to what "precivilized" life might have been like and to surmise that it probably did not involve the systematic oppression of women at all. Indeed, much of the energy that went into the forming of alternative communities like my own in those years arose out of the hope, fueled by what anthropologists were telling us, that you really *could* form communities that didn't replicate the hierarchical relationships of the ones we'd grown up in. Just knowing about the matrilineal structure of my own teacher's ancestral family in Kerala was significant for me and the other women in my own community, and meeting some of the confident and well-educated young women of that family (an electrical engineer, a pediatrician, a journalist, a linguist, a computer programmer . . .) had made it clear that a culture that honored "the feminine" could also honor real live women and girls as well.

Still, these impressions were only impressions. I'd never fit them together into a coherent way of looking at the past. I had never brought "they're bigger than we are" under serious question because I was aware of only rare instances in history when sheer force had ever been opposed successfully by anything except still greater force. It was inconceivable to me that an entire culture might look with real reverence upon the half of its own members who are notably smaller and less equipped for physical combat. Lacking the sense that such a thing was even possible, I was completely unready to take in something archaeologists have invited us to contemplate for decades: that, as Gloria Steinem loves to tell young girls, "for about ninety-five percent of the time human beings have lived on earth, every continent had cultures in which girls were as valuable as boys."[1]

The second reason why I found myself genuinely buoyed by what women's history has taught me is that the history of patriarchy is also the history of resistance to patriarchy. Women were not brought into line easily or swiftly at all. Steps had had to be taken: laws written, edicts issued, scripture reinterpreted. And every law and edict and every piece of misogynist scripture or liturgy represents a place where women were still thought to be resisting—where they still appeared to be, in some sense or another, "authorized." The version of civilization that was emerging seems to have required the full disempowering of women, but achieving that goal was a lengthy process that took about 2500 years. To realize that patriarchy was set in place, stone by stone, is to realize that it can be taken apart, too, stone by stone. It's also to realize, of course, that thinking it will ever take *itself* apart is sheer folly.

What's in a Word?

Women have always been fully active in history as it is lived, notes feminist historian Gerda Lerner, but they have had no active role in recorded history. Because they haven't appeared in it or had a hand in writing it, they have no idea what other women have accomplished in the past. For women who would shake off culturally construed notions of "woman," there has been no evident lineage and nothing they could hope to build upon. As a practitioner and teacher of women's history, Lerner has seen contemporary women galvanized by learning what women of the past have done.

Androcentric is an accurate and considerably less charged designation for our society than *patriarchal:* "male centered," that is, or, as psychologist Jean Baker Miller puts it, "organized in terms of the experience of men as they have been able to define it and elaborate on it." [2] I'll be using these terms frequently but will not drop the use of *patriarchy* altogether precisely because it is so very charged, reminding us that male centeredness cannot but result in effective male dominance, even if the intention to dominate is nowhere visible. Gerda Lerner is among those scholars who believe the term *patriarchy* is still applicable, but she warns against drawing from its use the implication that women have been primarily victims. What is, in fact, so very interesting to her about women's subordination is their complicity with the processes that brought them to this pass. A more accurate way to describe the arrangement, she argues, is as "paternalistic dominance . . . in which the dominance is mitigated by mutual obligations and reciprocal rights." [3] In an analysis of the beginnings of Western civilization that is far subtler and richer than I can even begin to convey here, Lerner outlines the process by which this arrangement evolved—how carefully it was fine-tuned, and yet how impersonally and unhurriedly. To follow her argument is to acquire an almost blinding new grasp of all the invisible mechanisms that operate still in contemporary life, at every level of society, across class and race, to keep women "in their place" and convinced, in the depths of their being, that they belong there.

As I became familiar with the broad patterns of change that Lerner outlines in her first book, *The Creation of Patriarchy,* it struck me that each of the particular "sensitivities" I'd been observing in contemporary women could plausibly be traced not just to patriarchy in a general sense, but to specific stages—three in particular—in its development.

The Onset of Patriarchy: Commodifying Women's Sexuality

In precivilized society, Gerda Lerner believes, women would likely have felt themselves to be at least the equal of men. If Neolithic women's lives resembled those of women living in gatherer-hunter cultures that can still be observed today, as anthropologists and archaeologists are inclined to believe, the foraging that they did, along with the children, provided between 60 and 80 percent, by weight, of what was actually eaten. Men would on occasion have pitched in, but would probably have spent most of their time hunting instead, for honey as well as wild game—quests that would have taken them farther afield than women could have managed who were carrying infants or accompanied by small children.

Contemporary anthropologists, an increasing number of whom are women, have refuted much of what was reported about these cultures generations ago. The term "gatherer-hunter," for example, is typically used now in place of the earlier term "hunter-gatherer," to emphasize that foragers supply more than half the food. It appears now that while division of labor along gender lines is a reality among gatherer-hunters, this division isn't a life-or-death matter—all kinds of exceptions can be observed—and it isn't understood to mean that one gender is superior to the other. The pattern is, rather, one of cooperation and mutual respect. Fieldworkers living among the !Kung, for example, describe the manner in which women gathering tubers, nuts, and berries are also gathering "intelligence" for the hunters—tracks and other evidence they've seen of animals in the area. And in fact, as anyone who has actually learned to forage recognizes, gathering foodstuffs is hardly a matter of simply plucking ripe fruit. It requires specialized knowledge of the properties of plants for food and medicine. From year to year, conditions change— one has to know which plants to fall back on in lean years, plants that may not be tasty, but that will sustain life.[4]

Whatever "edge" the males in a gatherer-hunter culture would have had—the glamour of risk-taking, the glitter of weapons, the excitement in camp when a hunt has been successful—would have been offset by the group's awareness of the remarkable nature of female experience. The mysterious synchrony between women's menstrual cycle and the phases of the moon would have been recognized, along with women's capacity both to give birth and to feed their young afterward. As givers and sustainers of life, *earth* and *mother* were almost cognate, and their near identity in turn gave rise very naturally to the worship of maternal deities. One needn't go so far as to imagine actual matriarchy (and Lerner does not) to recognize that the position of women would have been relatively strong within cultures with female deities. "Women must have found their likeness in the goddess, as men found theirs in the male gods," Lerner writes. "There was a perceived and essential equality of human beings before the gods, which must have radiated out into daily life. The power and mystery of the priestess was as great as that of the priest. . . . "[5] The work of archaeologist Marija Gimbutas and historian Riane Eisler has certainly substantiated Lerner's speculations in this regard.

Eventually, the nomadic gatherer-hunter way of life yielded to horticulture and then to agriculture, and somewhere in the shadowy, little-known period that preceded agriculture, particularly as physical strength became more important—to push the plow, and clear the land—the position of women began to weaken, as did the partnership model itself. Anthropologists don't see this development as inevitable. Division of labor along gender lines is seen in every known human society, but that division doesn't normally imply the subordination of women until and unless "specific kinds of social stress" begin to affect the society. "The most crucial factor seems to be pressure on the environment, which leads to competition within the group or with neighboring groups for diminished resources."[6]

Did women resist? Did they see what was coming? Lerner speculates a kind of long slide, much like the one that took place during the Industrial Revolution. "Things developed in certain ways, which then had certain consequences which neither men nor women intended. . . . By the time consciousness of the process and of its consequences could develop, it was too late, at least for women, to halt the process."[7]

Once land could be cultivated, nomadic tribes or extended families that had been accustomed to ranging around a particular area, gathering as they went, settled down and claimed land: an idea that must have seemed very peculiar at first, as it did to the American Indians when Europeans first settled on this continent. Diets that had been extremely diversified narrowed dramatically. Grains and pulses became the staple foods; the encyclopedic knowledge of plant life and food preparation that women had inherited from their mothers would thus have had decreasing value in their new situation.

A woman's worth would have been measured now primarily in her capacity to bear children to work the land. Kinship structures, often matrilineal, gradually gave way to more hierarchical authority patterns: the "big man" who could organize a labor force became a power broker, and a labor force could double as an army, as it would have had to, because the very notion of private property implies a willingness to defend it against other claimants. When one military force conquered another, the victor would have had the option of enslaving the men he had overcome. Running a farm with captured men is always problematic, though. Violent insurrections could take place, and daring getaways. Women were found to be a much simpler proposition—particularly once they had been raped. Knowing that even if they managed to escape, their own menfolk would not welcome them back, they weren't likely to try, and once they'd actually had children, their own maternality kept them in place—not as consorts, but as slaves, who could be bought and sold, too, or merely traded. "Their sexual services were part of their labor and . . . their children were the property of their masters. *In every known society it was women of conquered tribes who were first enslaved, whereas men were killed.*" [8]

Anthropologists have dramatized the tremendous shift these events brought about for women by declaring that in the minds of those who bought and sold them, women were in effect reified (literally, made into a *thing*). They were commodities now, interchangeable with parcels of land and herds of sheep. Lerner emphasizes that it was not the women themselves who were reified, but their sexual and reproductive capacities. Nonetheless, as a result of the "exchange of women," women were in a crucial sense dehumanized, and that alteration in consciousness would prove fateful. [9]

And I have to say that just learning about that momentous shift made for a powerful alteration in my own consciousness. It was as if all my life I'd walked around aware of a *bad smell* coming from someplace—now faint, now strong—and suddenly I'd turned up its source. I'm talking about that curious contempt for girls and women that is so pervasive in male culture—so destructive to all of us, and so unnecessary. It seemed to me now that it had directly to do with the idea that the central business in life is to build up power bases—fiefdoms, forts, and strongholds—and then make your name either defending them or seizing other people's. Women weren't particularly good at combat, and in the emerging "heroic" culture, that capacity was the sole measure. Not only were they physically "soft," women were vulnerable through their emotions as well: what could be more contemptible than someone who would adapt to the ways of "the other" merely to protect an infant who was in fact one of "the other's"? Where was her pride and her will and her tribal identity—her recognition that others really are *others?* For that matter, and this was the darkest suspicion of all, emanating out of buried memories of a time when women had been credited with mysterious powers and visible sovereignty, *could a woman even be impregnated if she didn't (secretly, maybe) want to be?* Given the emergent values of early Western civilization, there was no answer to that question that would have enhanced the standing of women. The very complex of skills and dispositions for which women had been revered in earlier times, those that equipped them to give and sustain life, identified them now as passive, inert, and quite possibly amoral. Recent political discussions of pregnant teenagers and welfare mothers reveal how tenacious such attitudes are.

So much was suddenly clear to me. Patriarchy was not just a way of organizing society, it was also a set of assumptions about what constitutes a self, the first being that there isn't enough to go around. For one group of people to be fully "authorized," others have to be subordinate to them—"commodified" and "reified" in one way or another: controlled, or simply silenced. The tensions I'd been observing in women with regard to self-naughting and its counterfeit or shadow version, codependency, were abundantly understandable now. For codependency is obviously only the tip of an iceberg that has been amassing for about four thousand years. Taught for so long to think of themselves as less than fully human, women appear to have internalized forms of control that were once external, setting in motion exactly the sort of compulsions that define codependent behavior, the inability *not* to put the desires of others before one's own. It is as if women had assented to being cast forever in supporting roles: the servant or helpful friend of someone else who is the real protagonist. On cue, they hand the hero his sword or hold the heroine's dressing gown, and on cue—conveniently, noiselessly—they vanish. The codependent personality is arguably the final triumph of patriarchy.

And if women find it impossible to think straight today about desire, it's surely no wonder. If Gerda Lerner is correct in tracing women's subordination to the appropriation of their sexuality and reproductivity that took place when agriculture and the city-state began to emerge, then *re*appropriating sexuality may well be the first order of feminist business. Historically, the primary job of women has been to produce offspring—for the tribe, the state, even the church—and to take pleasure primarily in the finished product. The price of male protection and support has been absolute restraint of one's own sensual desire. "All our eroticisms," writes feminist scholar bell hooks, "have been shaped within the culture of domination."[10] Hooks was speaking of African-American women in particular, but certainly her words are relevant to all women. Our desires, that is, have been "scripted." In a thousand ways, often subliminally, we are told what to want. And perhaps the most powerful force in this scripting is one most women never see. Pornography doesn't enter many of our lives directly at all. But just out of sight, and everywhere, it sustains a narrative that is horrifyingly misogynist and imagery that is even more so. Catharine A. MacKinnon has had the courage to read that narrative and the even greater courage to state publicly and passionately what she thinks of it and what she believes it does to shape the lives of women and children. Her conclusions are searing:

> The content of pornography is one thing. There, women substantively desire dispossession and cruelty. We desperately want to be bound, battered, tortured, humiliated, and killed. Or, to be fair to the soft core, merely taken and used. . . . Subjection itself, with self-determination ecstatically relinquished, is the content of women's sexual desire and desirability. . . . What pornography *does* goes beyond its content: it eroticizes hierarchy, it sexualizes inequality. It makes dominance and submission into sex. Inequality is its central dynamic; the illusion of freedom coming together with the reality of force is central to its working.[11]

Pornography (the term itself comes from a Greek word meaning "female slave") is an eight-billion-dollar industry, which probably makes it the ultimate instance of woman's flesh commodified. Organized crime—"The Family"—reaps most of the profits.

Patriarchy's Second Phase: Women Are Divided and Ruled

When I entered Stanford University as a freshman, there was a dean of women—someone I'll call Dean Arlen—whose job, as she saw it, was to keep close watch over the sexual conduct of women students. It was all managed very quietly. Someone would simply disappear. Her room stood empty, the bed was stripped, and while some gossip channel might have revealed what had happened, most of us weren't tuned in to them. Dean

Arlen felt she had a special gift that fitted her uniquely for her work. "I can tell whether a girl is a virgin," she maintained, "by looking her in the eye."

When I left Stanford nearly four years later, Dean Arlen wasn't there anymore. She'd gotten the boot a month or two earlier—was, rather more probably "asked to tender her resignation." The story made the front page of the *San Francisco Chronicle*. The student judicial council, of which my spirited and exceedingly astute friend Caroline was a member, had found out about the elaborate system of spies that Dean Arlen had put in place throughout the women's dormitories (women were not permitted to live off-campus at the time), and the flagrantly unconstitutional manner by which she had seen that suspected transgressors were expelled. This was the spring of 1965, and given what our friends in Berkeley were up to, it seemed the very least we could do was to end the flagrant abuses of authority enshrined in the University's *in loco parentis* rules.

What I've come to realize now is that Dean Arlen wasn't really appointed by the university administration at all: she got her marching orders, rather, about three thousand years earlier, when the ruling class of Assyria enacted a piece of legislation that would shape profoundly the lives of all Western women.

Once city-states had been established, certainly by the second millennium B.C., commercial prostitution emerged as a social reality, deriving initially, it is surmised, from the enslavement of women through military conquest and also from the pauperization of farmers and their subsequent slide into "debt slavery": to meet their debts, they would sell their children or wives. With the emergence of prostitution, it became increasingly important that, in contrast, the sexual lives of women in the propertied classes be closely regulated, for regulated or "sanctioned" sexuality yielded its own kind of profit as reliably as prostitution: the virginity of a respectable daughter was a negotiable commodity, as it would continue to be for the next several thousand years.[12]

To distinguish visibly, therefore, between women who were sexually available and those who were not, Middle Assyrian Law #40 required that wives, daughters, and widows of "gentlemen" must wear veils in public. Prostitutes and slaves, on the other hand, must not, and if they did they would be punished severely, as would any man who failed to report a violation of the veiling law. In effect, the veil was an extension of the "enclosure" of a respectable woman's home. It signaled that, properly speaking, she wasn't really in a public space at all. It followed from this understanding that for her to speak in public (allowing, we assume, for a measure of marketplace bargaining) would have been a serious impropriety.

The commodification of women's sexuality and reproductivity laid the foundation of patriarchy. With MAL #40, the walls went up. Prior to its establishment, control over a woman's sexuality was in the hands of her father, her husband, or the head of her extended family or kin group—of her owner, of course, if she were a slave. From this time forward, though, the state came into the picture.[13]

Again, we have lived for so long with the assumptions behind this piece of legislation that it's hard to imagine a time when they might have seemed absurd. When, for example, a woman's sexual availability or unavailability might have been something she decided for herself. Or when women might have aligned easily and naturally with other women, supporting one another without fear of consequence. Because the crucial effect of MAL #40 was to draw an all-important line between one woman and another. With the commodification of their sexuality and reproductivity, women had been disconnected from their own desires and from a sense of their own human dignity. Now, with their enclosure and veiling, they were effectively separated from one another as well—pitted against one another, ultimately, for there have never been as many places open on the "right" side of that line as there were women who wanted to be there.[14]

The stakes have always been high. Throughout recorded Western history, the distinction between public and private space has been crucial, maintaining that women are truly safe only inside a male-regulated enclosure and that safety outside the household or compound or convent involves wearing certain kinds of clothing that cover us well and mark us—particularly our sexuality—as belonging to someone. There doesn't appear to have been much of a middle ground, ever. By drawing the sharp distinctions it did between "respectable" and "disreputable" women, MAL #40 and its million subsequent variants have forced women to mistrust one another and stand apart from one another, lest by mere association (with someone whose husband has abandoned her, for example, or died, or someone whose father or brother has sold her) we might imperil our own fragile standing and safety.

And how that line has persisted! It redraws itself in the life of every girl and woman, starting, for most of us, sometime during junior high school, when we realize that the very floor of the classroom seems to have tilted and turned slick and that there is a new possibility—a new danger—in everyday life. The tilt is the force of your own desire and the danger is that you might yield to it and by yielding to it slide across that crucial line and be identified from there on out as someone who—

But you know all the phrases. Every woman does.

And the sad thing is how ruthlessly we have applied them *to one another.* How assiduously we have policed that border ourselves, making sure there was always a line and that some-body was on the wrong side of it: "the slut." The tale telling and sly speculation have been endless, and it speaks badly for us. But I do think there may have been something behind it besides sheer malice and the desire to protect our own standing. If we got the goods on enough of us—on nearly *all* of us—then wasn't it possible we could just forget the whole line-drawing business and get on with life?

Because in fact something like that did seem to happen when the Dean Arlens got sent down in the sixties and seven-ties, and briefly, anyway, it felt great. Suddenly you could laugh out loud at things that had had to be whispered . . . and staying out overnight with your boyfriend didn't put you at risk of los-ing your scholarship (nothing ever happened to his) . . . and for the first time ever it didn't feel actively dangerous to reveal, even to your closest friends, that you'd had any sexual experience at all. *No more secrets,* we gloated to one another. The "line," we pretended, had been erased.

But of course it hadn't been erased at all, it had just moved over, and the women on the other side of it now are at risk of losing much more than a scholarship. In *Promiscuities: The Secret Struggle for Womanhood,* Naomi Wolf records a conversation with a friend who had spent some time in the sex industry. She asks the friend what she thinks about films that glamorize "the life," and the friend answers, deliberately and slowly,

> "When men think a woman is a whore, it's open . . . season . . . on her. They can *say* anything to her they want, they can *do* anything they want. . . . They don't have to afford the woman *one ounce* of respect for being a human being. She's not a human being. She's a thing. . . .

". . . I was shocked. I thought that because of the progress that women have made in our society men would have a *clue* that prostitutes are human beings and that they don't deserve to be treated so poorly, but they don't. It's almost as if now they see sex workers as the only women that they can be so aggressive and cruel to." [15]

MAL #40 separated women in one more crucial regard. Insofar as it implied that public spaces are really no place for respectable women, it banished them also from political and economic goings-on and therefore from any real say in how things are run. It is part of the historical record that certain women of the propertied classes in the ancient world held property and wielded influence. But a woman's standing depended entirely on her connection with a man. In exchange for subordinating herself entirely to a man of her own race and class, a woman gained the privilege of exploiting both men and women of other races and the lower class. But her position was always tenuous and probably always linked to her sexuality. In ancient Mesopotamia, as in Henry VIII's England, even a queen could be set aside when she no longer pleased or bore no heir.[16]

To know something of the development of patriarchy is to realize that *harem* is not as exotic or exceptional an arrangement as we've pretended. Sociologist Fatima Mernissi's reflections on the cultural attitudes that produced it catch and hold our attention now:

Strict space boundaries divide Muslim society into two sub-universes: the universe of men (the *umma,* the world of religion and power), and the universe of women, the domestic world of sexuality, and the family. The spatial division

according to sex reflects the division between those who
hold authority and those who do not, those who hold spiritual powers and those who do not.[17]

Within this order, she explains, men have what amounts to
dual citizenship, while women are citizens of only the domestic
universe. Outside that realm, their very existence is "an anomaly,
a transgression."

Why, we wonder, was such a division deemed necessary?
The expressed rationale for enclosing women in Arab cultures,
Mernissi explains, is *fitna,* which signifies, on the one hand,
merely "woman," particularly a beautiful woman, but, on the
other hand, "disorder," or "chaos." [18] A man keeps his woman indoors, or veiled, not merely to protect her, but to protect the
other men in his community from the threats her beauty might
pose to their self-control.

And if you can't keep them indoors, and none of them will
wear a veil, you can at least hire a dean of women who will nip
chaos and disorder in the bud. . . .

The Final Adjustments

The foundation was laid, the walls were thick and high. There
remained but the installation of latches and locks and bars at the
windows. . . .

The third crucial stage in the development of patriarchy had
to do with the ways women are seen and see themselves, particularly vis-à-vis the sacred. It's hard to say exactly when the assault
on women's connection with the sacred actually began: it was
implicit, certainly, in the very earliest moments of patriarchy. I
place it last because it took the longest to be made final. Women's
hold on their spiritual identity was incredibly tenacious.

Even while they were fully subjugated both economically and sexually, Gerda Lerner observes, the women of the ancient Near East retained for a long while their connection with "metaphysical female power," mediating between humans and gods as priestesses, healers, and seers. It took thousands of years to dethrone the powerful female goddesses and replace them with warrior gods who replicated the warrior-king heads of state. Hebrew monotheism first emerged as an attack on the cults of various fertility goddesses. With the book of Genesis, procreativity itself was ascribed to a male god, and female sexuality outside procreation was identified as sinful. The Covenant, whose seal is circumcision, marked irretrievably the devaluation of women and their exclusion from the holy community. "Their only access to God and to the holy community," Lerner observes, "is in their function as mothers." [19]

Furthermore, in order for the subordination of women to seem natural to everyone concerned, the central gender symbols of Western culture had to reflect the fundamental inequity of the male and female, and thanks to the Greeks as well as the Hebrews they do. Aristotle's depiction of the female as a botched version of the male caught on, and the Hebrews' penchant for representing all women in the figure of a fallen Eve rounded out the picture nicely, confirming the existence, Lerner observes, "of two kinds of human beings—the male and the female—different in their essence, their function, and their potential." [20] What had begun as metaphor would swiftly take on "the life and force of actuality."

The assumption of women's inferiority that emerged out of both Greek and Hebrew thought became the basis for women's exclusion from all institutions. Whatever degree of equality women might have enjoyed in preliterate society, moreover, was rapidly eroded as the written word became increasingly significant, for women were denied even the most rudimentary education: "the right to learn," Lerner emphasizes, "the right to teach, the right to define."

With this final stage, patriarchy penetrated into the very interior of women, eroding still further the sense of self that had already been badly damaged and silencing them in ways far more extreme than their mere banishment from public places could have done. For it isn't merely that women have been gagged and muffled all these millennia, though there have been plenty of explicit pressures in that direction. It is also that in the domain of patriarchy only one sort of voice has any legitimacy; only one counts as a real voice. Because women were not allowed into universities—indeed, rarely into primary or secondary schools until quite recently—we never learned the language that men learned there and that they would go on using in government, business, law, the military, and churches. Assigned by default a tongue that was essentially domestic, local, and vernacular, we might as well have been walking around speaking Icelandic.

For millennia, Lerner concludes, "women have participated in the process of their own subordination because they have been psychologically shaped so as to internalize the idea of their own inferiority." [21] It doesn't need to be policed, this extraordinary machine, for it has achieved the perfect balance between force and finesse. The ancient threats, of ears cut off and pitch poured on the head, of beatings and hangings and burnings, are never voiced because they do not have to be. Indeed, it became gradually apparent that once an individual is robbed of her own strength, threats of violence aren't necessary, and patriarchy has managed to do this by imposing three kinds of separation upon women:

- By commodifying women's sexuality and reproductivity, it separated them from their own desires and feelings.

- By erecting barriers of race and class, and making enclosure the mark of respectability, it separated women from one another.

- By dethroning the goddesses and demonizing the religious practices of women, it closed off the wellsprings of their own spirituality.

CHAPTER 8

Cracks in the Walls: Resisting Patriarchy

A young girl on the cusp of womanhood, still and self-contained as the amphorae in her mother's kitchens filled with olive oil and honey, brings her father his breakfast, as she does every morning. She cherishes this moment and the pride in his gaze when he looks up. Always he greets her with a single word—her name, just that—and always he touches her cheek briefly with his fingertips, and always she sinks down next to him to talk, and from the next room her mother hears them murmuring together and smiles.

But "always" stops one morning. He doesn't look up when she comes in, she cannot catch his gaze, and his hand does not lift to her cheek. He remains silent, and finally she leaves the room, benumbed by the weight of what she fears.

Human beings crave etiological myths. We love to imagine a pivotal moment somewhere back in time that accounts for the present condition of things. Western religions ask us to believe in a primordial fall from grace—a peculiar narrative, sketchily told, of a woman who was curious and a serpent who egged her on and a husband who said "they made me do it." I've never *gotten* that story. It has never moved me. But if the crucial turning point in human history is the one that Lerner postulates, a very different rendering of the fall suggests itself. I've outlined the changeover in question in the broadest historical terms and noted that it happened gradually, over millennia. But what I realized now was that it could only have come about after a certain crucial adjustment had taken place within the structure of virtually every family. Before a man could look at his daughter or wife and see in her *above all else* the opportunity to acquire an adjoining field or a herd of goats, he had to have performed a kind of surgery on himself. The wordless tableau I've just described had to have been enacted a million times over. The first few times it happened, it must have felt unspeakable, but in time it was banality itself.

How did she feel, I wondered now, and what were her thoughts—the first girl who found herself turned into currency? History has kept the door slammed shut on that question. It's needed to, because patriarchy has required of women that they not have feelings that matter. We all know the story of Midas and his grief, but we don't even know the name of the daughter his greed turned to gold. And yet, thanks to the storytellers among us and their grasp of the truly timeless, we can reconstruct something of their experience. Because the sexuality of women is still commodified, though, the betrayal of the girl-child by her elders is still enacted, and today, because women who write and make films think it matters, her side of the story is being told, and because it is, we can begin to imagine what it must have felt like that first time, too.

In Isabel Allende's *The House of the Spirits,* for instance, the prostitute Transito plies her trade with every appearance of enthusiasm. "She was indefatigable and never complained. It was as if she had the Tibetan gift of placing her skinny adolescent frame in her client's hands and transporting her soul to some distant place." Transito, whose very name means "she who has crossed over," split herself intentionally as a survival strategy. Similarly, in the film *A Thousand Pieces of Gold* (adapted from Ruthanne Lum McCunn's book of the same name), a girl who has been sold by her father in China to a man who was supposedly bringing her to a husband arrives in San Francisco and is ordered to strip off her clothing so that potential buyers can see her. "Let your mind take flight, Lalu," whispers her friend. "Then nothing anyone says can hurt you."[1]

To remove oneself mentally from the site of affliction has always been the strategy of the oppressed. It is the way people endure hunger, grief, humiliation, even an hour in the dentist's chair, and thank heaven we can do it. But when it becomes habitual, psychologists call it dissociation, and they don't have much good to say for it, because it threatens the very integrity of self.

The protagonist of *Breath, Eyes, Memory,* by Haitian writer Edwidge Danticat, has been sexually traumatized as a young girl by her mother, who insists upon "testing" her each night with her little finger to determine whether the girl is still a virgin: if she has lost her virginity it will be impossible to get her a husband. The memory of being tested is so vivid and painful that years later, when Sophie has married a man of her own choice, with whom she is very much in love, she is unable to make love with him. She endures it, rather, by "doubling."

> I had learned to *double* while being *tested.* I would close my
> eyes and imagine all the pleasant things that I had known.
> The lukewarm noon breeze through our bougainvillea.
> Tante Atie's gentle voice blowing over a field of daffodils.[2]

The marriage, of course, begins to disintegrate, and Sophie struggles to fathom how it is that her mother could have done this to her—for the love she bore her daughter is plainly visible. Obliquely, Danticat has Sophie answer her own question:

> There were many cases in our history where our ancestors had *doubled*. Following in the *vaudou* tradition, most of our presidents were actually one body split in two: part flesh and part shadow. That was the only way they could murder and rape so many people and still go home to play with their children and make love to their wives.[3]

Once we begin to "double," in other words, we can become stony inside—as unfeeling of the pain of others as we are of our own. In *Warrior Marks,* Alice Walker reflects, in much the same spirit, on the anger of women who have been genitally mutilated.

> I think now about what that means in a woman's relationship to her child. Does it mean she's often abrupt, cold, withholding, abusive? Or simply that she never smiles, which might be the greatest abuse of all?[4]

Dissociation from one's own feelings and desires, in other words, *becomes* disconnection from others, a process that is among the primary focal points of feminist psychology. Traumatized by disconnection, we distance ourselves from the pain through dissociation; alienated from our own feelings, we become all the more incapable of forming authentic connection.

To have put every second human being born under a powerful anesthetic, persuading her by a host of stratagems that she is only partial—contingent, expendable—is so very wrong, so *vastly* wrong, that something in us understands it really could not have gone unquestioned forever, any more than slavery could have. One understands the persistence, now, in our fairytales and myths, of princesses frozen or put to sleep, held under glass, locked up in towers, their life functions brought down to as low a pitch as they could be without their dying altogether.

Understanding the history of patriarchy sheds a great deal of light on how we came to this pass. It reminds us, too, though, that the dissociation and the disconnection afflicting women today are system wide. Men who live out patriarchal scripts are just as disconnected from others as are women and at least as distanced from their own feelings. The story of King Midas would seem to be emotionally accurate, leaving him, as it does, in a terrible solitude and his daughter simply *stopped*—frozen by his touch.

Once I had come to understand how this process of massive disconnection had taken place—how pointed the various exclusions were, and how thorough—I saw, too, that for effective resistance to take place, something would have to have happened to reconnect women at each of those three vital points: with themselves and their desires, with other women, and with the sacred.

The Rise of Feminist Consciousness

During the Middle Ages and afterward the great women mystics of the European tradition made some astonishing discoveries.

Enclosed with one another, and unencumbered by husband or children, they found a scope for their energies and a freedom of expression women enjoyed nowhere else in the "civilized" world. They lived longer than their married sisters and developed their native talents fully, becoming artists, musicians, poets, scholars, playwrights, healers, and teachers. Freed from the clerical and pastoral responsibilities they'd have had if they'd been allowed to be priests, many gave themselves over entirely to contemplative prayer and discovered the mysterious beauties of *silence* that is freely chosen. In the depths of that silence they found voice, and the courage to speak—in prophecy or ringing calls for reform of church and state.

Turning their back on *self,* moreover, as patriarchy conceived it (that odd amalgam of separation and acquisition), they strove instead to see and serve Christ in themselves and in everyone around them. Mysticism represented for many of them, in Gerda Lerner's phrasing, "an alternative mode of thought to patriarchal thinking." Barred from schools and universities where they might have absorbed the elaborate structures and innumerable categories of scholastic theology, women mystics transcended the "othering" that is endemic to patriarchy and instead "saw human beings, the world and the universe in a state of relatedness, open to understanding by intuitive and immediate perception." [5]

And the fuel that powered the entire enterprise was *desire* itself, ordinary human desire, rescripted into something quite beyond ordinary human recognition.

For a long while before there was anything you could accurately call feminism, Gerda Lerner reminds us again and again, there were women who resisted patriarchy. The rise of what she calls feminist consciousness can be discerned long before an actual movement came into being. It was in fact this phenomenon, and not the history of patriarchy, that she set out to research in the first place. Specifically, she wanted to understand why feminist consciousness had developed so slowly. She was reasonably certain it had to do with the relationship of women to history—the fact that, as we've already observed, women *lived* history and *made* history but had no hand in recording it and are therefore pretty much written out of it. But before she could talk sensibly about women's relationship to recorded history, she realized she needed to look at the prehistoric process by which they'd been subordinated in the first place. In so doing, she arrived at a conclusion that astonished her . . . and that couldn't have been more compatible with conclusions I'd reached, coming at things from another direction.

"The most important thing I learned," she writes, "was the significance to women of their relationship to the Divine and the profound impact the severing of that relationship had on the history of women."

Lerner knew about the tremendous efforts Jewish and Christian women made for more than a thousand years to establish a connection with the divine—knew about the extensive feminist Bible criticism women had carried out and the various forms of religious revisioning. But it was only after she had come to see how systematically the goddesses of ancient Near Eastern cultures had been discredited by the architects of patriarchy that she saw the real significance of their struggle. "The insight that religion was the primary arena on which women fought for hundreds of years for feminist consciousness was not one I had previously had. . . . I listened to the voices of forgotten women and accepted what they told me." [6]

It's the oldest feminist trick in the book: she *listened* . . . and in the process she grasped for the first time the immense significance of what she was hearing—that, willy-nilly, regardless of the pressures women were under to be silent and submissive, they had regularly asserted the validity of their own experience, daring to speak of their direct relationship to the divine and of the feminine elements they had encountered there. Women like Julian of Norwich, Teresa of Avila, Clare of Assisi, and thousands of others had claimed "the right to define the Divine and with it the right to define their own humanity."[7] It's easy to look at them after the fact and say, Oh, well, they were exceptional— and of course they were, but so, I believe, were the circumstances within which they emerged. That they were able to experience silence, self-naughting, restraint of desire, and enclosure in the very positive ways they did had everything to do with certain aspects of women's position within the Christian Church. We need to look at those.

"If Indeed You Can Say 'a Woman'. . ."

The Jesus movement swept across the Mediterranean world in the first century after Christ's death, and in its initial phase it was neither hierarchical nor sexist. Although the institutional church came subsequently to mirror in many ways the Roman state that adopted it, the record of Jesus' actual life and teachings has allowed individual Christians to challenge regularly the idea that men were born to rule, and women to serve.

Women accompanied Jesus in his travels; they were part of his innermost circle. "In a time when a respectable sage was not even to converse with a woman outside of his family," says Bible scholar Marcus Borg, "and when women were viewed as both dangerous and inferior, the practice of Jesus was startling."[8] During its earliest years, the emerging church sustained this spirit. The apostle Paul was taking a politically radical position when he said, "There is neither Jew nor Greek, there is neither bond nor free, there is neither male nor female: for ye are all one in Christ Jesus" (Galatians 3:28, KJV). By canceling out the fundamental distinctions on which social institutions of his time rested, he was implicitly challenging the legitimacy of racism and imperialism as well as of sexism. Obviously, Paul was ambivalent where women were concerned—his strictures against women speaking in church are well known—but in fact he recognized women as leaders in the earliest Christian congregations, mentioning many of them by name, and warmly, in his letters.

Before long, of course, the cultural attitudes of the Mediterranean world overcame the radicalism of the early church. Historian Karen Jo Torjesen describes the gradual exclusion of women from positions of authority in the church as Christianity itself evolved from a persecuted underground movement to the official religion of the Roman state, and she relates that shift to the evolution of church architecture. Centered originally in the homes of its members, Christian worship was by the fourth century held in immense buildings patterned after those where Roman emperors and governors presided over public ceremonies. The Christian basilica had become the "throne room" of God, and "architectural space clearly defined Christian worship as public." [9] Public and, therefore, by the logic of patriarchy, off-limits for women unless veiled and silent.

(In fact, I believe one could plausibly argue that when the emperor Constantine made Christianity the official religion of the Roman Empire, Christian spirituality was commodified and enclosed by the state much as women's sexuality had been several thousand years earlier . . . a kind of leveraged buyout that resulted in a relationship much like the "paternalistic dominance" Lerner says women have experienced "in which the dominance is mitigated by mutual obligations and reciprocal rights." The parallels intrigue me, because they reinforce my hunch that spirituality and feminine sovereignty are both inherently subversive to patriarchy and have regularly, therefore, to be "dealt with" severely in order for patriarchy to retain its hold.)

Belief in the inferiority of women ran so deep by this time that church authorities really couldn't take in the possibility that women might embrace Christianity in a meaningful way. Historian Margaret Miles explains:

> For men, as for women, the development of a religious self required choice. Moreover, that initial choice had to be followed by active, vigorous pursuit of the new identity and membership in the new community. The models for such choice, in the social, intellectual, and religious world of the Roman Empire, were male. For women, then, courage, conscious choice, and self-possession constituted gender transgression.[10]

Since the very notion of feminine subjectivity—of self-possession—was a logical impossibility in the formative years of Christianity, women who did emerge as subjects were considered to have transcended the limitations of their gender and even "become man." Saint Macrina was such a woman, and Miles calls our attention to the way the church father Gregory of Nyssa wrote about her: "It was a woman who was the subject of our discourse, if indeed you can say 'a woman,' for I do not know if it is appropriate to call her by a name taken from nature when she surpassed that nature." [11]

While Macrina's biographer expresses all due reverence, one detects something else in his language as well—an ambivalence bordering on uneasiness. A woman who is "more than woman" is what, after all? She *cannot* really have become man. She must therefore be . . . well, *what?*

One can probably draw a direct line from the baffled male assessment of the first women saints all the way down to the anxiety that grips many women today when they undertake a serious, disciplined spiritual practice ("How can I make meditation my first priority? I already have a husband and four other first priorities right here in my house!"). However enthusiastically a woman like Macrina might have been received as an exemplar of the Christian faith, as a *woman* she would have been seen as a prodigy: a freak of nature.[12]

The Gospels themselves, on the other hand, had made it indisputably clear that Jesus himself loved women and took them seriously as spiritual aspirants, and if there had been any lingering doubt as to their suitedness for full membership in the church, the accounts of the early Christian martyrs would certainly have dispelled it. The names of women like Saints Ursula, Catherine, Barbara, Agnes, and Marcella were synonymous with the most extraordinary courage and resolution. Indeed, the story of Saint Perpetua, who died in the Colosseum rather than renounce her faith, is particularly pointed, because she was the mother of an infant son. In a journal she kept until her death, she speaks of how painfully engorged her breasts were until they brought the baby to her in prison. In other words, not even maternality itself, which patriarchy had always relied upon to keep women in line, could prevent her from acting on her conscience. Either that, or her concept of maternality had gone way beyond patriarchy's ken.

The fact that the Gospels and the stories of martyrs were accessible to Christian women meant that for them history was not womanless at all. They had role models. A young nun could take the name of Ursula, and a mother could name her daughter Catherine, and attached to those names were stories that would make your hair stand on end. In the Christian community, female heroism was an undisputed reality.

Having barred women from active roles in the congregational life of the church, therefore, the church nonetheless did have to provide for women who knew they had religious callings and the right to pursue them. Reluctantly, one concludes—

for there were rarely as many convents as were needed, and they were open for the most part only to the daughters of wealthy men, who could provide dowries—the church did make such a provision.

It was a fateful step. By providing even minimal facilities for even a few women to follow their callings, the church created conditions that actually allowed them to experience life outside patriarchy. As "brides of Christ"—the only identity that would have been acceptable in cultures where women had to belong to *somebody*—they were freed from the authority of fathers, brothers, husbands, and sons. Male clerics tried to fill the vacuum, but they were regularly rebuffed. Teresa of Avila insisted on the right of nuns to change confessors, and Clare of Assisi was unyielding in her refusal to accept any Rule for her order but the one she herself had drawn up. Mechthild of Magdeburg railed regularly and colorfully against corrupt clerics, and Catherine of Siena called the pope himself onto the carpet.

The irony is breathtaking. It's as if a secret recipe for empowering women had been kicking around from the beginnings of time, and the ingredients for it had gotten tossed together now completely by accident. For women to have had (1) explicit recognition of their full human dignity, (2) charismatic role models, and (3) the chance to build supportive networks and communities with one another was probably without precedent in Western history. In the atmosphere that resulted, suffused as it was with devotion and the spirit of prayer, women made astonishing discoveries. Convents were hospitals, schools, scriptoriums, centers for art and scholarship . . . sometimes, we're told, they were brothels. But over and over, they proved also to be places where women could become fully self-realized. These women didn't take on patriarchal institutions directly—they apparently were not even thinking about patriarchy. But in the course of their unfolding they shed almost effortlessly the "internalized sense of their own inferiority" that has sustained patriarchy down through time.

God lived *within* them. Julian of Norwich understood that. Christ was a king-emperor like his father, but his throne room was not some vast public hall built to intimidate, it was her own soul. "He sits erect there in the soul, in peace and rest, and he rules and guards heaven and earth and everything that is." Catherine of Genoa exulted in the discovery that "My *me* is God!" Women who knew what they knew, and had experienced what they had, simply could not be intimidated. They had acquired an immunity.

Over and over again, the drama is played out: the daughter of a powerful man slips out of his house at midnight to join a ragged crew of mendicant friars, or she cuts off her hair or rejoices at contracting smallpox, believing that pockmarks will render her unmarriageable. The father rages, the brothers fume, but the girl is adamant. The family priest might be shaking in his boots, but he knows where duty lies, and he supports her. She has made a decision, and her right to make that decision has been honored, and that is little short of revolutionary. She has experienced what it *is* to choose, and that is heady stuff.

Or maybe she doesn't even have to go to all that trouble. Her parents might have handed her over to God when she was just eight years old as a "tithe" (something that apparently happened rather a lot to tenth children), as Hildegard of Bingen's parents did, packing the little girl off to a holy woman, an anchoress named Jutta, who taught her Latin and the Benedictine Rule. Hildegard was a brilliant student, and the rest is . . . *women's* history.

Women religious were able to transcend patriarchy, I saw, because they knew themselves to be the subjects of their own biographies after all—individuals who could make meaningful choices and live by them, braving if necessary the stigma attached to women who made their own decisions—and also because convent life allowed them to form female cultures and communities. It was for sound strategic reason that patriarchy had erected so many barriers between women. Indeed, remarking the transformative potential of all-women communities even when they are not voluntary, Alev Croutier says of the *harem* that in certain ways it was "matriarchy incubating in patriarchy." [13]

This is not to idealize convent life: intrigue can flourish in the cloister, competition and cliques can be rife there, just as they can be in a harem. But the female communities that evolved in convents were also places where, quite unexpectedly, something could unfold safely that hadn't been seen for several thousand years, and when it did, it was like certain wildflowers not seen for years that suddenly take over a hillside and fill the breeze with their fragrance. Once Clare of Assisi was set up in quarters smaller than we can comprehend, sisters, cousins, friends, and eventually her own mother flocked to join her. She was to them exactly what the martyrs of the early church had been for other Christian women—living proof that women could be heroically decisive. Only she was *one of them*. One can imagine them telling one another over and again, proudly, the story of her fearlessness:

And there she was, barely eighteen, and her uncles rode their horses right into the convent, and she ran to the altar and pulled off her veil and wrapped herself in the altar cloth, and when they saw that her head was shaved they knew there was nothing they could do. Absolutely nothing!

Breaking the Hold

Thinking now about the women I'd met in workshops and of the unease so many of them displayed regarding spiritual disciplines, I wondered whether the secret of overcoming that unease perhaps lay someplace in the stories of women like Clare, Hildegard, and Teresa and their followers. It seemed to me that before contemporary women can give themselves over unreservedly to structured, systematic spiritual practices, they, too, must be able to see themselves as subjects of their own narratives—as capable of "courage, conscious choice, and self-possession." And it also seemed to me that we have just as much need as women living in the Middle Ages did to begin rebuilding the connections that patriarchy has shattered. We are easily as alienated as they were from our own feelings, from other women, and from the sacred.

I will say something here that is painful to recall. It has to do with my teacher and what it was like watching him discover how erroneous certain of his assumptions about Western women had been. Coming from a third world country, he saw us as enormously privileged, and said so. Wealthy by Indian standards, free to be university educated and have rewarding careers, possessed of voting rights and, more than that, good health, American women appeared nonetheless to be paralyzed: Why didn't they raise their voices, collectively, against injustice, greed, racism, and violence? Gradually—and I believe it had something to do with his watching a great many American movies and coming to understand something of the constructs of woman that permeate the media—he stopped asking.

His silence was painful to me, because I thought it meant he'd "given up" on us. Later, as I've mentioned, I would conclude instead that the "problem" of Western women could really be solved only by Western women, and that he knew it.

I'm not at all sure, though, that he would agree with my own reading of the situation—that women in this country are as profoundly undercut, as social and political beings, as Indians were under colonial rule and that their sense of self is as impaired. Gandhi understood that until Indians began to believe in themselves, both individually and as a people, they could not throw off British rule, and that even if by some fluke they did— if, for example, the British decided they didn't want to be colonists anymore and simply walked away—Indians would still be effectively colonized. To my mind, the position of Western women was—and is—comparable.

As I struggled to put this together, I was finding it increasingly difficult go on honoring the distinctions that are generally made between women's social and political emancipation, on the one hand, and their spiritual unfolding, on the other. It was becoming more and more evident to me that feminism and spirituality may actually *require* each other.

Water from a Deep, Deep Well

Paradoxically, feminism is currently performing for contemporary women many of the same functions Christianity did, quite inadvertently, for medieval women. It insists upon women's right and capacity to choose, it celebrates the acts of courageous, decisive women, and it fosters feminine community. Feminism, however, is not trying in any concerted or public way to reconnect women with the sacred, and for sound historical reasons. Religion as most of us know it is stunningly misogynist, on the one hand, and immensely divisive, on the other, and, as we've seen, even outside the context of formal religion systematic and structured spiritual disciplines can look, to women who are just breaking out of patriarchy, very much like "the enemy"—the enemy's excessive needs for control, its dualistic modes of thought, and its harshness toward "the flesh."

Insofar as feminism is strengthening women's belief in themselves and their capacity to be decisive, and insofar as it supports feminine community, it is certainly moving the cause of women's emancipation along. But so *slowly,* and unevenly. Feminism has remained, in the public eye, a movement that protests . . . that reacts . . . that is characterized at any given moment in terms of the latest media-orchestrated controversy. Feminists do have their own clear, positive, and compelling visions of the movement and its goals, but these separate visions haven't coalesced into a foundation for far-sighted and effective reform politics.

Certainly nothing in our own culture points us as powerfully in any one direction as religiosity itself did in the lives of women living in medieval and counterreformation Europe. When they were able to live out *in community* the positive messages about womanhood that their own tradition offered them, it was almost inevitable that many of them would take to contemplative prayer (in silence, enclosed, supported by ancillary disciplines that reduce self-will and indulgence in sensual pleasures). When they did, and when they had entered the deepest parts of themselves, the results were incredible: tremendous energy, creativity, stamina, resourcefulness, *ease,* wit, patience—and lovingkindness by the bucketful.

As a student of these lives, I knew very well what kind of impact these women had had on the communities and regions where they'd lived, and I wanted all of that for contemporary feminists—for the movement itself. And now that I had absorbed from Gerda Lerner some sense of how crucial the severance of women's connection with the sacred had been to their subordination, that desire seemed absolutely well founded. There had to be ways that feminism could open out to the sacred without compromising itself; there had to be forms of spirituality uncontaminated by patriarchy.

And clearly there were. Through contemplative prayer, the women mystics I'd so long admired appeared to have found their way to a stratum in consciousness where the prepatriarchal world still exists. Each time one of them completed her journey and returned to ordinary life, she exhibited all the qualities we associate with that world: inclusiveness, playfulness, affinity for nature, reverence for maternality. When we come upon such a woman unprepared, it can be like finding a chunk of lost Atlantis. In Julian of Norwich, the sharp divisions between things that characterize patriarchal thinking are nowhere to be seen. Everything *flows*—blood from the head of Christ crucified, the "bountiful waters" of God's grace, the blue and ample robes of the Lord seated before his servant—and everything is connected. The biographers of Saint Clare of Assisi employ phrases (quite unintentionally, we can be sure) that invoke a time when *mother, earth,* and *goddess* were all but indistinguishable. "Seeds of salvation" they called the women who were attracted to her—seeds that she herself brought to fruit, while Clare herself was seen as "a stream of heavenly blessings" too full to stay within its banks. Saint Teresa, who danced and sang with her nuns and even played a tambourine, fussed over marriage opportunities for a niece and found a place in one of her convents for the illegitimate daughter of a priest who was a good friend of hers. When she heard that one of her abbesses was ill, she sent marmalade she'd made herself from Seville oranges. She was utterly practical, immensely nurturant, and worldly wise, and none of this seemed to her to be at odds with a contemplative practice that presumed tremendous mastery over impulse.

In my heart of hearts, I've long suspected that Clare, Teresa, and the like would have had little patience with a great deal of what passes today for "feminine spirituality." And yet the atmosphere around them was clearly permeated with exactly that sense or spirit of the sacred feminine that women today are trying to reclaim when we join a drumming circle or walk labyrinths or create our own images of the Goddess out of clay or watercolor or silk thread or movements in a dance. Even if a mystic has had no prior inkling of the sacred feminine, it appears that when she enters the depths of her own being the missing half of human experience floods her awareness and permeates everything she says and does afterward, and because the feminine face of God is made visible through her, other women see new reason to believe in themselves. And when they do, enclosure, silence, and the like no longer feel like preambles to extinction but preconditions for reclaiming their own wholeness. Nowhere is there evidence that the followers of women like Clare, Teresa, or Hildegarde can achieve what their mentors did without having submitted themselves to the same disciplines, which are systematic, arduous, utterly interior. But they do seem to get a real jump start by sheer proximity with those splendidly human and beguilingly idiosyncratic exemplars.

So what is to become of *us,* who live in a time and place that has no particular love of saints or sanctity, not a great many living saints to rub up against, and only the haziest sense of the sacred itself? Is all of that vitality and brightness to remain forever out of reach, as if we'd lost the claim check in a fire?

On a farm down the road from the one where I lived as a child was a pump in the backyard that had to be operated by hand. Next to it sat a bucket of water, and if you forgot to leave the bucket full, my girlfriend told me, your name was mud, because if the well hadn't been used for a little while a hard, dry cap could form above the water source and you had to pour some water down the wellshaft to get the flow started again. This is called priming the pump, and I think it might be that way with this other sort of wellspring, too. Once everything's flowing it can flow all day, but if it's dried up and there's nothing on hand with which to start it again, you're in real trouble.

Fortunately, knowledge of the sacred feminine has never been completely eradicated. Like rainwater caught in granite formations up in the mountains, like airborne wild yeast for sourdough starter, it's there, and when thirst and hunger press hard enough, women have found their way to it. I'd like to look now at the relationship between the historic resistance to patriarchy that Lerner calls "the rise of feminist consciousness" and certain elements of prepatriarchal spirituality that have proven blessedly indestructible. Since most of us don't live next-door to a Teresa, a Clare, or a Julian, it's fortunate we don't have to rely on osmosis alone for access to the sacred feminine. Drawing from a great many places, little by little, women are putting together a portrait of the sacred feminine that is so persuasive and so beautiful that we begin to see ourselves, and our own capacities, in a dramatically different light.

It is time to talk much more explicitly about what actually comprises the sacred feminine and what the conduits are through which it is making itself felt today. I have found it thrilling to move gradually past my initial impressions and to discover at last that within this complex of values and motifs one in particular provided the very concrete links I'd been looking for between feminism and spirituality.

CHAPTER 9

The House Made of Dawn: Reinhabiting the Sacred Feminine

"A century ago," writes art historian Mary B. Kelly, "one could still quietly enter the low carved door of a Ukrainian village home and find there a treasure of soft light and warm color. The flickering lamp or candle in the 'beautiful corner' would attract attention first."[1] On a shelf draped with soft white linen cloths the woman of the house displayed ikons, family mementos, and flowers. The cloths were typically of her own weaving; on the ends she had embroidered bright red designs. "The splendor of the color, the soft glow, and the evocative aura of the objects left one with no doubt that this was indeed the most beautiful place in the house."

Several of us were in the garden one Sunday morning, transplanting chard and lettuce seedlings, and I was carrying on about the archaeological evidence for prehistoric Goddess worship and about how tragic it is that we have no direct connection with that tradition now, when I noticed my friend Helen, who hadn't said a word, looking decidedly pleased with herself.

"I have something for you," she said, but wouldn't tell me what. Helen is one of life's more gifted magpies: someone who picks up all kinds of things at thrift shops or flea markets even if she has no immediate use for them because she *sees the possibilities*. That means she's never caught short by anybody's birthday, and if she sees you dressed to go out, she'll tilt her head to one side thoughtfully and then disappear, returning with a brooch, a scarf, a belt, or a bracelet that transforms make-do into ensemble in one stroke. Since I'm of the opposite inclination, always throwing things away and wishing later I hadn't, our friendship has always worked out well for me.

So I really didn't know what to expect. That afternoon she slipped me an issue of a needlework magazine from nearly ten years earlier, one of a stack she'd found at a Friends of the Library book sale. It was opened out to historian Kelly's article on goddess cloths, and I learned that I'd been wrong in assuming nothing of that mysterious tradition had survived into the present.

In their "beautiful corners," Ukrainian women contrived to sustain down through time a connection with the sacred feminine that their ancestors had established more than five thousand years earlier. They embroidered favorite images on their household linens—not only on cloths under the ikons but also on curtains and bed hangings, shirtsleeves and hems, and, most significantly, on the six-foot-long "ritual cloths" that a woman used repeatedly during her life. During her wedding ceremony, one of these would be used to bind her husband to her. In childbirth, it was hung from the beam overhead for her to pull on during labor, and later it would swaddle her baby. When she died, her coffin would be lowered into the earth with these cloths, and each spring one of them would be tied to her grave markers in her memory.

The favored motifs were three: the sun, the tree of life, and the Mother Goddess, who bears a close resemblance to Neolithic goddess statues archaeologists have found in the same area. Everything that grows was under the Goddess's protection: fields, crops, livestock, and family. She was represented differently to reflect her various roles. In spring she held birds and sun disks; in the fall she presided over the harvest. Sometimes she was depicted giving birth, and sometimes her daughter accompanied her, riding on a large bird. Sometimes she is shown dancing. She has "familiars"—peacocks and smaller birds, but lions, too; she is on horseback at times, and at others she wears antlers (some women were believed to be able to attract deer to hunters). On borders produced for spring festivals her image alternates with that of the tree of life, and the two resemble each other closely, leafy branches bursting out of both of them in a way that conveys exuberant fertility. Each repetition of a particular image was believed to double its protective power. The wooden chest full of linens that a woman inherited from her mother and grandmother was thus understood to represent a cache of stored-away feminine power.

Paganism was outlawed in Russia in the eleventh century, but the display of goddess cloths nearly a thousand years later makes it clear that Ukrainian women never stopped looking to the Mother for assistance in everything having to do with sustaining life. One design in particular establishes the connection beyond any question. It is the fertile field symbol, a crossed square with a stylized seed in each quadrant. Visible as a kind of apron on the embroidered goddess figures, particularly in wedding and engagement textiles, the design was also impressed on the stomach of Neolithic goddess figures, a symbol of pregnancy and fertility. The design reflected an agricultural ritual that was carried out each spring as recently as the nineteenth century: after the fields were plowed across the center, they were recrossed from opposite sides and a seed was placed in each section.

Today, women have reason to be wary of the equation between woman and the earth that this sort of symbolism implies. In *The Death of Natures,* for example, historian Carolyn Merchant has described the crucial shift in thinking about nature that took place during the Scientific Revolution and pointed out the misogynist imagery with which it was rationalized.[2] But in the persistence of the cherished fertile field motif, and its association with the Goddess, one can glimpse something of the religious awe that the connection between woman and the earth must have evoked when both were seen as sacred.

The beautiful corner of Ukrainian women celebrates all the values of the sacred feminine, but more than that it reminds us how those values have always been transmitted—hidden away in the domestic interstices of life, encoded in symbols so familiar most people have forgotten their meaning.[3] Knowledge of the sacred feminine is a latency; a set of possibilities; a few seeds tied up in a pocket handkerchief and carried across mountains; a banked fire. What is remarkable is how deeply the seed-memory can be buried, and how indirectly sustained, without ever losing its potency.

In all kinds of ways, contemporary women are trying to secure for themselves something of what the beautiful corner provided. The friend who told me about goddess cloths is knitting a tree of life design into a sweater for her niece; another is planting an herb garden. Still another is hanging a picture of Black Madonna, while one more is poring over archaeological texts and flight schedules and wondering whether travelers to Crete can still see the island's ancient frescoes that depict no warriors and no conquering rulers but rather "multicolored partridges, whimsical griffins, and elegant women:"[4] We are improvising.

Cultural orphans, for the most part, barely connected to a living ethnic tradition, we are assiduous in our efforts, and as we gather our fragments, we're beginning to glimpse wholeness—an entire orientation toward life so different from what we've known that we can hardly take it in. And while in the Middle Ages it was primarily the mystic who bore witness to the power of the sacred feminine (men like Francis of Assisi and Bernard of Clairvaux no less than women like Clare and Julian), it is more typically the artist, particularly the literary artist, who is perform-ing that function in today's overwhelmingly secular atmosphere. To construct the usable past that women require, in other words, the resources of mainstream history are not nearly adequate. They reveal only the outermost look of things—the apparent se-quence of events, the names of those declared "winners."

"Or, Failing That, Invent"

"There was a time," writes French novelist Monique Wittig,

> when you were not a slave. Remember that. You walked alone, full of laughter, you bathed bare-bellied. . . . You say there are no words to describe this time, you say it does not exist. But remember. Make an effort to remember. Or, fail-ing that, invent.[5]

For anything like a revolution to take place, it must be imag-ined first. Before we can mobilize the energy to move toward a better world, we must have begun to envision it. A reform movement is continually fed by those who are good at writing songs and telling us a new kind of story and teaching us to be-lieve in ourselves.

As the silenced literary voice of half the human race emerges, we find that one of its central concerns is the generation of what I think of as countertexts: myths, folktales, and fairy stories that in one way or another correct the damaging ones patriarchy tells. Some are invented, but many don't have to be. They've been there all along, preserved, often, because nobody knew what they meant. We can find myths and stories, and we can find, too, the symbols around which the stories revolve—powerful feminine symbols that predate the swords and hammers and staffs and lightning rods that supplanted them: chalices, cauldrons, and vases holding and preserving the elixir of life . . . beehives, serpents, labyrinths, roses, and double axes "shaped like the hoe axes used to clear land for the planting of crops . . . a stylization of the butterfly, one of the Goddess's symbols of transformation and rebirth." [6]

The Arthurian legend, for example, which culminates in the quest for the Holy Grail, is rich with material that might have suggested, at any point in time, a reading very different from the one most of us know. But until Marion Zimmer Bradley published her immensely well received version of the story, *The Mists of Avalon,* that other reading never saw the light of day. Bradley recalls how as a young girl she read the story of Arthur and his Round Table over and over until she knew it almost by heart, and how again as a teenager she skipped school regularly to lose herself in the ten-volume edition of James Frazer's *The Golden Bough* and a fifteen-volume set of books on comparative religions, "including an enormous volume on the Druids and Celtic religions." [7] Years and years later, after the two works had simmered together untended, while she raised a family and wrote a long string of potboilers, the day came when her husband urged her to follow her heart and offered the financial support she needed to do it. In other words, when Bradley wrote a radically new version of the story, placing a wonderfully appealing Morgaine le Fay at its center as a high priestess of the Goddess, she does not appear to have done so as a deliberately feminist act or "statement." Rather, the story almost seems to have come *through* her, just because it was time. And for hundreds of thousands of women it has come, indeed, at the right time, teaching us to look with new eyes at *all* the old texts and to imagine what they leave unsaid. To remember, "and failing that, invent."

Similarly, a couple of summers ago a one-act opera called *The Seal Woman* was performed at Berkeley's Julia Morgan Theater. Its composer had never written an opera before. Her inspiration was a vivid, recurring dream of a "selkie," the creature ubiquitous in North Sea legend who is woman on land and seal at sea. When a selkie removes her sealskin to rest on a beach, says the tradition, she can be captured and kept as a woman by whomever seizes the sealskin. The story has many tellings, but in most the selkie lives on land and bears a child, maybe several, and has entirely forgotten who she really is. But one day she finds the sealskin, and, overwhelmed by longing for the sea and the liberty she'd known there, she slips it on and disappears, leaving a grieving family behind. John Sayles's film *The Secret of Roan Inish* draws upon selkie legend, too, and of course so does A. S. Byatt's magnificent *Possession*. It doesn't require a Ph.D. in anthropology to grasp the power such a legend holds for women, for it renders vividly the contrary pulls exerted by the world of intimacy and the world of utter sovereignty that we've seen described as "the common divide." With respect to patriarchy, it is implacably subversive, for it refutes the conventional belief that maternality is the single strongest force in female consciousness. In one of the most recent reworkings of this theme, *Leaning Toward Infinity* by Australian novelist Sue Woolfe, mathematics represents the longed-for alternative universe—of imagination, ultimate truths, *vision*—toward which a mother and then her daughter are drawn as inexorably as the selkie to the sea and almost as disastrously for their own domestic arrangements.

In countertext literature like this, women refuse, finally, to be pitted against one another and instead find ways to support one another and rebuild the broken female lineage. In Edwidge Danticat's *Breath, Eyes, Memory,* for example, Sophie confronts her grandmother with the suffering imposed upon the women of Haiti—the terrible betrayal that "testing" involves, since it is one's own mother who imposes it. Her grandmother defends her actions: "You must know that everything a mother does, she does for her child's own good." But a few minutes later she gives Sophie her own statue of the goddess Erzulie, "hot-blooded Erzulie, who feared no men," and says, "My heart, it weeps like a river for the pain we have caused you." [8] And of course by doing so, she is at last weeping for the pain her own mother had caused her and the pain her grandmother had caused her mother. . . .

We are re-establishing female lineage, but we are also shattering the wrong kind of female lineage. A woman who is a school principal in a town near ours was speaking to my husband one day after she'd heard him give a presentation on the loss of confidence that young girls undergo somewhere around the sixth grade (more on him, and those losses, later). Rachel told him a story, and even the telling of it reflects an extraordinary cultural shift, for she seems to have felt no inhibitions. When she was twelve, and her periods started, her mother came to her in the bathroom and slapped her across the face—hard. The girl looked back, dumbfounded, and her mother said, "This is to teach you that a woman's lot in life is pain and suffering." Years later, when she had a daughter of her own, Rachel returned to her mother and asked why she had done that, and her mother answered that *her* mother had done it to her. "Well, Mom," Rachel rejoined, "this is where it stops."

When the sacred feminine can take root and bloom, everything that patriarchy has put aside blooms with it: inclusiveness, for example, in place of obsessive separations; laughter in place of solemnity. Painstakingly drawn lines of authority give way to creative partnerships, and everything that has been frozen thaws and flows and dances. Walls come down. There is a moment in the film *Fried Green Tomatoes* when Evelyn Couch's husband comes home and finds her swinging a sledgehammer around in a house full of plaster dust and exposed studs. "What in God's name are you doing now?" he asks, because it's been like this for weeks—every night a fresh piece of midlife eccentricity, and this time it looks as if she's going after the house itself. Their son is gone, he won't need his bedroom anymore, so down come a couple of walls and the living room is that much bigger. Distracted, dusty, she glances up and flashes a radiant smile. "Oh, just . . . *air* . . . *light!*"

Above all else, perhaps, when the feminine is sacred, the body is not left out. Flesh is not demonized. Birth is holy, and birthing bodies are sacred, and because this is true, every woman is much more than she appears to be—a goddess sprouting leaves, with birds hovering about her head. In *Sassafras, Cypress & Indigo*, novelist, playwright, and poet Ntozake Shange introduces Hilda Effania, weaver of extraordinary fabrics, and her three daughters.[9] They are "rainbow children." Indigo is the youngest. She will be a violinist and a midwife, but here is how she is introduced:

> Where there is a woman there is magic. If there is a moon
> falling from her mouth, she is a woman who knows her

magic, who can share or not share her powers. A woman
with a moon falling from her mouth, roses between her legs
and tiaras of Spanish moss, this woman is a consort of the
spirits.

Indigo seldom spoke. There was a moon in her mouth.
Having a moon in her mouth kept her laughing. Whenever
her mother tried to pull the moss of her head, or clip the
roses round her thighs, Indigo was laughing. . . .

"Mama, if you pull 'em off, they'll just grow back. It's my
blood. I've got earth blood, filled up with the Geechees long
gone, and the sea."[10]

Wherever the sacred feminine is honored, the central imagery is of birthing, but also of rebirthing. In cultures where individual achievement and aggrandizement are crucial to one's
experience of self, the very notion of death evokes immense
anxiety, because mortality limits one's opportunity to make a
mark in life. Where identity is experienced in terms of connection and relationship, one might assume the idea of death would
be just as terrifying insofar as it disconnects us from those we
love. But, in fact, another dynamic comes often into play. The
little boy's smile is so like his father's, and his eyes are those of his
grandmother. He laughs like his mother's sister, and so, probably,
will his grandchildren. The continuities are so evident we can
rest in them, feeling ourselves held securely in a web of intricate
design. Life is not snuffed out when one individual dies; it gathers itself in and reconfigures from one instant to the next.

This kind of awareness, antithetical in so many ways to our
own, is intrinsic to many traditional cultures, and it is certainly
one of the reasons those cultures exert the powerful draw upon
us that they do. It is nowhere more powerfully evident than in
the feminine initiation rites that anthropologists working in a
great many different traditions have been able to reconstruct or,

in some cases, observe directly. I've described women's efforts to reinhabit the sacred feminine as a form of scavenging—pulling together bits and pieces from various cultures and gluing them together into something usable. But in the female initiation rite we're about to look at, we see the sort of find that archaeologists wait for all their lives: a whole and coherent representation of the Divine Mother, unbroken, unchipped, radiant with meaning. We discover, too, that of the four motifs around which I've structured my inquiry, enclosure is the one to watch. . . .

Contained, Transformed, Emergent

A thirteen-year-old Navajo girl sits quietly in the semidarkness of her family hogan close to an older woman who is murmuring instructions to her. The girl wears a ceremonial sash and jewelry made of turquoise and white shell. Her hair is fragrant with yucca shampoo: heavy bangs cover her forehead, the rest is held back in a buckskin thong. Before her is a basket full of roasted corn and a set of ancient stone tools for grinding it. Her cheeks are flushed, because she has just returned from a vigorous run with her friends—a race she was foreordained to win, accompanied by special songs:

> *Black Jewel Girl,*
> *the breeze coming from her as she runs is beautiful,*
> *Her black jewel moccasins,*
> *the breeze coming from her as she runs is beautiful. . . .*
> *Before, behind, it is blessed,*
> *the breeze coming from her as she runs is beautiful.*

There is a moment in a young girl's life when the child is slipping away and one can catch glimpses of the woman she will be, hovering behind her smile, prefigured in her gestures. It is a magical and indeed a *liminal* time, for sometimes you seem to see both the girl and the woman at once, and that very oscillation, along with the curious radiance that can settle over girls at that moment, suggests still another possibility: that it may be neither girl nor woman standing before you but rather the Girl of girls and the Woman of women. In cultures that consciously revere the feminine sacred, this fleeting intuitive awareness is honored and becomes the basis of initiatory rites. We might imagine that these are carried out primarily for the girl's benefit, but in fact they are times when her entire community rejoices, for each time a girl becomes a woman, the Goddess is reborn into her family and community. She is regenerated, and because She is the giver and sustainer of life, so everyone else is regenerated along with her.

Mystery writer Tony Hillerman has performed a great service by familiarizing ordinary readers with the beauty and power of Native American religious practices. In *The Listening Woman,* Detective Joe Leaphorn's key informant is an elderly woman who is assisting at a *kinaalda* ceremony, marking a Navajo girl's initiation into womanhood. To hurry the old woman, or pressure her, is absolutely out of the question; Leaphorn will learn what he needs to know only if she is persuaded that he is not asking as an outsider. He can do this easily enough, because in fact he is not an outsider at all. He takes part in the *kinaalda* itself with evident delight, singing the ancient songs, whose words, "down through the generations, had become so melded into the rhythm that they were hardly more than musical sounds." [11]

Ceremonies and rituals are like the genetic material of a particular culture: the medium in which its deepest values are preserved down through time. Central to women's rites, particularly the rites that initiate a young girl into womanhood, is the theme of regeneration, of the creative and recreative forces of the natural world. Resiliency itself. In every instance with which I am familiar these ceremonies involve ritual enclosure, and in these contexts enclosure connotes, not imprisonment or limitation of any sort, but a symbolic gestation.

Citing the work of anthropologist Bruce Lincoln, Jungian psychotherapist Virginia Beane Rutter observes that in contrast to male initiation patterns, which reflect "a process of separation, liminality (transition), and reincorporation," feminine rites tend to follow a threefold pattern of "enclosure, metamorphosis (or magnification), and emergence." [12] She interprets those three stages in psychobiological terms and observes that in fact they recur over and over again throughout a woman's life:

> Containment, transformation, and emergence form a ritual pattern of renewal for women. The pattern has both an inner and outer place in women's lives. . . . Initially, as a girl child, she is self-contained. Her body is hers and closed to the world. Menarche "opens" her physically, emotionally, and psychologically to external influence or intrusion. With each menstrual cycle, she undergoes a bodily transformation. Each month brings periods of containment, changing, and emerging. Her sexual receptivity fluctuates with her changing moods. During pregnancy a woman finds herself in a deep state of inner-containment while creation and transformation take place in her womb. Emergence comes when the blood flows in childbirth and the baby is born. During lactation her milk flows, opening her physical boundary into the world, into relationship in a new way. Later in life, when her blood ceases, she returns to another state of self-containment. Transformed once again, she emerges into old age and an identity as a grandmother. [13]

Ceremonies like *kinaalda* have proven a richly meaningful resource in Rutter's therapeutic work with women. "Depth-oriented psychotherapy," she maintains, "is an experience of initiation—a rite of passage from one stage of consciousness to another." When a woman seeks a woman therapist, she explains, it is typically because "an initiatory threshold has been reached, or life has been dammed up at an old stage. A new developmental task requires attention to inner reality." She compares such a moment to early adolescence when "longings press for realization from within" and notes that elements from rites like *kinaalda* have turned up regularly in the dreams of her own clients as they themselves moved toward greater wholeness. Rutter feels now that she has presided over their unfolding in much the same way that an older woman mentor does over the initiation of a young Navajo girl in *kinaalda:* "The therapeutic enclosure . . . provides the ritual container for development that our culture generally lacks . . . a quiet, closed, sacred space with the attention of a single woman focused completely on her. It is a place of self-attunement; it can be a place of self-realization." [14]

In *kinaalda* a young girl really *becomes* Changing Woman, the foremost Navajo deity, "the power of change and fecundity in all things."[15] What goes on during the ceremony between a young girl and her mentor forms the foundation for the girl's entire life as a woman. Directly, but vicariously, too, with her own daughters and nieces, she will experience over and over that threefold pattern of containment, transformation, and emergence, and she will come to know its power—to know that continuous renewal is what it means to be Changing Woman. Every aspect of *kinaalda* works to reinforce this knowledge. Let's look at the ceremony now a little more closely, noting as we do the importance attached implicitly not only to enclosure but also to silence, restraint of desires, and a very interesting variation on the theme of self-naughting.

⌒

Ritual enclosure is signaled very simply by the hanging of a blanket across the door of the girl's hogan, but the hogan is made holy for the purposes of the ritual by the singing of traditional songs:

> *Here at this house, it is a sacred place . . .*
> *The house made of dawn is a sacred place . . .*
> *Now it is the house of long life and everlasting beauty.*[16]

The girl herself chooses her Ideal Woman—someone who is strong and beautiful, a good cook, a mother, and a skillful weaver. In the first stage of the ceremony, Ideal Woman washes the girl's hair with yucca root shampoo and brushes it with ceremonial grass. She washes the girl's turquoise and white shell jewelry and dresses her, singing all the while. After the girl has been dressed and ornamented, she lies upon a pile of blankets lent by guests and family members (her very touch will bless them), and is massaged by Ideal Woman from toe to head. Because a girl is believed to be malleable during menarche, she can be reshaped through massage into Changing Woman. Because she is considered to be particularly vulnerable during this time, both physically and emotionally, she must stay away from evil places, and everyone around her is careful to model attitudes of kindness and generosity. At the same time, she knows herself to be growing in strength. Twice a day, followed by her girlfriends, she runs, a little farther each time, understanding that the farther she runs, the longer she is likely to live in health.

Over the course of her enclosure the initiate roasts and grinds corn—as much as thirty pounds—for an enormous corn cake. She grinds it with stone tools; the work is meant to strengthen her "soft bones." Her father will help dig the earthen pit where it is to be baked; her grandfather may keep the fire going. Once the batter is in the heated pit, she sprinkles it with corn pollen. She herself will be blessed with sacred pollen before the all-night sing. She stays awake throughout the night listening attentively to the songs.

At dawn the girl's hair and jewelry are washed one final time, and she leaves the hogan for a final run. When she gets back, she will cut the cake and serve it out, refraining from eating it herself. The cake is huge and round and deep gold in color. It looks like the sun—the very emblem of bounty and brightness. And *she* glows, too: this is her day. She has been re-created, and so have those who participated in her initiation. To look upon her is a blessing. The Mother has returned. This is what regeneration looks like—tastes like.

See how differently female experience is depicted here. The girl is silent, but only so that she can hear with her whole being timeless songs that portray her to herself as "the subject of her own epic."[17] Her sense of self is not assaulted; it enlarges, rather, as she feels herself becoming one with Changing Woman. She curbs her own hunger, but does so in the context of becoming one who can feed and heal others. In point of fact, she is acquiring *power*. And finally, she is enclosed, but only for a time, and with a female mentor *of her own choice,* and their enclosure serves only to intensify their communion.

CHAPTER 10

To Construct and Inhabit Our Airy Spaces

It must be the result of the painstaking reconstructive work women have been carrying out this past couple of decades that several friends of mine who are otherwise fairly conventional speak of the Goddess now quite without self-consciousness. What I believe this says is that the sacred feminine is in a curious way *pressing in* upon us all so unrelentingly now—as archetype, as salient principle, as alternative way of being in the world—that many of us are feeling it, and feeling *Her,* as a real presence in our lives. The sensation intensifies as we become more and more conscious of the hunger and aridity associated with living under patriarchy.

Once I became familiar with the three-stroke cycle Virginia Beane Rutter and others see as being so crucial to women's full unfolding—of enclosure, magnification (or metamorphosis), and emergence—it seemed to me that it was among the most important ways that awareness of the sacred feminine communicates itself to us. Just as women experience it over and over again in their physical lives, so the pattern occurs in our imaginative lives as well. It shapes our dreams, our paintings, our stories. And each time we experience or witness it, particularly when we're conscious of it, it is as if we'd worked one more figure of the Goddess into a linen kerchief. Something in us amplifies.

I believe that the dilemma within feminism known as the "common divide" has directly to do with this three-phase cycle and our culture's utter failure to honor it. To reiterate, feminists are deeply divided over what kind of meaning they should attach to feminine biological experiences. Some would prefer to minimize their significance: "equality feminists" for example, ask only the equivalent of a level playing field, fearing that any allowance for "difference" will only perpetuate the second-class status of women. Others, among them the "cultural" or "difference feminists," think it's vital to celebrate the positive values that have been carried along in feminine culture and to introduce those values into the public sphere. Two different perspectives on identity and self are associated with these positions. One maintains that gender is entirely a social construct and that one's real identity or selfhood is established by rejecting gender identities seen as false because they are defined and imposed on women by patriarchal culture. The other perspective attaches rich significance to gender and holds that the intensely "connected" mode that characterizes women's psychological development constitutes a path toward selfhood that is at least as reliable as that of systematic separation.

I hadn't been able to resolve this dilemma. I'm not sure it can be resolved. I'd found myself drawn to both perspectives at various times. But it seemed to me now that the two perspectives can be bridged, and the values inherent to both preserved, when the full significance of that three-phase cycle is recognized. In cultures where the sacred feminine is revered, that cycle is seen as central to a woman's biological life, her emotional development, and, eventually, to her full spiritual unfolding. But it is also regarded as a kind of wellspring for the entire community.

If a young girl is taught, for example, that menstruation is a time for inwardness and solitude and deep pondering as well as a time for her female body to rest and restore itself, then both versions of selfhood are honored. And if her culture genuinely treasures its children, at least as much as it does, say, corporate earnings, she will not experience menstruation or pregnancy as a handicap or humiliation, and no one around her will regard it as such. Everything she learns *as a mother,* "enclosed" for a time in that relationship, will be seen as wisdom useful to the whole community. If over and over again she experiences the cycle of enclosure-magnification-emergence in a positive way and associates it *simultaneously* with the well-being of those around her and her own full self-realization, the way is paved for her to undertake uninhibitedly the profound sort of enclosure that is associated with the mystical experience. As a Western woman, I grew up without any inkling of what that sort of recognition might feel like, but I think the hunger for it guided me at crucial junctures.

At some point during the construction of a usable past, one finds herself drawing not merely on collective history or even imagined reconstruction of that history, but on personal history as well, and these bright bits of one's own remembered experiences as girlchild or woman complete the work. This happened to me now, as I reflected upon the ways in which traditional cultures regard the transition between girlhood and womanhood.

My own periods began when I was thirteen and a half. It was summer and I was picking beans on my granddad's farm. All my girlfriends had begun to menstruate months before, and I was feeling like a real laggard. I was working a good quarter-mile from the house when I felt a warm trickle between my legs and realized something was happening. After I'd walked back to my grandmother's and been fitted out, it was assumed I'd go back to work. Nobody made a fuss, nobody suggested I might like to curl up with a hot water bottle, and absolutely nobody stepped forward to hang strings of turquoise and white shell beads around my neck. Not a word spoken. I might as well have been getting a Band-Aid. My mother had left a book by my bed some time earlier that purported to explain everything; it was about as intimate and magical as the Montgomery Ward catalogue, and even so I read it only when I was sure nobody else was in the house because the whole subject was for me so very. . . clandestine. I guess that's how the fifties were.

A Bare Shell of a Cottage

In fact, though, I believe I did manage to envelop myself in a certain aura that summer—a sense that I was indeed becoming a woman and that this quite possibly had spiritual as well as physical significance. The right books came along, as they always seem to have done—in this case, Anne Morrow Lindbergh's *Gift from the Sea,* which my mother and I read together. I still read it every couple of years, particularly when I'm getting ready to lead a meditation workshop for women. When I know that I'll be talking with women who have children, I like to let Lindbergh have the first word:

> The pattern of our lives is essentially circular. We must be open to all points of the compass; husband, children, friends, home, community; stretched out, exposed, sensitive like a spider's web to each breeze that blows, to each call that comes. . . .

With a new awareness, both painful and humorous, I
begin to understand why the saints were rarely married
women. I am convinced it has nothing inherently to do, as I
once supposed, with chastity or children. It has to do primarily with distractions. . . . I want a singleness of eye, a purity of intention. . . . I want, in fact—to borrow from the
language of the saints—to live "in grace" as much of the
time as possible.[1]

Which is pretty much what the women who come to these
workshops want, too, though they're rarely in a position to act
upon the desire in the way Anne Morrow Lindbergh did. *Gift
from the Sea* grew out of a period of several summer weeks the
author spent alone on an island set with pine trees, dunes,
herons, and seashells. It's the measure of her accomplishment
that her account of that period has inspired more gratitude than
envy. Vicariously, we are right there with her, especially when
she describes the intense pleasure ordinary solitude holds for
women who are rarely alone:

I walked far down the beach, soothed by the rhythm of the
waves, the sun on my bare back and legs, the wind and mist
from the spray on my hair. Into the waves and out like a
sandpiper. And then home, drenched, drugged, reeling, full
to the brim with my day alone; full like the moon before
the night has taken a single nibble of it; full as a cup poured
up to the lip. . . . Let no one come—I pray in sudden
panic—I might spill myself away! (45)

"That may be it," one among us murmured one night, the
mother of three: "A beach all to yourself. The ultimate erotic fantasy for mothers." Perhaps there's a little Seal Woman in all of us.

When I first read *Gift from the Sea* I was just a girl, way too young, at thirteen, to be fretting about the competing pulls of family and inwardness. But as the eldest of four children I saw how rare the moments were for my mother when somebody wasn't clamoring for her attention, and it did chill me. She couldn't get away, but I could and did and usually with her connivance: I was always finding new places on the farm where I could hide from my siblings with a book and an apple, and the appeal of Lindbergh's "bare sea shell of a cottage" was not lost on me at all. Seashells were the focal point of her meditations, delicate enclosed spaces that yielded the meanings she sought, by way of metaphor.

> Channeled whelk, I put you down again, but you have set my mind on a journey, up an inwardly winding staircase of thought. (35)
>
> Moon shell, who named you? Some intuitive woman I like to think. . . . I can take you back to my desk in Connecticut. You will sit there and fasten your single eye upon me. You will make me think, with your smooth circles winding inward to the tiny core, of the island I lived on for a few weeks. You will say to me "solitude." (58)

Was I feeling fragile when I first read this? I know I was. Transitional, and extremely vulnerable, like a sea creature between shells. Lindbergh's depictions of enclosure helped me understand my own insistent need to keep taking flight: to a dusty stillness in the midst of stacked hay bales upstairs in the barn or to a branch high up in a cherry tree where green leaves or pale pink petals (gloriously, briefly) sheltered and concealed me.

There was a story I loved equally well about that same time, a short novel called *The White Room,* by New England writer

Elizabeth Coatsworth. It worked for me in much the same way that Anne Morrow Lindbergh's talk of seashells and solitude did. I was able to lay hands on it again recently and happy to find it as enchanting as I remembered. Coatsworth's heroine, Laura Treadwell, has always lived at High Farm, and she is there with her husband and family when the story begins. To Laura, the farm is intensely alive.

> Here the sun shone brighter, the well water tasted colder, and the wind came and went like a familiar. Here if one looked about one, the eye learned a taste for distances, for far horizons, for the unknown. The real and the imagined became indistinguishable. Fact and dream walked side by side.[2]

Over the years, Laura's marriage and her relationship with her two children has been eroded steadily by the machinations of a sister-in-law who has moved into the home under the pretext of helping out. "Sometime Laura felt like a ghost. When she said something, it often happened that no one answered" (53). Things have been deteriorating steadily, and one day, during a sudden snowstorm, Laura is caught outside and stumbles into "the white room." It is the lee of a stone wall, arched over with branches so weighted down with snow that she cannot escape. Frightened at first, she settles in—finds some figs and walnuts in her pocket, and realizes that "in a house of snow, thirst was no problem" (122). It is dark, and she sleeps.

"And when she woke, perhaps on the second day, she found that, after all, there was light, a glowing blue light, lovely though faint. She could see nothing by it but the darkness of her own body like a shadowy bee in a blue morning-glory" (122).

Laura realizes soon that her cell of snow is remarkably peaceful. "There is nothing I need do but sit here and think quietly of whatever I want to" (123). Her fears—of starvation, smothering, freezing to death—begin to dissipate. For "here am I like a bulb safe in the darkness of the earth, or the bees in their hive. . . ." (123). She sings to herself, hymns she remembers from her childhood, "buzzing away very much like a bee, she thought."

Drifting in and out of sleep, half frozen, steadily weakening, she is able nonetheless to use her very imprisonment to think through everything that has happened to her and her family. Four days pass in this way, and at last, even as the drowsiness of death is beginning to overtake her, she sees—really sees—the whole course of events for what it has been and her own unwitting complicity in it. Realizing that it may not be too late to set things right, and that she *wants* to, she realizes also that she is wearing a red scarf and that if she can tie it to one of these sticks, and push it up through the crusted snow. . . .

Red the scarf is, the red of birthing, bright against the white snow, and her son sees it and digs her out, and the mistress of High Farm takes back her rightful place. It's a wonderful story, deliciously archetypal, faintly redolent of Daphne du Maurier's *Rebecca*, and it strengthened my sense that whatever my own version of womanhood was going to be, whatever bargains I struck with life, I would never be without my *space*. Years later I would copy out the words of Luce Irigaray and pin them up over my desk:

> Once we have left the waters of the womb, we have to construct a space for ourselves in the *air* for the rest of our time on earth. . . . To construct and inhabit our airy space is essential. It is the space of bodily autonomy, of free breath, free speech and song, of performing on the stage of life.[3]

As Gerda Lerner traced out the historical processes that had brought women into subordination, she was impressed at how complicit women had actually been with those processes. I think that complicity is more than comprehensible when we recognize how crucial some form of protective enclosure is at certain junctures in a woman's life—a bare shell of a cottage, a leafy surround, a translucent "white room" made of snow. Historically, we must remember, the choice placed before women has almost never been between enclosure and freedom but rather between enclosure and *exposure,* and the only dependably safe enclosures available to us have been those offered by patriarchy. Every once in a while, under the right circumstances (a sympathetic partner, a decent income, manageable offspring), just often enough to keep us all optimistic, ordinary domesticity *has* permitted women an interior life relatively free of interruption and the consequent opportunity to unfold deliberately and fully. Only quite recently have women been able to enjoy such an opportunity without the direct protection of a father, brother, or husband.

There is of course one traditional form of feminine enclosure with which patriarchy has coexisted that is not altogether under direct "paternal dominance," and it has always exerted a powerful tug on the imaginations of young girls and women— many of us not even Catholic. The very fact that it has been available as a point of reference at all has been more important than is generally acknowledged.

Where the Silkworm Dies

"I cannot be a nun in the midst of family life," Anne Morrow Lindbergh protests to herself in *Gift from the Sea,* "I would not want to be." Yet she can't help introducing the possibility, either, precisely because in the secular industrialized West, we have almost no other way of imagining what it might be to "live in grace." I had no other images at thirteen, and for that reason I read everything I could get my hands on about nuns. Now I think I understand why—and I recall with great fondness that the same grandmother who didn't have anything particularly elevating to tell me about menstruation used to take me with her whenever a play or an operetta was performed at nearby Mount Angel College where she'd gone to "normal school" decades before. She made no secret of her abiding affection for the Benedictine sisters who taught there. Not in a million years would she have become a Catholic—what a scandal that would have caused in our Willamette Valley farming community!—but she loved, I think, the dedication of those lives, and the idealism, and I believe I must have absorbed something of the way she felt.

In the life of Catherine of Siena, the fourteenth-century visionary and prophet who used to take the pope to task as if he were an errant nephew, the three-stroke enclosure cycle can be seen repeatedly. As a young girl Catherine spent hours in her own room, praying and drifting rapidly away from the future her father had planned for her. Alarmed, he made her share a room with her sister, whereupon she discovered that she could construct for herself "an inner cell no one could take away from her" and remain in it all the time. Eventually, seeing a white dove flutter above her head while she prayed, her father gave in and allowed her to have her room back. Over the next several years, that room would be the site of extraordinary interior adventures: long hours of prayer but terror, too, in the form of demonic voices that wheedled and cajoled "like a maddening swarm of flies," mocking the idea that she might have a vocation. Like Julian, she learned she could drive them away with laughter. Later she would receive Jesus as a regular visitor; they would walk together in her room or on the roof of her family house. Sometimes Mary would come along, or Saint

Dominic. . . . At last, though, shortly before her twentieth birth-day, Jesus came to her door one evening and refused to enter the room. She must come out, too, now, he said; from this point on she could love him only by loving others. "Your neighbors are the channel through which all your virtues come to birth."

In the writings of Teresa of Avila, sixteenth-century reformer of the Carmelite Order, the motif of enclosure is explored with particular force through the metaphors she uses to explain contemplative prayer. At twenty-one, Teresa had chosen to enter the Convent of the Incarnation deliberately, knowing it was not the most closely regulated community she could have joined, because she imagined herself unready for the austerity of a genuinely enclosed life. In fact, the choice could hardly have been more disastrous. The story of her long, painful struggle to establish inwardness in a situation almost diabolically constructed to prevent it is as moving as anything in the literature of mysticism. Later she would devote herself to securing for other young women the opportunity she had *not* had to live fully and securely enclosed. As if anticipating that some of them might be as apprehensive about real enclosure as she had been, she writes about the interior life like someone holding jewels to the light, invoking hauntingly beautiful images of containment: "If we make the effort, practice this recollection for some days, and get used to it . . . we will understand, when beginning to pray, that the bees are approaching and entering the beehive to make honey" (*Way of Perfection,* 28.7).

Call in your senses, she urges her novices. Be very still, and slowly the inner recesses of your own being will fill with sweetness. You are beehives, you are *palaces:*

> Let us imagine that within us is an extremely rich palace,
> built entirely of gold and precious stones. . . . Within us lies

something incomparably more precious than what we see outside ourselves. Let's not imagine that we are hollow inside. (*Way of Perfection,* 28.10)

From the worldly perspective, a woman vowed to chastity *is,* of course, "hollow inside," for no child is taking form within her womb, and none will be. By the standards of ordinary folk culture, she is not "fruitful"—not really, therefore, *womanly.* Teresa would have understood the anxiety a young nun might feel around this question—better, probably, than they would have understood it themselves. Brilliantly, therefore, she defuses it, expressing her wonderment that "He who would fill a thousand worlds and more with his grandeur" might enter something as small as a human soul, as well as seeking "to enclose himself in the womb of his most blessed mother" (*Way of Perfection,* 28.11). The soul of the Carmelite and the womb of Mary are mysteriously, therefore, one and the same, full and fruitful after all.

Teresa's imagery of enclosure culminates in *Interior Castle:* "Consider our soul to be like a castle, made entirely out of a diamond, or out of very clear crystal, in which there are many rooms" (I, 1, 1).

If this is enclosure, it is like no form of enclosure women normally experience. The number of rooms is in fact all but infinite, and all is light and brightness, increasing as we move inward. It is the ultimate version of Luce Irigaray's "airy spaces."

At the fifth dwelling place in the interior castle, the soul, Teresa explains, is like a silkworm. It spins a cocoon for itself by "getting rid of self love and self will" (V, 2, 6). The object of spinning this cocoon is that the silkworm/soul can then die to everything that is not God, and when she does she finds herself enclosed entirely in God: "Somewhere I have read, or heard that our life is hidden in Christ" (V, 2, 4). Inside the cocoon that is

God, when the silkworm soul has died to its old self, it is transformed and reborn as a white butterfly. *Psyche.*

We know something about cocoons that Teresa didn't. When the larva enters the pupa stage, it actually dissolves completely, turning into a kind of broth. While it is in its liquid state, the firm walls of the cocoon are vital to its survival. Over time, safely contained, it configures itself into a chrysalis, and at last it cannot *be* contained. The cocoon falls away, and the moth spreads its wings and flies. It has become "the butterfly, one of the Goddess's symbols," as Riane Eisler reminds us, "of transformation and rebirth."[4]

It's a pity Teresa didn't know this detail, because I think she'd have found it clinched the metaphor perfectly. That one's very identity should dissolve into an undifferentiated "broth" is all but unimaginable and, if imaginable, terrifying. And yet from what Teresa and others tell us of the mystical experience, something very like this is exactly what takes place at a certain point in spiritual unfolding. To become what we would be, we must let go of everything we have been.

Teresa's enclosure metaphors were lyrical, but within their cultural context they were also subversive. For they bring to mind all the traditional poetic comparisons of young women to walled gardens or treasuries, but they go on to maintain that all of that interior wealth does not belong to anyone but the young women themselves. The splendor is theirs, the palace their home. To take that position where and when she did was a revolutionary act on Teresa's part. No less so was her establishment—in the dead of night, in utter secrecy, in a small, shabby building across town from the Convent of the Incarnation—of a community of reformed Carmelites. At the Convent of Saint Joseph, the nuns would be veiled, silent, and fully enclosed, not out of deference to anyone's authority, but *because they chose to be,* and they chose to be because those were the conditions that would enable them to move steadily inward, undisturbed, and eventually attain full self-realization. Paradoxically, Teresa tells us, it is at the innermost chamber of the interior castle, where we are most profoundly enclosed, that we experience utter freedom. It's fascinated me to see that perception, or some semblance of it, working its way out into the most apparently secular works of popular fiction.

"A Dot in Motion, Heading South"

In her splendid 1995 novel *Ladder of Years,* contemporary novelist Anne Tyler picks up exactly where Lindbergh and Coatsworth left off, raising the same questions they do about women's struggle for identity and selfhood. In the process, to convey the real seriousness of what her heroine is going through, she, too, invokes the atmosphere of a cloister: obliquely, though, and humorously.

Cordelia Grinstead, inveterate reader of romances, has three nearly grown children. Her husband is a physician, and Cordelia is his secretary as well as his wife. Like Laura Treadwell, she has gradually slipped into the position of all 'round household *schlepp.* "When did this start happening to me?" she asks her teenaged son. "When did sweet and cute turn into silly and inefficient?" (23). The family is severely out of joint, but Cordelia is the only member who knows it, and for all she can tell it's her doing. The boiling point comes on the first morning of the family's annual stay at the beach. Feeling more extraneous by the minute, infuriated by the condescension of her husband, her

sisters, her children, Cordelia looks out across the water and feels
something snap. It's a truly *selkie* moment:

> She snatched her tote bag from the blanket, spun on one
> bare heel, and stamped off down the beach. . . . After a few
> yards she changed course till she was marching alongside the
> ocean, on wet packed sand that cooled the soles of her
> feet. . . . Delia pictured a map of the entire East Coast from
> Nova Scotia to Florida. . . . She herself was a dot in motion,
> heading south. She would keep going till she fell off the
> bottom of the continent. . . . She would keep on the move,
> like someone running between raindrops, and they would
> never, ever find her. (75)

In deliciously seriocomic fashion, Delia has acted upon the
premise of *Gift from the Sea*. It's almost as if Tyler were replying
to Lindbergh's reverie from forty years back: *The shell in my hand
is deserted. It once housed a whelk, a snail-like creature, and then . . . a
little hermit crab who has run away, leaving his tracks behind him like a
delicate vine on the sand. He ran away, and left me his shell. . . . I too
have run away, I realize, I have shed the shell of my life, for these few
weeks of vacation* (21–22).

Delia Grinstead, of course, has run away from the vacation as
well as the life. Striding along the beach, she veers inland finally
and by a series of coincidences finds her way to a new life in a
small town called "Bay Borough." She has the five hundred dol-
lars that would have paid for her family's groceries for the rest of
the week, and with part of that she replaces her damp bathing
suit and beach wrap at a women's clothing store, pulling a dress
off the rack without really seeing it. Her normal taste in clothing runs to round collars with lace trim, but "normal" is back at
the beach. Her reflection in the dressing room mirror surprises

her: "She had assumed she would resemble a child playing dress-up, for the hem nearly brushed her ankles. What she found, though, was someone entirely unexpected: a somber, serious-minded woman in a slender column of pearl gray. . . . " (88).

A few blocks away, Delia finds herself standing in front of an older home with a "Room for Rent" sign. And yes, of course, she takes it: "a long narrow room, its outside wall slanting inward under the eaves, a window at each end. A metal cot extended from beneath the front window, and a low, orange-brown bureau sat against the inside wall. . . . the cot, which was made up with white sheets and a white woolen blanket washed bald.

In the bathroom Delia slips off her wedding ring. "Then she made a brief return trip to her room. She didn't go inside but merely stood in the doorway, claiming it—reveling in its starkness, now that she had it completely to herself" (93). She is virginal, a novice without an order in a cell without a crucifix. "So. She was settled. She could look around the room and detect not the slightest hint that anybody lived there" (97).

The new Delia has a new job, because near the dress shop where she had shed the garments of her former life there is a lawyer's office with a sign in *its* window: "Secretary Wanted." The dress, the room, and the job are made for one another and for Delia. She is "Miss Grinstead" now, coolly competent, gracious, but very private.

> She took to sitting on her bed in the evenings and staring into space. It was too much to say that she was thinking. She certainly had no conscious thoughts, or at any rate, none that mattered. Most often she was, oh, just watching the air, as she used to do when she was small . . . an infinity of air endlessly rearranging itself, and the longer she watched the more soothed she felt, the more mesmerized, the more peaceful.

She was learning the value of boredom. She was clearing
out her mind. She had always known that her body was just
a shell she lived in, but it occurred to her now that her mind
was yet another shell—in which case, who was "she"? She
was clearing out her mind to see what was left. Maybe there
would be nothing. (126–27)

"... *What is the shape of my life?* ... *I want* ... *to be at peace
with myself. I want a singleness of eye, a purity of intention, a central
core.* ... *I want* ... *to live 'in grace.'.* ..."

To watch the descent of grace upon Delia Grinstead is pure
joy. The change is barely even a change—only the slightest, sub-
tlest, most negligible kind of *realignment* you could imagine. She
really only becomes herself, and anchored there; but once she
does, everything and everybody has to reposition itself around
her. They really have no choice. ...

Like Anne Morrow Lindbergh, Laura Treadwell and Delia
Grinstead are wives and mothers, and the outcome of being effectively cloistered for a time is that they emerge strong, clear-
eyed, and able to take charge again of their own households.
Only that, nothing more. Yet on a subliminal level, the possibility
of another and more far-reaching sort of outcome is at least
raised. Pushing up through the surface of these entirely mainstream novels are some very searching questions about the nature of consciousness itself, questions that declare themselves
ever so quietly through the imagery of religious enclosure. "It
occurred to her now that her mind was yet another shell—in
which case, who was 'she'?"

"Give Me All That Thine Is ..."

From the perspective of the mystic, then, Delia Grinstead's
months in Bay Borough and Laura Treadwell's four days "like a

bulb, safe in the darkness of the earth" represent a kind of re-hearsal for a far more radical separation from ordinary life and a metamorphosis that is commensurate. More radical, yet *on a continuum,* and it seems to me imperative that this be recognized. If the Teresas and Clares and Catherines are correct, the ultimate transformative act—the half-knowing desire for which is the *reason* we keep burrowing into cottages, caves, and anchor-holds—is to still the mind.

When I first studied Julian of Norwich, I imagined her in stark, almost Gothic terms. In my mind's eye her cell was small and cold and hewn out of stone, and she was absolutely by her-self in there, thin and pale from fasting and vigils. It took years and years for me to absorb the likelier picture—that she had two rooms, a maid, a cat, and a window where people came to get her advice. I seem to have needed to keep a real distance from Julian and others like her. Needed to keep at arm's length the possibility that their lives might be more relevant to mine than was obvious. That I revised that feeling much later had to do with my revised understanding of spirituality itself.

When mystics speak of renunciation and sacrifice and tell us that in the final stages we must renounce every attachment, something in us does protest. Women have so little to begin with, surely that little is not what's standing between them and God-consciousness! "Give me all that thine is," God says to Mechthild of Magdeburg, "and I'll give you all that mine is." And our first impulse is to read that in material terms.

But close reading of the mystics suggests that the sacrifices at issue really have very little to do with fasting, vigils, flagellation, and dark cold cells. Living with a contemporary mystic has left me in little doubt on the subject. The whole business is much subtler than conventional assumptions suggest. Subtler, and yet simpler. And much harder. The object of every renunciation made along the way is to remove anything you can that agitates the mind: like the desire to have the last word; like the need to read at least one literate murder mystery a week; like a hankering for chocolate *biscotti*.

In other words, silence, self-naughting, enclosure, and training of desire are not ends in themselves. They are valued by the mystic only insofar as they help bring about a mind absolutely free of turmoil. In Sanskrit there is a term for the mind in its undifferentiated state: *citta,* or mindstuff. Every thought we think, every desire we entertain bends *citta* into a particular form. In deep meditation, though, when all thoughts are stilled, *citta* becomes formless. . . . Broth. The mind that is undifferentiated is like a mountain lake without ripples. We can see to the very bottom—can see our very selves.

In *Way of Perfection,* responding to her nuns' request, Teresa sets out to explain contemplative prayer. The first third of the book, though, is given over to a discussion of detachment, humility, and love of one's neighbor. The reason one cultivates these states, she explains, is that their opposite numbers, selfish attachments, pride, and envy, keep the mind stirred up, making it impossible to pray attentively.

The brilliance of Teresa's writings on contemplative prayer is that she talks always in terms of gradations and stages. The scheme she adopts in *Interior Castle* is one of several she develops that help us see that just as there are deepening levels of consciousness, so also there are deepening capacities for renunciation. An individual might make a sacrifice that an outside observer would assume to be inconceivably painful, but that is because she has moved within tasting distance of something invisible to that outside observer, something inconceivably desirable. *Over and over she has undergone that three-phase cycle of enclosure, magnification, and emergence, and she has learned to trust it.*

Initially she experiences it only in "psychobiological" terms, and this is why feminine spirituality insists that the body be given the respect that most religions have denied it.[5] The experience of living in a female body can teach a woman that each time she encloses herself (voluntarily, on her own terms), embraces silence and darkness, and emerges only when she knows it's time, she is a little more herself for having done so. With increasing abandonment she can give herself over to a process that culminates eventually in full self-realization . . . in full *freedom,* for that matter, a paradox that Teresa fully appreciated.

It is something to ponder that, like Delia Grinstead, Teresa of Avila was in her girlhood an inveterate reader of romances. She loved the very idea of falling in love. Contemporary essayist Vivian Gornick could be speaking for Teresa when she writes, "Romantic love was injected like dye into the nervous system of my emotions."[6] The reformer of the Carmelite order, "La Madre," didn't really manage to disentangle herself from the assumptions of the courtly love tradition until she was well into her forties. One can trace across her writings evidence of a kind of prolonged adolescence—the sort one often sees in particularly gifted girls—and I suspect this was one of the reasons she was so effective as a leader of women. She could always empathize fully with younger women who were still struggling with illusions she herself had shed only recently and with considerable effort.

What I'm trying to suggest is that by keeping the enclosed contemplative or the recluse at the imaginative distance we generally do—indeed, by allowing a kind of penumbra to encircle her, of "weirdness" and pathology—contemporary women may also be keeping ourselves distant from our own full unfolding. It strikes me that it is not in the inclusive spirit of feminism for this sort of distancing—of "othering"—to be tolerated indefinitely.

A powerful continuum arcs out across the liberation writings of all women, and women like Teresa and Julian are on that continuum. Making room for them there, giving them their rightful place in feminist discourse, is the first step toward gaining access to what they were able to do.

Yet even as I say this, I feel self-conscious about having said it. And I think that has to do with the particular stage the women's movement has reached. Steadily, on all sides, women are gathering the strength to oppose the cultural forces that have oppressed them, and they're going about it in a million and one different ways, and from what I can observe, they all have their own timetable. They're not going to be rushed. They're not going to be *anything*ed, in fact, by anybody. That's the whole point. As filmmakers and composers, novelists, poets, and politicians, as cookbook writers, for that matter, and health activists, theologians and homemakers, women are at a great figurative swap meet, informing one another, filling in blanks for one another, presenting ourselves *to* ourselves in a new light . . . making some new choices, experimenting in a very open-ended way, and finding courage together. It's tumultuous and exuberant, and it's very much like something that happens twice a year in my own Petaluma in an establishment called Mishi, which is both a clothing store and the factory where the clothing is made.

Mishi offers a line of natural fabric fashions featuring lovely, uncommon colors and artful styling with a lot of flow—designs women my age like to call "forgiving." They are pricey, because they are made by people who are paid considerably more than the ten to twelve cents per hour they'd be getting stitching up jeans or name-brand designer clothing in Indonesia. Mishi has terrific semiannual sales, and everyone who can't afford to shop there the rest of the time pours in. We crowd into the large communal dressing room in the back—electric fans keep the oxygen moving around—and the ensuing scene borders on the Breughelian, but unless you're subject to claustrophobia, it can be marvelous. Babies are there, in and out of strollers, so you tread carefully, and even if you didn't come with a girlfriend you're absorbed quickly into what is an essentially relational process. You put on a mauve jumpsuit, and several other women help you assess. You put on a skirt and wish out loud for a matching top, and someone tosses it to you from across the room.

"That needs a scarf."

"Here, try this one."

"Coooool."

You go back to the floor for another size of something and take a couple of orders with you. And when it's all over, you come out with one, two, maybe even three new looks, some you'd never have imagined yourself wearing, and the next week, standing in line at the bank, you find yourself looking at another woman, each trying to figure out where you'd seen the other, and then start grinning as you remember you'd both been in your underwear.

It's consciousness raising on a whole new scale, and all the living rooms in the country couldn't contain it. . . . And surely the only reasonable stance to take in the midst of this lovely melee is one of immense and uncritical nonchalance. Harriet doesn't like the jacket you think would look great on her, fine. Back off.

To press, therefore, as I'm pressing now in urging that serious feminist attention be given to the likes of Julian and Teresa and the sort of disciplines they followed, feels, in a certain sense, discordant. Part of me wants to just sit still, be quiet, and let things take their course. To explain why I can't do that, I must back-track and acknowledge that the period I've been writing about in my life was not just a time of soul searching and hard thinking and poking around in bookstores and libraries. Certain things happened in my own immediate world that put the whole in-quiry in a particular light. Because of them, I came to believe that the struggle women have embarked upon is going to be so much more fierce and unrelenting than I'd imagined that noth-ing short of the admittedly extreme measures to which women like Julian and Teresa resorted will carry us through. It's time to talk about those events.

Magic Circles: Island Time

In Shakespeare's *As You Like It,* a delicious reverie on gender, pastoral conventions, and true romance, a pivotal moment occurs when Rosalind finds a bloodstained piece of cloth and hears that Orlando, with whom she is "giddy in love," has been hurt fighting with a lion. Rosalind had been disguised as a man—initially, for her own safety, later as a contrivance so that she could probe the depth of Orlando's affection for her and hold forth to him about the real nature of love and lovers. In fact, dressed as a boy, she proposes to him that she pretend to be "your Rosalind" in a kind of dress rehearsal of courtship. Since Rosalind would have been played by a male actor in the first place, the deception is actually three layers deep. She's been having glorious fun with the situation, but now the sight of his blood shocks her, and in a comic reversion to traditionally constructed gender, she faints.

Until that moment, time has not mattered: The Forest Arden has been a magic circle within which lovers have all the time in the world to imaginatively fine-tune the perfect romance. The torn and blood-soaked cloth is the very image of mortality and tells Rosalind unequivocally that the time for playacting at love is over: *life* is calling.

I've always loved that device and have been sure that Shakespeare meant its ripples to be felt beyond the context of Rosalind's and Orlando's courtship of each other. For there are many magic circles we can step into that remove us from the clocks and calendars of ordinary life and allow us to begin feeling our way toward what our real desires are. Scholarship is one of those, as surely as monastic life is, as surely as even the right kind of sabbatical is. One thinks of Anne Morrow Lindbergh and her reverie on "island time." Of Alice down the rabbit hole. Robinson Crusoe, Annie Dillard up Tinker Creek.

And it is always understood in works of this genre that "island time" loses its meaning if we stay there forever. The Forest of Arden, like Prospero's Island in *The Tempest,* is a transforming medium for its visitors: identities can dissolve there and reform. One can take some risks, try a few things. . . . But at last we are recalled to the time-bound workaday world, with its obligations and institutions, where we have identities we are expected to sustain from one day to the next, responsibly. The insights of island time are to be applied in "real time."

The world of scholarship is one of these magic circles that many of us slip into at regular intervals and bring everything we've thought we thought into question, and it can feel timeless and freeing—even magical. My own immersion in women's history and related literature had for me something of that feeling.

And I probably could have gone on indefinitely, because as anybody knows who's "done" scholarship, it is one of the ultimate drugs. Every intriguing article has an equally intriguing bibliography, and every lead branches into six more, and there hovers over you all the time this delicious feeling that any minute you'll have explained Everything.

But in fact, all along, there was another dimension to what I was doing. Something quite terrible had happened not long after my interest in Julian had been reawakened. This was the second instance of synchronicity that I mentioned initially. I could put it aside for hours at a time, but it never went away, and it kept my inquiry shaped and urgent.

BOOK TWO

Draupadi's Dance

Too many hours have passed. No ordinary dicing match has ever taken this long. Her husband is wealthy—a prince—but even if he has lost everything he owns, it should all be over by now. The women's quarters are at a considerable remove from the court itself, but even back here one senses that something has gone terribly wrong: the silence is heavy as the monsoon cloud.

She is a princess and a woman of great distinction and beauty—"fragrant as the blue lotus," chaste and devout. Her hair is unbound, and she wears nothing but a single piece of fabric wrapped loosely and barely secured.

Suddenly, she hears running footsteps and the protesting cries of her maidservants, and before her is a breathless emissary from the court.

"Impossible," she answers, bewildered and angry together. "Can't you see . . . ?"

He quails and vanishes, and in moments the sequence repeats itself. But this time there are no words. Strong hands seize her rudely, and when she resists, they bury themselves in her long black hair and drag her along as she clutches at her wearing cloth and tries not to fall to her knees.

She is in the court, the sabha, where a woman of her class would rarely be, and one in her condition never, and she knows before she is told that her husband has indeed lost everything. Lost everything he'd owned—but then kept on gambling. He has staked his four brothers and lost them, staked even himself and lost himself, and finally, sure his luck would turn, he has staked *his wife. The man who has won the toss (luck could not have turned in this game, for the very dice were crooked) hates her and the whole clan she's married into. With lewd gestures he mocks her now and boasts of how he will use her.*

"Impossible," she whispers, as her eyes search the room. On every side are men she knows revere her and love her, but none of them moves. Frantically, she calls upon each of them by name—cousins, elders, brothers-in-law—and many of them are visibly anguished, but an unspoken understanding keeps every man's hands at his sides. No one will come to her defense, no one will look at her. Something dreadful has been released in this room that is proof against any appeal.

"Strip her!" comes the order, and again the powerful hands close on the woman—a warrior's hands, callused and brutal—but this time they seize the cloth she is wearing and tear at it roughly, and still no one moves, and mingled with their anguish and their shame is something else that is more truly their shame and that has to do with the loveliness of her and their inability to look away.

One sound she makes—throws back her head and hurls it at the heavens. Her eyes close, and she stops struggling, and her whole being is prayer—one prayer, one word, a name—her very self. Insensibly, she lets go of the wearing cloth, and rough hands pull at it now with growing excitement. They pull—as the princess stands unresisting now, and utterly absorbed—and pull, and pull, and the fabric piles up around her feet and his feet, and

he begins to sweat with the effort he is making. For something ex-
traordinary has happened.

There is no end to this fabric. And she doesn't need to open
her eyes to know it. She feels her freedom and dances it. Spins
around the room, oblivious now to everything but a song she alone
can hear.

CHAPTER I

Hindu Myth and Petaluma Reality

If that first instance of synchronicity felt like a gentle nudge—the coincidences around Julian's age and mine when we wrote and rewrote—the second was more like being mugged.

I had been invited to take part in a conference on the Berkeley campus that was to commemorate Mahatma Gandhi's birthday. The planners of the conference were faculty members and students from a variety of backgrounds who had come together the previous spring, heartsick at the murder of a student, a young woman who had thought herself safe working late one evening in the Associated Students' offices. (Her killer is still unidentified.) The conference had been envisioned as a means of extending Gandhi's teachings on nonviolence out into the campus community—a kind of "seeding" operation. As it took shape, however, its focus had become broader and broader and more and more cerebral. The stated topic was "Finding Unity in

Diversity: A Dialogue Between Religion, Science, and Social Action." High-minded, but hardly relevant, it seemed to me, to the concerns of women students fearful about leaving their dormitory rooms after dark and angry at having to feel that way. I wasn't sure what I was doing there until I discovered that I had been invited because a friend who had founded Berkeley's Peace and Conflict Studies department, and who speaks knowledgeably about Gandhian nonviolence, had begged off and suggested I be asked to speak in his stead, presumably because I'd thought a lot about nonviolence, too, especially with regard to women.

Not My Shining Hour

The conference was scheduled to begin Friday afternoon, October first. Gandhi's birthday was actually the second, but it was already that in India. I would be speaking in illustrious company: Huston Smith, perhaps the most respected scholar of world religions around, and Professor Marian Diamond, renowned authority on the brain and director of Berkeley's Lawrence Hall of Science. It was more than a little embarrassing to be representing the "social action" point of the triangle, since I had spent the past twenty-some years in a remote corner of West Marin County meditating. Fortunately, Dolores Huerta, executive director of the United Farm Workers, was scheduled to speak the next day, so that base actually would get covered—in spades.

My copanelists were lucid, riveting, and exceedingly polished. If I'd actually heard them, I'd have been even more intimidated than I already was, but as it happens I misunderstood the timetable and thought the whole thing got under way at four o'clock. In fact, it had begun around one, and when I slipped in at four, my own slot was just ten minutes away. So my grasp of what went on before I got there has had to be constructed from audiotapes that I received some months later. Discovering my error, I felt doubly overwhelmed—first by my appalling, if unintentional, rudeness, and second by the consequent fact that I would be speaking "cold start" in a context that had been taking shape over an entire afternoon.

It was not my shining hour. And it didn't help matters that the room itself, the law school auditorium, was furnished with desks in the front several rows rather than single seats, so that everyone sat at a formal remove from everyone else. It felt more like a senate or judicial chamber than a classroom—as different as it could possibly have been from the genial circles of chairs where I was used to meeting with my own students. And as I'd feared, the number of other women was really very small.

There is a trick I have learned since then that smooths the way somewhat when I find myself talking about feminism—or even broaching it—with a male or mostly male audience. It's very simple. I just ask at the beginning how many of them have daughters: would they hold up their hands and keep them up? I ask about granddaughters, nieces, wives, and sisters, and soon all of them have at least one hand in the air. Then I explain that when I use the word *feminism* I mean nothing more than what they mean themselves when they think about the women and girls they love—the safety they want them to enjoy and the good health, the simple respect, and the fair crack at becoming everything their own gifts and hard work will permit. This at least lets them know *I* know they aren't raving misogynists. It puts us all on the same side.

Of course that really works only if I'm talking to men who won't be insulted by the inference that they might even think I *thought* they were misogynists . . . if you get my point. And this *was* Berkeley, so I was probably better off just plunging in. The impassive stares, though, were daunting.

The Sari That Had No End

"Spirituality and the Women's Movement" was my topic. I began by explaining the meaning of the word *satyagraha*. (Only much later did I learn that Professor Smith had begun his talk by chanting, in a tremulous but deep and resonant voice, a Sanskrit invocation from the Upanishads that he translated to mean "Lead us from the unreal to the real," noting that the Sanskrit word *satya* meant "that which is real." We were actually in fair sync, all things considered.) The ultimate truth of Hinduism, I explained, its *satya,* is that all of life is one. Satyagraha, a fierce clinging to truth, was the basis of Gandhi's political vision. Satyagraha wasn't so much a political tool, I said, as a way of looking at life so that you saw the unity rather than the differences. And you didn't acquire that view by joining a particular party. Rather, you trained your senses and mind—"made yourself zero," in Gandhi's words—so that you could see truth clearly without any distortion from self-will or the senses.

The special value of "soul force" for today, I added, is that it permits human beings to be fully religious without confining themselves to a particular religious tradition. In Gandhi's words, "Religions are different roads converging in the same point. In reality there are as many religions as there are individuals."[1] I pointed out that for Gandhi politics had been inseparable from religion. "My devotion to truth has drawn me into the field of politics, and I can say without the slightest hesitation that those who say religion has nothing to do with politics do not know what religion means"(Gandhi, 76). For Gandhi, I emphasized, no human being was the adversary, or could be. The real adversary, always, is *asat,* untruth—the lie that one person can ever be justified in exploiting another.

I wanted to suggest that there are in the lives of nearly *all* mystics political dimensions we tend not to recognize. Few feminists had shared my own interest in the Catholic women mystics, I explained, because they saw them as having submitted unprotestingly to an institution that was patently—blatantly—patriarchal. If you looked at their lives in context, though—I gave several cases in point—you saw that within structures that were indeed oppressive, most of them had had occasion at one time or another to be what Gandhi called "professional resisters." They were not pale and silent brides of Christ at all; they were passionate and vivid, eloquent, resourceful, funny—and impressively stubborn.

I turned then to contemporary feminism and the mood of discouragement that had settled over much of the feminist community. I cited an observation Susan Faludi had made at the end of *Backlash:* that at the end of the 1980s women seemed curiously "unaware of the weight and dynamism of their own formidable presence" and of the "vast and untapped vitality"[2] they possess. I had wondered about this myself: Why aren't women using the power that is available to them even now? Why, for example, have we not exercised our most basic right as citizens, the vote itself, to reduce the level of violence that surrounds us by demanding adequate gun laws? Why are the United States Senate and House of Representatives still dominated so overwhelmingly by men? How could we have permitted military spending to become so bloated it eats up money that belongs to children, and the poor, and the elderly, and the mentally ill?[3] What *are* we waiting for? Why the paralysis?

I proposed a partial answer to such questions in the form of a story.

Draupadi is a prominent character in India's great epic, the Mahabharata. She was a princess, we are told, whose five husbands were brothers, princes of the Pandava clan. (The stories that explain this rare instance of regal polyandry are several, and some are very funny, but this didn't feel like the time or place to relate them.) Draupadi was singularly beautiful, competent, and wise. She was in addition so devout and so proficient in spiritual disciplines that she was known to have an inside track with the powers that be.

The Pandavas were the righteous branch of a family divided in a bitter dynastic feud. The eldest of the five brothers, Yudhishthira, was, in all respects but one, an exemplary man. His weakness for gambling would prove to be the chink in the whole family's armor, for it led him to agree one day to a game of dice with the family's sworn enemies, the Kauravas. Just before the game began, it was announced that instead of playing against his cousin Duryodhana, he would be playing Duryodhana's stand-in, a man known for his sharp practices.

From the first roll of the dice, Yudhishthira saw only defeat. He lost his land, his palaces, his horses and chariots, and his army, lost his armor and everything in his treasury. Stripped finally of all his possessions, he was still unable to stop, and to the horror of everyone watching, he bet his own brothers, lost them, and finally gambled even himself away. He thought he was through at that point, but his opponent said, "Wait," he could still redeem his losses. Just one more throw of the dice. If Yudhishthira won, he could have everything back. If he lost, he would lose all that was left to him to lose—the beautiful Draupadi.

And of course this is exactly what happened. The dice were thrown, Yudhishthira lost, and Draupadi fell into the possession of Prince Duryodhana.

The ensuing scene is a perennial favorite in Indian dance-drama. Draupadi is not present in court when the game is played, so when Duryodhana wins her, he sends an emissary to the women's quarters ordering her to come forth. When she refuses to come, Duryodhana's brother Dusshasana drags her out by the hair. With lewd gestures, he seizes her in front of everyone and begins to tear off her wearing cloth. Distraught, holding on desperately to her clothing, she calls out to her beloved Lord Krishna. It looks for a moment as if the vile Dusshasana will have his way with her, but suddenly Draupadi stops clutching her wearing cloth. Her eyes close as she falls into a state of rapt meditation, and her hands fly upward in a gesture that conveys both entreaty and utter abandonment to the will of God. It is understood that she is now entirely united with her Beloved. Her assailant grins rapaciously and starts to tug in earnest, and her garment begins to unfurl. It has become a sari, and it goes on unfurling—on and on and on—until you realize that this sari has no end. Draupadi spins about now in a dance of ecstasy, while the evil prince pulls and pulls, collapsing at last, sweating and exhausted, upon a billowing pile of bright silk.

I told the story because it conveys a point Gandhi himself used to love to make—that there is a kind of "wild card" within each of us, a well of courage and creativity we don't even know is in there until we learn how to tap into it through spiritual disciplines. In fact, Draupadi's story provides the perfect metaphor for Gandhi's nonviolent revolution. One of the key components of that whole movement was the production of *khadi,* the homespun cotton that women all over India made and wore, breaking the hold of the British textiles industry and rendering village economies viable again. The bolts of *khadi* spilling off the looms of India's women were more than a symbol for the women of India; they really *were* Draupadi's endless sari.

The reason I loved this story, I explained, was that it inspired me to think that when today's women's movement reconnects with its spiritual lineage, it will have the authority, strength, and momentum it needs to accomplish all its objectives.

What would such a movement look like? On the surface of things, I volunteered, it might not bear much resemblance to Gandhi's satyagraha movement, because like all of Gandhi's own various campaigns it would take shape on several fronts at once, as a specific response to a particular wrong. It would be local, that is, vernacular, and diverse. It would be nonviolent and permeated with a spirit of self-sacrifice, not because that is the womanly way to be, but because it is the supremely human way to be. It would be rooted in the silence of interior prayer and meditation, but it would be vociferous in response to injustice, confusing no individual or group with the adversary, identifying as the one real enemy the very idea that anyone could justifiably impose his or her will over another. It would recognize materialism itself as one of humanity's most damaging adversaries.

Draupadi Didn't Gamble

People generally like the story of Draupadi, and these people did, too, but this was, after all, a Berkeley audience, and I had been speaking in the same breath about women and nonviolence, so there was no reason in the world to be surprised when someone asked, "Are you saying that when a woman is being attacked she should go limp and pray?"

I knew I wasn't saying that, but, more important, was the Mahabharata? My trust in the ultimate validity of traditional epics is very strong, so I wasn't about to say something superficially conciliatory about different times and different places. I struggled for a moment but at last found my answer. It had two parts.

One was that in fact Draupadi had not gone limp. When she throws up her hands there is nothing despairing about her gesture and nothing particularly reckless. Her husband may have been a gambler, but Draupadi really wasn't. She has good reason to trust her Beloved because they have a relationship of long standing. Through austerities and charitable acts performed since she was a little girl, she has already been *letting go,* systematically, for years, of ordinary human attachments—to comfort, pleasure, vanity—and thus has accumulated what the Hindus call *tapas,* which she knows very well to be a better defense than anything in the physical realm. It's a magnificent spiritual allegory: As long as she holds on tight to ordinary measures, nothing out of the ordinary can happen. But when she stops trying to do it all herself, emptying herself of everything but trust and love, she opens the way for the miraculous. In the words of Meister Eckhart, "God expects but one thing of you: that you should come out of yourself insofar as you are a created being and let God be God in you."

The second part of my answer had to do with context. To understand the story fully, you had to know what preceded it and what followed it—which, for the sake of simplicity, I had omitted. Draupadi's story is the pivotal moment in the entire epic. Up until this episode, one might have entertained hopes that a cataclysmic war could be averted. Things might work out. But when Draupadi is humiliated as her menfolk sit by paralyzed, bound by a code of honor that will not let them intervene, we know that nothing short of a terrible cleansing will set things right. Indeed, in the war that constitutes most of the epic, not only her assailant and all of his clan but also the entire warrior caste would perish.

What the Mahabharata means us to realize, in other words, is that the desecration of woman—of the feminine principle, for that matter—is the sign and symptom of a civilization that has absolutely lost its moorings. It has no moral ascendancy. Draupadi's story, placed where it is in the epic, is thus an encoded message to the reader: "Things can get no worse." To extend the parallel with contemporary realities: a woman might choose to fight off a rapist, or she might be too frightened to put up the needed resistance. Either way, she will undergo severe and lasting injuries, both emotional and physical. That she should even have to decide which course to take—that she should even be subject to assault—is already a disaster, whatever the outcome. By calling on God (and in a subsequent discussion deploying her own dazzling juridical competence), Draupadi managed to extricate herself before the very worst could happen, but the appalling fact remained that nothing and nobody in the court itself worked on her behalf.

Why do we take it to be a given, I asked, that women are courting assault unless they've placed themselves under conspicuous male protection? Does violence against women and children have to be regarded as a force in nature, ineluctable, like hurricanes and earthquakes? When we jump past these more fundamental questions and worry about whether Draupadi should have fought back, isn't it like pretending that the remedy for the violence women face today is for them all to study karate or carry cans of pepper spray everywhere?

I read them a traditional Sanskrit teaching (it actually comes from an epilogue to the Mahabharata) that I believed put the issue in the right perspective: "That is a well-governed state where women, adorned with all dress and ornaments, and unaccompanied by men, can move freely and fearlessly in its roads and lanes."[4]

Clearly, I said, by this measure our own society is in dire straits. The roots of our malaise go so deep that most of the proposed solutions are mere stopgaps. One of the lasting strengths of Gandhi's teachings, I said, was that he stoutly rejected stopgap, short-term solutions. He wasn't just trying to get the British out of India but rather to build an Indian civilization that would make it impossible for India to be colonized ever again. . . . I told them something I suspected nobody in the room knew: that Gloria Steinem had spoken about Gandhi at length in her most recent book as an example of someone who had managed to end a cycle of violence not by reacting violently himself, but by challenging the whole structure of Indian society, which presumed oppression not merely from British colonialists, but also from higher caste Indians (toward untouchables) and from men (toward women). "Having experienced the humiliation of hierarchy," she observes, "he stopped identifying with the oppressor." [5]

I was grateful for that question from the audience. It had given me permission—obliged me, really—to say some things I'd felt too inhibited to broach initially. On the whole, I was feeling pretty pleased with things.

The conference was over around seven, and my husband and I had dinner in Berkeley before we drove home. The change to standard time hadn't taken place yet, so it was still twilight when we drove through Petaluma, and I wondered later whether, if we hadn't been so absorbed in talk, I might have seen the sullen, thickset man with the yellow bandanna around his hair whose likeness we would come to know as well as the President's in the months that followed. If I hadn't been so intoxicated with my own bright ideas, might I have noticed him and somehow known that something was wrong? Done something? Irrational as it was, this thought would recur, because the drive through Petaluma took us within a block of Polly Klaas's house no more than an hour before Richard Allen Davis entered it, and it

appears now that he wandered around for a while first, disoriented, drugged, struggling to remember whether one of these
houses might be his mother's, and deciding what he would say
to her if it was.

The next afternoon I was coming out of the movie theater
with my son, and we saw that since we'd gone in a couple of
hours earlier, someone had posted a flyer on the glass door. The
photograph was of an uncommonly pretty twelve-year-old girl
last seen with a man who had a dirty yellow bandanna around his
head. By evening new flyers had gone up, and more of the story
had begun to emerge. She had been taken at knifepoint from her
own bedroom, where she'd been playing board games with two
girlfriends who were sleeping over. Her mother and sister had
been asleep in the next room, and they'd heard nothing.

Draupadi Seized, Polly Abducted

Days passed, and no one received a ransom note.

It was numbing. It couldn't be. This little girl was one of our
own. Everybody knew, at the very least, someone who knew her.
We warded off what we feared by concocting elaborate scenarios
that would explain her absence but keep her unharmed. A
strange couple somewhere with unlimited resources who'd lost a
daughter just her age . . . Or maybe a trick she'd devised herself
in order to run away from home, for she was a very bright girl,
we understood, creative, and restless . . . A prank, perhaps, to get
publicity, because she did want to be an actress. We could forgive
her that. Only meanwhile, you couldn't drive out of town in any
direction without seeing somebody walking along gazing into
ditches or across fields, looking for scraps of fabric, a headband,
a shoe—(no, *not* a shoe, you reminded yourself, because she wasn't
wearing shoes when she left her home). You'd see off-road

vehicles, camouflage painted, full of National Guards with dogs, heading out to check the wilder wooded areas near the coast— and you knew in the middle of yourself, felt your stomach contract with the knowledge that in the end somebody would find something in a field or near a road and that Polly Klaas hadn't run away at all, hadn't been forcibly adopted by anyone.

The town was altered unbelievably. Parents of small children kept them very close; nobody had slumber parties; everybody installed dead bolts on all their doors and made certain no one could see into their windows at night; a vacant storefront was turned into the headquarters for a citizen-run effort to solve the crime; a "Polly Come Home" banner was stretched across Petaluma Boulevard with notes scrawled all over it from her grief-stricken classmates.

For my own part, I kept going back to everything I'd said that evening—about spirituality and feminism, about violence against women and children and what had to be done about it. I had presumed so much, been so glib. . . . What had I thought I knew, anyway?

When something like this happens, the response is instinctual: we all ask ourselves what resources we can bring to bear. A terrible drama is unfolding, it could still have a happy outcome: What part am I supposed to be playing? One prays, if that is something one does, or meditates, and does it in that special spirit of "offering it up" for another. And I did both of these. But it seemed to me also that in some mysterious way what had happened there in Petaluma was profoundly connected to the questions I'd already undertaken. I needed to read it, or *construe* it. Once again, I felt the weight of a kind of assignment settling upon me.

I tried to grasp the mysterious conjunction of the two stories—Draupadi seized and Polly abducted. I pondered the same mythic parallels many other women were feeling, particularly with the story of Demeter, whose daughter, Persephone, was seized and carried off to the Underworld. In private, with trusted women friends, I looked at questions too painful for public discussion. It was not a time for delivering feminist analyses; I remember my fourteen-year-old son murmuring one evening, "This makes me so ashamed to be a man," and he wasn't alone in feeling that way, and one wanted to honor those feelings. But as one friend observed, in barely a whisper, "What's happened to her—the silencing of her—it's too much like what happens to *all* girls," and those feelings, too, had to be honored.

It seemed imperative to me now that my two deepest commitments should flow together. Certainly I'd never believed that my spiritual practice could or should exist in a social or political vacuum. And for that matter, feminism had never been to me merely a social or political movement but an expression of spiritual hungers as well. Under the pressure of what had happened that fall, my questions were becoming clearer and more pointed. What does spirituality *look like* when it coexists with feminism's sharp critical faculties? And what does feminism *do* when it is steeped in spiritual perspectives?

In the first place, I needed to come to grips with my feelings about violence against women and children and what I thought was its relationship to patriarchy. Which really means that the anger that had slowly been gathering itself all these years was by now formidable and was going to have to be squared somehow with my spiritual practice.

Second, I realized after telling Draupadi's story that I had never brought my feminist concerns to bear in any systematic way on the Indian spiritual tradition. I'd loved the wealth of that tradition for so long, but I'd also been aware of elements I didn't love at all, and it was time to clarify my relationship to it.

Third, I was certain that this particular act of violence weighed as heavily as it did on so many people because, indeed, it did mirror something that was happening to girls that same age all across the culture. What could we do that would mitigate that other crime, and what are the real connections between the two?

Over the next few months that feeling of assignment, amorphous at first, began to clarify. I've never spun yarn out of wool, but I've watched a friend with her spindle, and what I was doing during October and November of that year was much like I imagine spinning to be: in one hand you have this coarse, thick wad of fibers, all tangled in on itself—the raw material of unmediated experience—and in the other a spindle. And little by little, as the spindle turns (as the days pass and you walk quietly through your routines and don't force anything), a coherent thread begins to form—a strand of meaning, strong and pliant. It seemed to me that this was taking place in several areas of my life at once: three distinct skeins all declaring themselves independently and at the same instant reaching out toward one another and weaving themselves into larger patterns. Patterns of remarkable beauty, in which the distinctions I'd been feeling obliged to make between feminism and spirituality finally vanished, supplanted by figures of strong, dancing goddesses and trees of life.

The first tangle remained untouched as long as there was still any hope at all that Polly Klaas might still be alive, but the day came when I had no choice but to take it up.

 *A War Against Women*

We were coming back to the house from evening meditation the night of December fifth, and my son came out to meet us.

"They found her, Mom, it was on the radio. She's dead."

A man had confessed to killing Polly Klaas and had led investigators to a pile of scrap wood outside the town of Cloverdale where he'd hidden her body sometime before dawn on October second. Slowly we took it in. When the first flyers went up the morning after her disappearance, we realized, the child had already been dead for hours. Everything anybody had done to try to bring her back had been after the fact. The phone banks, the door-to-door canvassing, the consultations with psychics—all of it after the fact.

Everybody absorbed the news, and responded to it, a little differently. There was a great deal of soul searching. All of us knew we'd have done anything to prevent what had happened,

so to protect the children who were still with us, it felt imperative to do everything now in our power—if we only knew what
that was. And of course a lot of people did think they knew and
that it was all about dead bolts and yard lights and neighborhood
cops walking regular beats. Or longer jail sentences for violent
criminals and electronic monitors for parolees and even surgical
or chemical castration for known sex offenders. I managed to
slip out of most of these conversations, though there were others
I found almost as hard to take: the ones in which everybody
commiserated over how there's all this senseless *evil* out there,
and how you can't hope to fathom it, and you can't address it in
its particulars, all you can really do is try to counteract it by creating a lot of *real* positive energy… and how for sure if we
could just put some limits on media violence it would help a lot
… but of course that gets into censorship, and you know where
that leads, so I guess. …

The media-fueled public obsession with the tragedy made
me uncomfortable. Privately hardheaded in response, I kept
noting how many brief and cursory newspaper reports appeared
during that time of other crimes against children that were no
less unspeakable but that apparently didn't meet the criteria of
"good copy" that this one did. Since I hadn't known Polly Klaas
personally, it felt wrong to grieve any less over these dozens of
other deaths than over hers.

I found, though, that I really couldn't put this local tragedy
out of my mind. Gradually I realized that it wasn't the murder
itself that had me so preoccupied or the circumstances surrounding it or even the fact that it had taken place the very
evening I had presumed to suggest there might be more of a
certain kind of sense to "senseless violence" than we like to believe. What was holding my attention was the very strong feeling
that I had been here before.

We're in school, the mystics tell us: that's what the human context is. Miss the point of a particular kind of experience, and it will keep replaying itself for you, over and over if need be, until you get it.

Years before, once in 1969 and again in 1976, a young woman I knew and cared for deeply had been killed as brutally as this girlchild had been. I had pretty much sealed off the memory of both those deaths, but now—for such is the power of things that come in threes (wishes, boons, curses)—I remembered vividly what I'd felt both times. It had seemed pointless then, too, to spend any emotion at all on the men who were directly responsible but just as pointless to refer everything to "evil" in the abstract.

Karen

Karen Sprinker was the eldest child of two of my parents' closest friends. She was just a little older than my sister Wendy, seven years younger than me. Strikingly pretty, smart, and willful, she spent most of her time on horseback. It was her voice you remembered first: it was improbably, almost comically, husky. After high school she enrolled at Oregon State University, where her boyfriend was already studying. I had been in California for years, but I remember seeing her for just a few minutes on a visit home to my parents sometime in 1968. She and the boyfriend careened briefly and noisily through the house on their way to work, or a party, dressed nearly alike in white jeans and bright T-shirts.

She must have been eighteen then, because she was nineteen in March of the following year, when she disappeared. She'd arranged to meet her mother in downtown Salem but never arrived. The police found her car in the parking structure of the department store where they were to have met, and their best guess was that she had run away. So many other restless young people were heading to San Francisco that year that it didn't seem out of the question ("I just wish she'd call," said her baffled father to mine).

A few months later, fishermen snagged the body of a young woman from the Long Tom River near Corvallis, and then police search teams found another. The second was Karen's. At that point, aware that two other local girls of about the same age had disappeared the year before, police began looking for a serial killer.

The man who destroyed Karen and three other girls was arrested not long afterward and is serving a life sentence. His wife was also tried and convicted of abetting him. It was during her trial that we all learned that none of the young women had been killed outright—nowhere near.

Within two years Karen's father suffered a cardiac arrest and died. "It broke his heart," my dad wrote to me. "The s.o.b. that killed Karen got Luke, too."

Lucille

I met Lucille Towers in 1976. She was only a year or two younger than I was. I don't recall what had kept her out of school until then, but now that she was there, a sophomore at Berkeley, she was there with eight cylinders. She was one of those students who don't take anything for granted: curious about everything, bursting with idealism. She took my course in the literature of mysticism and came to most of my office hours. We *talked*. I had included Gandhi in the reading list, and not only did she love what he said, she saw its relevance to the lives of the kids who came to the public library where she worked in Richmond. One of the last times I saw her was when I stopped in at the library on my way home to see the display of Gandhi photos and quotations she'd put up in the children's section.

Lucille was smart and funny and very good looking. You knew within minutes that she was from Texas and knew that she was not to be trifled with. I remember especially her long, strong stride, and that is especially painful to recall, because it was late one night when she was walking from the campus library to the parking lot—fast, you can be sure, but probably too taken up with the paper she was writing to be alert—that someone leaped out of the darkness and took hold of her. She struggled fiercely, and a couple of students actually saw them, but by then her attacker had a hand clamped over her jaw.

"It's okay," he yelled, "she's having a drug withdrawal!"

The students kept walking but changed their minds and ran for help. By the time the campus police got to Lucille, though, her assailant had struck her head repeatedly with a rock and she was unconscious. Her would-be rapist lunged at the police, who shot him in the stomach.

She never regained consciousness. She lay in the intensive care unit for eleven days, and her husband, Fred, sat with her until the end, having to endure the knowledge that her assailant was hospitalized one floor down under police guard, recovering from his bullet wound before he stood trial.

Lucille's death was for me the turning point in my commitment to staying on the campus. I would have had to scramble to keep getting teaching assignments (when you've gotten your doctorate at Berkeley they like you to teach somewhere else before considering you for a real position), but I could probably have kept reinventing myself, now as a religious studies lecturer, now as a women's studies instructor, and continued to find temporary part-time work, as many of my women friends did, for at least a few more years. In fact, though, I didn't try.

I actually did teach one more quarter. I remember this distinctly because Lucille's husband, Fred, signed up for my class. He sat near the back of the room. He knew how much she'd liked the course, and I think being there made him feel closer to her. I taught the same material I'd taught several times before, enhancing my lectures with new illustrations. It should have worked, but it really didn't. I could not get past what had happened any more than Fred could. I could not find in Teresa or Gandhi or Francis or anybody else anything that would begin to address what this quiet, fair, stricken young man in the last row had endured those eleven days at Herrick Hospital. Something was finished for me. I think I'd come to grasp the full irony of the word *professor.*

Adjusting the Focus

I did not want to think long and hard about these three tragedies. I understood the wisdom of withdrawing one's attention from certain things. "All that we are is the result of what we have thought," the Buddha said. "We become what we meditate upon," my teacher has paraphrased. Dwell on darkness and all your thoughts grow dark. You can lose your way.

But in fact I wasn't feeling lost as I struggled to make my own sense of Polly Klaas's death, and I wasn't feeling darkness close in on me at all. On the contrary, the anger that had been so diffuse when Karen and then Lucille died—so undercut by bewilderment—was focused now, and vigorous. The difference was, of course, that in the intervening years feminism had taught me there was a place to direct my anger that actually made sense. I had put on corrective lenses: everything that had been blurry before and indistinct was crystal clear.

What I felt I could not ignore, or even allow to be ignored, was the basic shape of these crimes—this *one* crime. This was not violence in general or in the abstract, it was violence in a particular and concrete form: a man overpowering and then destroying a young woman *with whom he has absolutely no acquaintance*. No emotional nexus, no drug deal gone awry, no personal score to settle. Certainly this is not the only violent scenario that gets played out in our culture. Indeed, I believe that more men are murdered each year than women—more boys than girls. But there is in this recurring configuration something that is pointedly and chillingly consistent with other aspects of women's and girls' ordinary, everyday experience.[1] Each of those girls had been deeply cherished, and not as a possession or an asset, but for the vibrant, lovely, intelligent being that she was and for all the promise her life held. But in the eyes of the man who destroyed her, she was absolutely nothing. She was, in fact, an object—a thing. Here was the logical endpoint of that process I'd seen traced out by feminist historians that began when women and girls first became negotiable tender.

It was with enormous reluctance that I came to believe I had to read these deaths not merely as acts of violence in an increasingly violent culture, but as crimes committed *by* men *against* women. The causes of violence are many, and so are the forms. Men are not the only ones who hurt and kill. Women hurt, women kill, women "abet" in hurting and killing; these are documented facts. But in my own experience, and among my acquaintances, throughout my entire fifty years, I had known nobody who had been killed by a woman—and no woman I'd known had killed.

I blurted all of this out to a friend one day, a longtime, dedicated advocate of nonviolence and a fellow meditator, and he recoiled. Focusing on male violence in particular, he argued, is exactly like targeting particular racial groups for blame. I couldn't agree with him. Men are not like members of a particular race or religion, I insisted. They are not a minority population whose rights are at risk, they are half of every racial group, half of every religion, and within each group they are the half that is responsible for far and away most of the violence. This isn't about blaming, I emphasized. It's about getting the clarity you need to identify root causes and to address them. To tiptoe around the gender dimension of societal violence is like living with an alcoholic and pretending there's really no problem. The illness in question—the addiction, if you will—has to do with the deeply rooted belief that difference justifies dominance, and that, I felt absolutely certain, is not a social or political problem at all. It is, surely, a spiritual issue of huge consequence. To be opposed to violence in a general kind of way without looking specifically at male violence against women made no more sense to me than if Gandhi had traveled around India talking about the evils of colonialism without ever bringing up the relationship between India and Great Britain.

My friend still looked troubled, so finally I made him an offer. Recognizing that he was worried about leaving female violence out of the equation, I offered to take full responsibility for addressing its causes and effects: I was willing to get to the bottom of why women commit the violent crimes they do if he would just see what he could do about men. For just a second his face cleared in relief, then he realized I was teasing.

And I guess I felt a little mean, a little heavy-handed. But I sat watching my son eat breakfast soon afterward, and I got to thinking about all the movies he'd seen and the recordings he'd heard and what they've told him about women and how men are supposed to relate to them, and for just a minute it seemed to me as unspeakably awful, as if someone had put strychnine in his orange juice.

In the past, my "spiritual" response to acts of violence had been to avert my eyes from what I couldn't change. I'd retreated into the "enclosure" of my community and family. But I didn't feel as if I could do that anymore. If *for no other reason* than that I was the mother of a man-in-the-making, I knew I had to do everything within my power to oppose what was happening. I did not have the luxury of withdrawing my attention or remaining silent.

My feminism was insisting that I look at things squarely, unblinkingly, but my spiritual practice steadied me, meanwhile, allowing me to begin imagining what effective resistance might look like but reminding me, too, over and over, that nothing of consequence would be accomplished quickly. The two perspectives were strengthening one another, and it felt very good.

A War Against Women

I had come to see that regarding young women as objects, and therefore disposable, is not, after all, the most wildly aberrant idea a boy or man might entertain today. It is the unspoken subtext of a great deal of what passes for entertainment and what works remarkably well as advertisement. And that, I now understood, is a direct inheritance from patriarchy. I knew that many would disagree. These young women were not killed by misogyny, they would insist, they were killed by sociopaths—bent, twisted, truly sick individuals. Patriarchal ideas about women had nothing to do with it.

And ten years earlier, I might have bought that line or at least tried to. Women get into a lot of trouble when we draw connections between things that are normally treated as unrelated phenomena: between foot binding and high spike heels, for instance, or the international sex trade and slavery, or fashion photography and pornography, or pornography and rape, or defense budgets and sexual performance anxiety. But what I'd come to see was that refusing to draw those connections takes a heavy internal toll, as any woman knows who has resisted her own feminism or merely lets it simmer away at the wordless level.

I saw Alice Walker's powerful film *Warrior Marks* about this time—her impassioned indictment of the practice of genital mutilation—and I heard her speak quietly but unequivocally there of "an ongoing war against women." She describes how a young girl who has just been "excised" takes into herself the knowledge of that war during the surgery itself. Walker's own window into the experience is the memory of the day her brother shot her in the eye with the air rifle he'd gotten for Christmas. She lost her sight in that eye, and although it was plain to her that the act was intentional, her family spoke only of "the accident." When the stares and questions of her classmates became so intolerable that she began to flounder in school, her family sent her off to live with her grandparents. "It was a patriarchal wound," she sees now, compounded by being exiled from the family, forcing her to conclude that in some way the fault had been hers.

When feminists describe the condition of women as a form of colonization, and when Alice Walker or Susan Faludi speaks of an "undeclared war against women," they are often rebuked. War and colonialism are specific kinds of experience, they are told, different from one another and different in important ways from other kinds of human oppression. When you maintain that something else *is* war or colonialism, you flatten out the meaning of either term: you harm language itself. As a sometime literary scholar I'd honored that line of reasoning in the past. Now, though, I'd come to see that at critical junctures language regularly fails women for the simple reason that in male-centered cultures language just isn't set up to speak for women or to carry women's meanings. This is the one of the subtler aspects of the silencing of women. (Advocates for the surgical removal of the clitoris and/or labia, for example, do not call it "genital mutilation" but rather "cleansing.") To characterize the condition of women as one-sided warfare, or colonization, is to state with real force what it can *feel like* to be a woman. When conventional language offers no literal or accurate terms for what a woman has experienced, she is forced to employ metaphors and similes—comparisons that will seem exaggerated and parallels that will sound strained to those who have no idea what she is talking about. The alternative is silence.

I had kept such a silence for some time, and the effort had cost me dearly. Polly Klaas's death was a real watershed, because I simply could not look at it, as I once might have, in isolation. Its resemblance to the only two other violent deaths that had ever touched my life was just not to be denied. The truth that forced itself upon me now involved a connection that I'd been close to making for some time but had resisted. It was that the men who deal out violence upon women and children—the rapists, the kidnappers, the molesters, the pornographers—are the unacknowledged but systematically groomed "enforcers" of a system of values and priorities that it seemed to me inaccurate to identify as anything but patriarchy.[2]

This was a profoundly disturbing conclusion, giving rise to a real firestorm of emotion. I would have been even slower to reach it if my husband had not been working his own way, by his own lights, to much the same position. Looking back now, I realize that the intimacy of our relationship—the "therapeutic container" in which our conversations took place—steadied us both as we struggled with these painful insights. Tim teaches fifth- and sixth-grade "gifted and talented" kids in Petaluma, and he hadn't known Polly Klaas, though many of his students had (his school is on the other side of town from hers). One morning as he stood before his class trying to talk about galaxies and black holes, the hum of twelve-year-olds all around, he went absolutely blank. For a moment all he could hear was a voice inside: *It could have been one of these girls, one of my own students.*

That first insight set off a kind of chain reaction that he would describe later in his journal: "When her body was found, and we learned what had happened, and I felt the devastation in the faces of my girl students, the voice got more insistent: she *was* one of my students. What happened to Polly, that night, it was clear, *had* happened to them all. They would never be the same again."

But his grasp of things enlarged still more: "During the week after Polly's body was found, and details concerning her alleged kidnapper and murderer came into focus, I realized that *he was one of my own, too.* I wasn't prepared for this. . . ."

Tim experienced his connection with Davis in two different ways. As a teacher, he knew firsthand that "Richard Allen Davis is sitting right now in fifth-grade classrooms all across the country, alienated, abused, angry, helpless, with little sense of right and wrong, and with nothing to lose." Teachers see these kids, they know what direction they're headed, and they know what it would take to redirect them—know, in fact, that in many cases it wouldn't take that much. They know of such kids, and know how poorly our educational system is equipped to intervene.

But the connection was not just that of a teacher to a student; as an adult male, Tim also knew "that Davis was on a continuum with every other man in the culture." The utter contempt for women that had allowed him to destroy a young girl was abnormal only in degree. Like me, Tim had been reluctant to read this crime as an expression of patriarchy: we'd all rather have classed it with earthquakes, meteor showers, bolts of lightning. . . . We'd rather have demonized the act and distanced it from everything familiar. But then he saw a quotation attributed to Polly's alleged kidnapper, describing a violent assault on a woman Davis had abducted several years earlier: "We both got something out of it."[3]

This is the timeless, terrible rationalization Tim recognized, of men who rape women: the great lie that justifies not just the serial rapist but the college boy, as well, who just decides to "push things along." Try as we might to place Davis outside the norms of human behavior, he is not the utter aberration we would like to believe. "He is part of a male culture," Tim wrote, "that bolstered his feelings, however bent they might have been, however distorted or self-serving or even irrational. At the center of that culture, driving it, is the understanding that sex is domination and that women want it to be. And whenever any man tells a lurid joke or rents a pornographic video or brags about last night's conquest, we've done our little bit to perpetuate it."

Unrestrained now, my feminism had picked up momentum, tearing illusions away at a great pace and forcing me to see things I really didn't want to see. I think I was experiencing what many women do. You keep wanting to feel—well, innocent, and surrounded by innocence. You hate to be one of those people who read sexism or male oppression into every little thing. You want to be able to laugh with your kids at formulaic Hollywood movies, blind and deaf to the subliminal misogynist messages. But in fact there's no going back. Once the blinders are off, you do see and hear, and the whole of yourself has to take it in.

My husband was not the only man who would provide me with insights into male experience that I would have been happier not receiving. Mike Messner is a sociologist and sportsman who believes that boys and young men learn "from each other and often from pornography" a "sexual script" that he summarizes as follows:

> Through this script, young males essentially train their own minds and bodies to become sexually aroused through a three-stage process: objectification of a woman, fixation on one or more of her erotically charged body parts, and conquest through real or imagined sexual intercourse. In this process, the girl or woman, in the male's mind, is reduced to a manipulated object and fragmented into a set of body parts that the male uses to excite himself. Importantly, the sexual act is most erotically salient for the young man in terms of his status vis-à-vis his male peers—not in relation to his actual sexual partner. Though she is physically present, the girl or woman, as a thinking, choosing partner, is obliterated.[4]

Here was the strychnine, isolated, as if in a laboratory beaker. The verb *obliterated* was chilling, but it seemed accurate. Could anyone seriously question the relationship between this figurative obliteration and the real destruction of young women like Karen and Lucille? I didn't think so, and the process Messner outlined seemed particularly horrific in the light of everything I knew now about cultures where women are cherished, instead, and the feminine is revered.

Wars That No One Wins

There are so many reasons not to bring into clear focus the violence that is daily enacted upon women and children, and I have adopted them all at one time or another. "Do not get mired down in the horrors," whisper the admonitory voices, "and don't underscore the disempowering text of woman-as-victim. Speak if you must about violence, and how it can be diminished, but do not single out whole categories of crime and characterize them as male violence. No good will come of that."

And I would have to agree: not much good *would* come of that in isolation. But as the first step toward setting things right, it is indispensable. Mohandas Gandhi never confused the British people themselves with the cruel policies of colonial government. The real adversaries, he knew very well, were colonialism itself and the racism that rationalized it. On the other hand, he knew very well that British men and women were implementing those policies. Human beings had enslaved India, and it was to human beings that Gandhi addressed his nonviolent campaign for India's freedom. And basic to that campaign was a clear "mirroring" of the wrongs that would have to be set right. "Expose the injustice" was ever and always the byword of satyagraha. Set wrongdoings out in the strong light of day.

Is it an exercise in male bashing to draw the dark picture I have of a society held hostage under the tacit threat of male violence? Surely not. The men in our lives today didn't invent this culture, they've only inherited it. They're only culpable if they do nothing to change it. And of course there *are* men who are trying to change it. Mike Messner is one; another is his coauthor, Don Sabo, who writes, "There is something rotten in the ways that manhood has been defined and the ways that men relate to one another, to women, and the planet. Increasingly, men are beginning to reconsider their identities, their sexuality, and the violence they have shown toward women and toward one another." [5]

Suggesting that something like a war against women is going on, and pointing to the ways in which women are being hurt by that war, has been taken by some critics to imply that men are correspondingly victorious and therefore happy. Since men are plainly not happy—are more likely than women to become addicted to drugs and alcohol, to be homeless, to commit suicide or spend time in prison—then either they are not in fact victorious *or* there isn't really a war at all.[6]

But did Alice Walker say that anybody was winning this war? Did she say, for that matter, that any war has a winner? When a war is fought, particularly a long, drawn-out war, everybody loses. After a hundred years, or a hundred days, one army may walk away with certain spoils. But what has typically happened, in the meantime, to its economy, its government, its arts, its system of education, its *sensibilities?* What has the cost been to the United States, for example, of becoming and remaining the world's dominant military power? What has the cost been to American men of their long-standing efforts to keep women subordinated?

Behind the deaths of the three radiant young women that concerned me now were three men one might best describe as "benighted"—full of darkness. Sociopaths, to use the clinical term. Not just ordinary guys who were having a bad day, but individuals with severe and long-standing disorders. When I insist upon underscoring their gender, it is not with the intention of suggesting that the men and boys we interact with each day are all potential rapists or murderers. It is rather to remind us that *as males,* men like Richard Allen Davis have worked from scripts that are not merely available to men in this culture but *are pressed upon* them. Damaged during their childhoods, individuals like Davis, in every case I know of, are in a very real sense wound up and set loose by the imagery of male violence against women (as well as children, homosexuals, and "others" of every kind) that is so stunningly pervasive in this culture. It is as if a certain kind of instruction, or permission, were being beamed out at all of us, all the time, not merely from X-rated videos or "adult books" but from ordinary Hollywood films, television programs, and advertisements of all kinds—so effective and relentless that eventually the most impressionable among us cannot but act upon it.

I am not suggesting that anyone is consciously deciding to fill our streets with potential bad apples. I *am* suggesting, though, that the will to be sure this doesn't happen is not overwhelmingly evident. Although our elected leaders could direct federal funds to drug rehabilitation programs, family services, job training, more schools with smaller class sizes and adequate counseling staffs, neighborhood gymnasiums, boys' and girls' clubs, mental health facilities, early intervention programs for troubled and abused children, and any number of other programs that are *known* to reduce crime as well as the human misery it springs from, they spend our money instead building more prisons and developing increasingly sophisticated methods of criminal detection and pursuit.

"Don't worry," is the apparent motto, "we'll get them at the other end." And they do, more or less, with undercover sting operations, high-speed chases, SWAT team deployments, and neighborhood surveillance by armor-plated helicopters. And because so few efforts are made to reach troubled kids, we are assured of a steady supply of reasonably desperate criminals, so that there is every apparent justification for building more prisons; hiring more police and arming them more heavily; hiring more judges and lawyers, for that matter, and building more courtrooms; writing more stringent laws, imposing the death penalty with increasing frequency . . . *sustaining, that is, the punitive model for life that has always been fundamental to patriarchy.* The end result is that we *all* live in an atmosphere that feels increasingly like socially sanctioned warfare. Women are once again impounded almost as effectively as they were under

Mesopotamian law: not individually but collectively, by men who don't even know us.

Through his village uplift program, Gandhi showed India that the path to freedom wound its way through all kinds of areas that might have appeared irrelevant to getting the British out of the country: mass literacy campaigns, abolishment of child marriages, construction of safe water supply and hygienic latrines, and of course the manufacture of *khadi* and the concomitant refusal to buy British textiles. By the same token, I was coming to understand now how many issues are of serious concern to feminists that don't necessarily appear to be. I saw more clearly now how patriarchy actually works—invisibly, that is, and so far-reaching in its effects that it is very difficult not to envision a malign and calculating genius behind it. Silently it persists, much like the electronic perimeter fences many dog owners install around their homes. The fence is underground—you never see it—but the dog very quickly gets an idea where it is because her collar gives her a good sharp *ping* whenever she starts to cross it.

CHAPTER 3

A Circle of Beauty, a Wall of Strength

"Alice," he says after a long silence, "do you know what I believe? I believe that if the women of the world were comfortable, this would be a comfortable world."

—SAMUEL ZAN,
GENERAL SECRETARY OF AMNESTY INTERNATIONAL IN GHANA,
QUOTED BY ALICE WALKER IN *Anything We Love Can Be Saved*

In 1994, federal legislation was enacted declaring that violent crimes committed against women are a violation of their civil rights. This means that rape or wife beating is actually a federal crime. The Violence Against Women act was well intentioned, but its passage didn't fill me with optimism. All it was really likely to mean, if indeed it held up in the courts, was that more men would go to jail, most of whom would come out of jail more disposed to violent behavior than ever. Worse still, adoption of the act signaled to everyone: There, now. We've taken care of it. Discussion finished.

When a woman is raped or beaten up, recognizing that her civil rights have been curtailed does serve notice that she is a full citizen before the law. But it's a singularly limited way of responding to what has actually taken place. Realizing that laws can do no more than declare something illegal and mete out punishments for wrongdoers, I struggled now to find words for what I felt really needed to be addressed.

And words didn't really come. Images did, though, in profusion. Images of young girls walking about, dancing, playing together hilariously or sitting alone, lost in thought—at home, every one of them, in the "airy spaces" Luce Irigaray evokes so movingly: "the space of bodily autonomy, of free breath, free speech and song."

But almost at once I find myself wondering what freedom they can enjoy, of song or speech or movement, if their spaces—their "boundaries"—are not honored, and as soon as I do I find myself taking another step, imagining that around every girl child there might extend a zone of real safety, invisible, but absolutely impenetrable. And as soon as that happens, I realize I'm coming full circle, conjuring up something dangerously like patriarchal enclosure: safety at a price we shouldn't have to pay.

The paradox is one that every mother of a girl confronts: you want her to be fearless, take risks, make her own choices. But as soon as she steps out of the safety zone marked out by convention for "good girls," she is genuinely and terribly imperilled.

The solution, it seemed to me, lay in imagining a different version of safety and a different kind of guarantor. Let's look at that for a moment. . . .

In the first place, we need to bring the status quo itself under question. In anything approaching a truly human community, built upon even a modest reverence for life and spirit, the girl child is safe.

Why girls in particular? What about little boys and old men and shell-shocked Vietnam veterans? And the earth itself? Doesn't everyone need protection?

Of course they do.

But a girl who is just becoming a woman is, I will insist, particularly defenseless precisely because she is turned inward, absorbed in a momentous transition. And a society's willingness to recognize this and guarantee her safety is a good index of *everybody's* safety: a society that's wise enough to draw a protective circle around her will do the same for everyone who is vulnerable. That is, of course, the logic behind the description I've referred to earlier of the "well-governed state" as seen by India's ancient sages. In order for women "adorned with all dress and ornaments, and unaccompanied by men," to be able to move about freely and without fear, a great many other good things would also have to come about. The streets would be broad and well lit, and there would not be desperately poor or crazed individuals trying to make their home there. Wealth would not have piled up in the hands of a few. Little boys wouldn't be growing up unloved and unguided. The laws of the land would be working for everybody. All of this is implied.

But the sages were also implying, I believe, that for women to be truly safe, good laws are not enough. There must also be, ambient in the culture, some sense of connection between women and the sacred. The unseen force field I'd been trying to imagine would in fact be a kind of sacred zone—one that doesn't exist in the external world at all, but in minds and hearts. For this, ordinary laws are the frailest possible substitute.

To honor the sacredness of girls and women is not to elevate women over men, or girls over boys, but rather to honor life itself—procreativity, and nurturance; generosity, abundance, laughter. But all of this requires in turn that the very word *sacred* must mean something, too. And this is, of course, why the sort of safe space I kept trying to imagine was so problematic. Spiritual principles can't be legislated. Maybe they can't even be taught. Maybe, as some say, they can only be *caught*. Like measles . . .

And this was where my feminism turned empty-handed to my spiritual practice: "Okay, well and good. But how do we make *that* happen? Where are our Typhoid Marys?"

It is almost impossible to imagine, in a culture as thoroughly secular and diverse as our own, how one might go about creating or recreating even a semblance of the sacred zone. There is so little in Western myth or literature that supports it. Quite the contrary, in fact. Over and over during the winter of 1994 various women friends would recall the story of Demeter and Persephone. Writer Noelle Oxenhandler put it so well:

> Kidnapping has to do with the invasion of the "bright" world in which children chatter and play in their rooms, and wait for school buses and swing in playgrounds, by another world, the dark world of unspeakable sorrows, the underworld. Part of the horror of Polly's story is how swiftly these two worlds connected, how easily the dark world made its claim—as when, in the ancient myth, a crack opened up in the earth, and golden haired Persephone, who had been happily playing with her companions, vanished with the dark figure of Hades into the ground. . . .[1]

It was a terrible myth—I'd hated it as a young girl—and when I went back to the sources I found it was even worse than I'd remembered, because the whole plot against mother and daughter had been carefully set up. Zeus himself had been a co-conspirator. Demeter in her grief could render the whole earth barren, but all she could get for her troubles was a compromise.[2] By the time her story had taken the form in which we know it, patriarchy was firmly in place, and all the narratives that made a different kind of point had been carefully suppressed or reworked.

When I was first trying to come to grips with the grief and anger that flooded my thoughts after Polly Klaas's death, I hadn't yet come to understand the place—and the power—of countertexts. Not explicitly, anyhow. In a kind of blind, instinctive way, though, I was reaching out for imagery, for *stories,* or "scripts," that would incorporate the full range of things I was feeling and that would allow me to move forward. I was feeling agitated, on the one hand, and drained, on the other. I knew what I wanted to do—Gandhi had talked about it so much, the transmuting of anger into the capacity to change things. But how does one actually do that? Where do you start?

There is a saying among practitioners of folk medicine that when something in a forest has poisoned you—an insect, a reptile, a berry—the cure is nearby. Look around and you will find close at hand the plant whose leaves or bark or root will offset the life-threatening toxin. Gandhi always focused on the work at hand: he didn't go looking for causes, they came to him, walked in his front door. And he addressed them right there, too—locally. Instead of bringing in experts or influential big guns, he drew greatness out of the ordinary women and men in the affected communities. And it seemed to me that something of that spirit was visible in the grassroot responses to violence that I was seeing all around me in my own Sonoma and Marin Counties and that I could learn from them.

Born of Woman

Kristi Moya Zoog lives just a few miles away from me, so we arranged to meet at a bakery that is located midway between our respective homes. The establishment is one of the better kept secrets of the North Bay: its champagne tea buns and apricot tarts, its calzones and focaccias and cheese Danish, are as good as anything you'd find in San Francisco. In fact, several photographs decorate its walls of friends standing in front of the Eiffel Tower eating croissants they've brought from home. Bicyclers fill these backroads every weekend, and like flocks of tropical birds they descend on the place Sunday mornings in wave after neon-bright wave. This was a particularly balmy Sunday, so as Kristi and I sat outside and talked, traffic in and out of the tiny business never let up.

Kristi is one of nine West Sonoma County women who are the core of an organization that first came together to protest the Gulf War. Many of them fell away when the war ended; those who stayed on wanted to understand, in Kristi's own words, "how it had gotten to be okay to have that war." Each of them took one area, like economics, education, and health, and asked that question. The conclusion they arrived at startled them.

"It came down to rape. It seemed to us that in a society where it's okay for women to be raped, then other kinds of violence were okay, too, right on out to invading other countries and dropping bombs on civilians."

I had heard Kristi and her friend Diane Hart being interviewed on KPFA, Berkeley's independent radio station, and had sensed that in some very important way their orientation was much like my own. They weren't talking about rights or changing the legal system. For them male violence against women and children isn't just a matter of crimes committed against individuals; it goes much deeper. It amounts to a far-reaching assault on the sacredness of life itself and on women as the bearers of life.

Kristi had never heard of Gerda Lerner or the historic circumstances around the commodification of women's sexuality. She and her friends had arrived at their belief in the connection of one kind of violence to another through reading and discussion, certainly, but their personal experience weighed in heavily. Certain that they understood some of the cultural roots of violence, but baffled still in many regards and eager to translate what they did understand into effective resistance, they formed an organization they called "Born of Woman." They pulled together a library of books and films that they made available to others, they gave workshops and talks, they published a newsletter, and they held public vigils—ceremonies that were designed to replicate the long-range transformative process to which the members of BOW had committed themselves.

I am not drawn to rituals by and large. Maybe it's just the Scottish Presbyterian in me; the quiet inward focusing of meditation has always suited me better than external observances. Under the pressure of everything I was feeling now, though, I was much more open than I'd have been in the past to the ceremony that members of BOW carried out at their public vigils. There was nothing merely formal about this particular ritual; every element was meaningful, and I sensed that the women who had designed it had an end result in mind—a kind of alchemy of the heart and will—that was very close to what I was trying to work in myself. Anthropologists have taught us to see that behind every ritual there is a narrative. The Eucharist reenacts the Last Supper. A Seder meal reenacts the Jews' escape from Egypt. Behind this improvised ritual, too, I saw a kindred sort of narrative: a countertext, and an antidote.

The ceremony requires a large, beautiful altar cloth, a bowl of seawater with a sheaf of herbs, three low round planters with soil, three stone Goddess sculptures, one large basket of cut flowers, and three bowls of mixed flower seeds. Alongside these tokens of a nurturant, fruitful earth and of the sacred feminine are two other essentials. One is a public address system, and the other is a number of media reports of assaults against women and children that have taken place within one's own county.

The men and women participating in the vigil form a circle around the altar cloth. Someone dips the bunched herbs in the water and shakes them gently over the circle in a seawater blessing. Afterward there is a song, and then someone declares the intention of the vigil:

"To make visible the war on women, to break through our numbness and despair, to transform our rage and grief into action, to reclaim our potency and value as women."

Three women take turns reading accounts of violence. The narratives are inevitably graphic and hard to read. They are about teenagers and infants, wives, mothers, elderly women, and children. It is one thing to pass the eye quickly over these stories in the newspaper, quite another to read them aloud like this. With each account, a woman steps forward and places flowers on the altar.

When the last story has been read, the group joins hands and shouts a clear, strong "No!" repeated several times. "This has to stop because we say so: Because women say so." Participants are invited to step forward at this point, take seeds from a bowl, and scatter them in the soil in the planter. Finally, they hold hands and sing songs of celebration. "Open the circle," someone says, "and take the seeds in the planters and the seeds in our hearts home."

So here they were, the same two ideals, reconciled symboli-
cally, that I had been struggling to reconcile in my own life: the
fearless truth-seeing that feminism demanded of me, and the
inner calm and balance I'd always sought through meditation
and that, if lost, would have meant the end of me as well. The
ceremony seemed to me to have a certain initiatory quality.
Many of the elements of *kinaalda,* the Navajo ceremony for
girls, were evident.

In the construction of that "circle of beauty," I saw something very like the "safe space" I had been imagining—protected from within by the presence of images of the sacred
feminine and protected around the perimeter by individuals
who "know how to hold energy" (like the *discreti* in Clare of
Assisi's convent).

It is vital, I saw, that the circle be strong because of the force
of the emotions discharged within its bounds. It is almost as if a
bomb were to be defused there. The images of feminine divinity
that are placed within the circle during a vigil are not a casual
gesture. As Kristi herself explained, becoming aware of the Goddess traditions was what first allowed her to understand *why* she
felt so very angry at how women are regarded today.

In the second phase of the ritual, the truth is told—without
compromise, no matter how harsh it is, *because* it is true. "We
create a field of beauty," Hart explains, "so we can listen with
our whole body and mind, letting ourselves fully feel our rage,
despair, and grief." It did worry me, for reasons I've already
touched upon, to think about the effects of inscribing stories of
inhuman cruelty more indelibly into consciousness than they already are, but in fact truth telling is not the ultimate endpoint
of the ritual. Having acknowledged one's anger—and this is
the ceremony's third phase—participants commit themselves to
transforming it.

"We believe that by paying attention to these stories," says Hart, "we will discover what we need to change to create a world where women are honored and nothing will ever be done to harm the children." Tracing cultural violence to its sources, Kristi told me, has turned up surprising connections.

"You know, you just start looking at all those choices. What you eat, the movies you see, the music you and your kids listen to, what you wear and who made it and what kind of conditions they live in. It's all connected."

In practical terms, what sort of defense against male violence can we imagine women might be able to wage who reach way inside, who rely on their connection with one another and with the sacred? Sustained down through time, in folk belief, there is a strong sense that we could do a great deal.

When church authorities were deliberating the canonization of Saint Clare of Assisi, people who'd known her came forward with all kinds of stories that attested to her sanctity. Two of these had to do with her successful repulsion of hostile assailants. In one episode she was believed to have saved the convent of San Damiano and in the other the city itself. In the first case a roving band of mercenary soldiers was actually scaling the convent walls. Consoling her sisters, telling them they needn't be afraid, "she turned to the help of her usual prayer," and the troops departed "as if driven away." When an entire army was about to invade Assisi, word was sent to Clare. This time she called the sisters together, had ashes placed on her own and everyone else's head, and ordered them all to pray. Once again, the assailants departed, and the city celebrates the event every year on June 22.

What the people of Assisi recognized in Clare and her companions was that their very presence at San Damiano signaled their willingness to renounce every ordinary comfort. The Poor Ladies lived entirely on alms, refusing to buffer themselves against deprivation with any sort of endowment or cottage industry, and it was understood that this very way of life endowed them with a certain leverage against the demonic forces in life. When Clare gathered her sisters together and placed ashes on their heads, the gesture itself called up the capacity for sacrifice that all but defined the life they shared and also the mysterious power that in every time and place has been associated with that capacity.

When women like Kristi Moya Zoog and Diana Hart construct a ceremony that helps them give form and voice to their opposition to male violence, they are working within a tradition—a *lineage*. And as I thought about these circles of good women and their mysterious power, I began to think more clearly about the two young women in my own acquaintance whose deaths had made the issue of violence against women real for me, and urgent. I saw now that by immersing myself as I had in the teachings and lives of women mystics for the past several years I had been preparing—quite unconsciously—to take up the challenge to my spiritual practice that those deaths had posed. By building a circle of beauty and a wall of strength of my own, I hoped I might somehow "contain" stories like these and, eventually, respond to them effectively.

Women who believe, with Alice Walker and Diana Hart and Kristi Moya Zoog, that something like a war is being waged upon them and their daughters are not easily dissuaded. They have dressed the wounds, healed the traumas, buried the dead. But what must be understood regarding women like Alice, Diana, and Kristi is that they do not stop with calling a spade a spade, and a war a war. No more than Rigoberta Menchú stopped when her father and mother and brother and sister were all murdered, with unbelievable savagery, for their efforts to organize a resistance movement on behalf of the indigenous people of Guatemala. No more than the members of Women Together, composed of Irish women, Protestant and Catholic, who organized to oppose the violence that has made Northern Ireland a war zone . . .

No more than Eve Nichol, mother of Polly Klaas, who maintained a silence so complete throughout that agonizing October and November that you found yourself thinking about her all the time and breathing wordless prayers in her direction . . . and who found the strength to write, only a few days after her daughter's body was found:

> It is with unspeakable sorrow that I must let go of the dream we all shared—the dream of our sweet Polly coming home again. My heart tells me that she is safe in a place filled with light and love. . . . I wish I could be with my beloved community to share our grief, but for now I need solace and the strength of my family and closest friends. My heart is broken, so much life unlived, but your miraculous outpouring of love brings me comfort, and time will bring us peace.
>
> . . . For now, let's grieve together for our hope lost, for our faith betrayed. When we can, let's open our hearts to forgiveness and healing. . . . We must have mercy ourselves. And Polly would want us to thrive on the love we have created, not the hate. . . .

When I spoke last with Kristi Moya Zoog, Born of Woman was in a dormant period. Its members were catching their breath, assessing, and asking themselves what direction their work will be taking.

"Initially, you know," said Kristi, "so much of what you're doing is fueled by anger, and after a while you've moved beyond the anger, and it isn't clear what you'll be drawing on instead, and what direction to go with it. . . ."

First, it seems, there is that long, steady look at what we would infinitely prefer were not there to be looked at. And, second, a resolute gathering up of oneself *into* oneself, a refusal to be conquered or defined by what one has seen, no matter how daunting it might be . . .

"You find yourself moving into this huge space," Kristi murmured.

And I thought I knew what she meant. As you look more and more deeply into the sources of violence, back through time and the immensity of wrongs perpetrated, there are no more villains. None you can touch. No *other*, finally. Only oneself, one's own consciousness, one's own capacities and relationships, the depth of one's own desire to begin setting things right, and the opportunities that one's own situation affords. And that will be different for every individual.

Participating in a ceremony like the one designed by members of BOW is not meant to be seen as an end in itself. It's rather a kind of rehearsal for life. It can help us impose some kind of structure on powerful emotions and perceptions and prepare us to at least *want* to respond appropriately. But it is no substitute for a response. When I read those stories about Saint Clare and the would-be invaders, I kept having to recognize that Clare and her companions didn't just sit in a circle, they *prayed*. I felt certain that the effectiveness of their prayers lay in their ability to transcend distractions—to empty out the mind—and that it was this emptying out, for which the abandonment of material goods was really just a preparation, that explained their power over adversity. By the same token, I cannot imagine how one could even begin to oppose violence effectively without a steadily deepening commitment to the practice of meditation.

Feminism had opened my eyes to a vast web of terrible connections I'd been slow to recognize, and feminist spirituality had insisted that I own the anger I experienced when I did recognize it. But I knew feminism alone couldn't help me transmute that anger into the kind of steady, unflinching determination I thought it would take to make substantive changes, and I didn't think the more loosely conceived forms of feminist spirituality could, either. I was reasonably certain that only meditation could do that: meditation supported by all the ancillary disciplines—one-pointed focus, the "enclosure" of consistent practice, the diminution of egocentricity, and the harnessing of desires.

To the endlessly repeated story of young girls seized and silenced, I had begun to construct a fragile countertext, but I'd really only begun. In lives like Saint Clare's one can see moments when the West has experienced the power of the sacred feminine and even celebrated it, but I needed much more than isolated moments. I was certainly familiar with India's far more fully developed tradition of reverence for the sacred feminine, and I might have turned to that tradition anyway at this point for the spiritual sustenance I was craving, but the afternoon I spoke in Berkeley I learned something that would make that tradition newly and immensely significant for me. It seemed there was one a small piece of Draupadi's story that I hadn't told because I hadn't known it, and learning about it now would have far-reaching effects, the first of which was to draw me much more deeply into the Mahabharata itself. . . .

CHAPTER 4

The Endless Sari

I'm sure I'd told the story of Draupadi's sari dozens of times without ever thinking much about Draupadi herself. This time, though, because of what had happened in Petaluma the next day and the parallel I'd sensed between fiction and fact—Draupadi seized and Polly abducted—thoughts about her lingered with me for some time afterward. As I reflected on the other bits of her story that I could recall, it struck me that she might be a very useful touchstone for the questions I was trying to answer about spirituality and women's lives, and before long I found myself trying to "draw her down" as eagerly as I had Julian of Norwich.

It felt very right and very timely to be doing this, because I was feeling in need of a fresh point of entry into the culture that decades before had become my second home. When I'd first met Easwaran, I was feeling as disaffected from mainstream American culture as most Berkeley students were in the late sixties, and everything about India had seem constrastingly wonderful. I'd plunged in eagerly: learned to wear a sari and pile my hair into a chignon and make a *tilak* mark on my forehead; learned how to make *chappatis* and chutneys; saw my first Satyajit Ray films and heard Ravi Shankar in concert. Once I'd begun to study Sanskrit a little, and come to understand the depth and the beauty of the Indian spiritual tradition, I was enthralled, and for years I don't think I really looked up.

Eventually, though, that had changed. It's a function of middle age that the parts of ourselves we've undertended come back: feminism, in my own case, had certainly reasserted itself, but so had my sheer Americanness, strengthened no doubt by the hours I was spending now at Little League games, or watching movies with my son that were a far cry from the Apu Trilogy. The drift was gradual, but very real. By my fiftieth year, the intimacy I'd once felt with India and Indians had faded considerably, and I was conscious of a sense of real loss. With my rekindled interest in Draupadi, a door back into that world had swung open, and I found myself peering through it hungrily. I had always known about India's Divine Mother tradition, but I had kept it carefully compartmentalized. It hadn't occurred to me to bring it into active conversation with my feminism or any of my other contemporary Western notions.

Huston Smith has described tellingly the value of looking at life through the lens of more than one culture:

> Until sight converges from more than one angle, the world looks as flat as a postcard. The rewards of having two eyes are practical, they keep us from bumping into chairs and enable us to judge the speed of approaching cars. But the final reward is the deepened view of the world itself.[1]

I wanted to bring this kind of "deepened view" to bear on my struggles to reconcile feminism and spirituality, and renewing my appreciation of India's vision of things seemed an ideal way to do this.

Draupadi spoke to me now precisely because she was *not* a nun or an anchorite. She was "out there" quite literally—granted no shelter or respite from even the cruelest forces in life. A wife not once, but five times over, and a mother whose sons all would die in the Great War. Brought up a princess, thrown into poverty and exile, she would even be obliged to make her way disguised, for a time, as a lady's maid. And through all of this, a spiritual aspirant of tremendous capacities: for it's one thing to achieve oneness with God in a monastic cell, seated alone in stillness, and quite absolutely another to do this under the circumstances she did. In the figure of Draupadi one sees unitive awareness tested in the thick of life—thinking on its feet, and breaking out in prophetic utterance.

I'd always loved Draupadi's story, but now I saw in it the lives of women I knew. Tracy, who gets up a little earlier every morning to meditate and finds her three-year-old is still climbing onto her lap to play before she's even got her eyes closed. Or Barbara, who thought she'd raised her kids and could finally resume the threads of her own life and interests, only to find they were back—one with a drug problem, the other with, oh, call it vocational ambivalence. Or my Berkeley students, for that matter, whose visions of university life hadn't really included having to hold down twenty- to thirty-hour-a-week jobs while they studied or living in apartments that were broken into regularly—by burglars, if they were lucky, who wanted only their stereos and computers. A couple of years ago I kept seeing a book titled *Girl, Interrupted,* and whenever I did I'd think, "Yes, well, it starts early and doesn't stop." For as contemporary women we are all *Woman, Interrupted:* "open to all points of the compass," as Anne Morrow Lindbergh put it, "stretched out, exposed." This is our condition, and any semblance of a spiritual practice we undertake has got to move us along in spite of it.

I'd have thought long and hard before telling that Berkeley audience about Draupadi and her endless sari if I'd known Bob Goldman was present. Professor Goldman is one of the foremost Sanskrit scholars in the country, and my rendering of the story probably made him wince in a dozen different places. He brought up only one, though. Had I known that Draupadi had not been dragged merely from the women's quarters, but from a special room set aside for women who were menstruating?

I can't honestly remember anything that anybody said for the next several minutes. I was stunned. I realized at once that all the versions of the story that I'd read or heard or seen performed had been altered for Western sensibilities. One can imagine the consternation of the first European translators: "Oh, but you can't say *that!*" Even more, though, I realized that my tentative reading of the episode had been correct. Draupadi's assailants had not just humiliated a particular woman, they had in a very real sense violated womanhood itself. The full significance of their act would become clear to me only later, but even the glimpse I received that afternoon was enough to send me directly to the Mahabharata, focused and intent.

The poem's sheer luxuriance didn't trouble me this time as it had before (it's considerably longer than the *Iliad* and the *Odyssey* combined), because now I wasn't a slack-jawed sightseer. I'd brought serious questions with me that would keep me on track—questions about womanhood itself, centering around the intriguing person of Draupadi. The most urgent of these now was a question someone had asked *me*.

Epic as Though Women Mattered

The bare-bones plot of the Mahabharata is as follows:

Two groups of cousins, five Pandavas and one hundred Kauravas, are vying with each other for sole possession of a central throne. Fatherless, the Pandavas live with their mother. Disguised as young Brahmins, they visit the court of a great king who is offering his daughter in marriage to the best archer. One of the brothers wins, and afterward he and his brothers—jointly—marry the princess Draupadi. In addition, they form an important alliance with Krishna, a neighboring prince who is also a divine incarnation.

The jealous Kauravas scheme to win everything from the Pandavas in a rigged dicing match, and finally Draupadi herself is gambled away and assaulted. After shaming the court and winning her husbands' freedom through a brilliant legal maneuver, she joins them in twelve years of forest exile, dressed still in the cloth she'd been wearing that day—bloodstained, I learned now—her hair unbound as if she were a widow and vowing not to put it up again until the widows of the Kauravas had let down theirs in mourning. The war of wars is finally fought (it takes up a good two-thirds of the epic), and the casualties are horrendous. All five of Draupadi's sons—one by each husband—are killed, along with nearly all the warrior caste on both sides. The Pandavas do prevail, however, and the eldest brother, Yudhishthira, is crowned king.

The Mahabharata is a compendium of spiritual wisdom that's meant for ordinary folk. Over and over, we are shown the frightening ease with which a good person can commit a terrible mistake or a weak one can slip sideways into outright evil. Every imaginable life situation is mirrored there, and by the time the work reaches its end and the consequences of all the errors and all the heroic acts are manifest, one understands that in the vast reaches of time, each of us will learn what must be learned, however many lifetimes we must pass through in the process. The carnage will stop, and peace—*Shanti*—will be achieved. "All shall be well," it is understood, "and all manner of thing shall be well."

What struck me immediately as I read my way into the poem now, though, was not its profundity so much as its wit— its surprisingly light touch. Take the story (one of them, for there are several) that explains how Draupadi ended up being married to five brothers.

Arjuna was an archer of great skill and good looks to match. It was he who won Draupadi's hand in marriage, and afterward he and his brothers took Draupadi home with them. Arjuna called in to his mother, who was inside cooking, urging her playfully to come look at what they had won. Without looking up, Kunti told him to be sure the five of them shared their gains equally among themselves. Hearing a gasp of collective dismay, she turned around and saw the lovely princess. Too late. The words of a woman of Kunti's stature (her story is also riveting, and the whole plot of the epic hinges on it) could not be called back. Indeed, in the words of the eldest brother, Yudhishthira, "The word of a guru is Law, and of all gurus the mother is the first."[2] Draupadi would have to marry them all.

The second quality of the epic that impressed me right away was that unlike the Western epics I had studied and taught at Berkeley, it appeared to have been produced by a culture that was genuinely interested in women—in their experience as well as in their impact on the male principals. The questions I had been formulating about what it means to be female and a seeker were not at all out of place in this milieu. I couldn't help thinking, in fact, that the poem must have been composed in a time when the prehistoric world, with its higher valuation of women, was still alive in collective memory. (Indeed, Draupadi's polyandrous marriage could be read as direct evidence of that continuity.) For all its obsession with martial combat and dynastic formation, it is permeated with the sense that women may well "hold up half the sky." In contrast with the *Iliad* or *Odyssey* or *Aeneid,* this was epic as though women mattered, and the primary reason it felt that way was its characterization of Draupadi.

Unlike the women who flit ghostlike across Western epics, Draupadi is a fully drawn subject. She doesn't just turn up for the dicing scene and then vanish. She has a past—presented mostly in flashbacks—and she has a future. When the Pandavas go into exile, Draupadi goes, too. She takes care of them, she deliberates with them, and she has her own harrowing adventures. And she is not a one-dimensional or idealized figure: she has certain very human shortcomings. One is a lingering partiality for Arjuna (who was, after all, The Guy). The other is, according to one school of thought, anyway, the depth of her anger. Draupadi can't forget what has happened, and she won't let her husbands forget, either. One of them promises to bind up her hair with his own hands, when he has soaked them in the blood of her assailant, and she really doesn't do all that she could to chill his ardor.

As I made my way through the poem, stopping awhile at each episode that involved Draupadi directly, I found I was almost automatically thinking about each one in terms of the four issues that had come to seem so problematic to me, silence, self-naughting, restraint of desire, and enclosure, along with their feminist counterparts, finding voice, establishing self, reclaiming both desire and freedom of movement. And to my genuine surprise I found that those issues appeared to have been as pertinent to ancient India's ongoing conversation about woman (for it is really that, a conversation, open-ended and sometimes fractious) as they are to women today.

Silence and Speech

In the first place, there is palpable tension around the question of Voice. Is it *okay* for a woman to speak in public? The assembly hall where the dicing match took place was off limits for women, so it was completely unseemly for Draupadi to speak there. But what choice did she have when the law, or *dharma*, was being violated while her menfolk remained silent? For it is clearly this that concerns her as much as her personal suffering.

"Go to the game," she had instructed the emissary who had first come for her, "and ask my husband, 'Whom did you lose first, yourself or me?'" And now, after she has foiled the men who'd tried to humiliate her, she raises the question again. If he had already lost himself, she reasoned, which he had, then he did not have the right to gamble her away. Draupadi's knowledge of *dharma* wins the day, and the king offers her a boon. She asks that Yudhishthira be freed. Offered a second boon, she asks that her remaining four husbands be freed. Offered a third, however, she declines. Asked why, she delivers a terse and pointed summation of everything that has taken place and everybody who has permitted it.

"Greed kills law, sir."

By speaking in the assembly hall, Draupadi breaks with tradition, but when she speaks—impassioned as a prophet but restrained as a yogi—she reawakens her audience to values that are clearly more fundamental and more ancient than the one she has transgressed. Indeed, the episode reads almost like a collision between the prepatriarchal world, where women were fully authorized to speak, and the patriarchal "warrior" culture in which they were not. As I realized this, I found myself thinking about contemporary women who still find themselves in the middle of this sort of collision.

Of Carolyn McCarthy, for example, lifelong Republican from New York State. After McCarthy's husband was killed in 1993, and her son maimed, by a man wielding a semiautomatic weapon on the Long Island Railroad, she learned that her congressman had voted against the 1995 bill to ban assault weapons. This even though the incident, in which six people were killed and seventeen injured, had taken place in his own district. Stunned at his indifference, realizing how colossally her trust had been misplaced, she translated her anger into action. She ran against him and won: won as a Democrat, however, who is pro-choice and who supports increased spending for education, environmental protection, and welfare reform—and who opposes the death penalty.

Unto Herself

Closely linked to the perennial wrangle over the acceptability of female speech is the deeper question: Can a woman be or have a self in the same sense a man can? Draupadi is living proof—and has been for thousands of years, to Indian women and men alike—that to think otherwise is sheerest folly. She is fully a subject in the sense I've already described. That is, she makes her own choices. The ceremony in which Arjuna "wins" her hand, I should emphasize, is actually called in Sanskrit a *swayamvara*— "her own choice." In other words, it is understood that his arrows would not have come anywhere near the target if she had not already selected him and let him know this, egging him on with a devastating glance or two (contemporary film and television renderings of these scenes make the princess's active encouragement more than evident). And as for the fact that she appears to have gotten more husbands than she'd bargained for, there is another story, as we'll see in a moment, that alters that impression significantly.

But the question about self would really only have meant one thing in ancient India. It meant, "Can she know God?" And that question in turn has really meant only one thing to Indians. What is her capacity for sacrifice—for letting go of everything that *isn't* God? Draupadi demonstrates that dramatically when she lets go of her sari, risking, to all outward appearances, the utter loss of her honor as a woman. But she has demonstrated it already by submitting to a marriage that exposes her to public ridicule—guided, of course, by her own inner lights. And in fact the very circumstances of Draupadi's birth signaled to anyone who lived in that culture that she was the embodiment of the spirit of sacrifice upon which all of life depends.

For Draupadi was born out of the earthen altar in her father's palace. On such an altar, which represented the earth, householders would place offerings of oil, honey, milk, and grain and feed them to a sacrificial flame that represented hungry deities. The gods would in turn feed those who had fed them, providing the earth with rain and sunlight. The earth's fertility was believed to depend upon this cycle of giving, in which all human beings must participate according to their place in the scheme of things: "Through sacrifice," say the Upanishads, "life is sustained."

All of this, of course, was lost upon Draupadi's assailants, so benighted they treated her like a thing. There is a moment just before the attempted disrobing when their folly is disastrously evident. The prince who has won her leers at her and pulls his own clothing back, exposing his thigh in a gesture that is blatantly sexual and so offensive to her husbands that it effectively seals his doom.

Desires

The Western ideal for women has so much to do with desirelessness that I was fascinated to see that Draupadi is *not* presented as a woman without strong desires. Not at all. It turns out that she had a strong hand in bringing about her odd marriage. In a previous life, as beautiful and accomplished as in this one, she had been unable to find a husband who answered all of her requirements. An ardent devotee of the god Shiva, she had impressed the god with her austerities, and he had offered her a boon. "I wish a husband who has all virtues," she exclaimed, and she enumerated them: he should be able to dance and ride splendidly, he should be immensely wise, courageous, handsome, and strong. . . . In her enthusiasm she repeated herself—five times altogether. Well, said Shiva, mischievously, there is no way any one man could be everything this girl requires. She would, therefore, have five husbands *(next time),* with all those gifts distributed among them.

Despite her spiritual attainments, then, Draupadi shows no particular inclination for the celibate life. "Fragrant as the blue lotus," she is adored by all five brothers. Could a woman with five husbands be regarded as chaste? Not an ordinary woman, perhaps, but this one clearly is not ordinary. The poet tells us, for example, that she is a virgin for each of her husbands in turn. And as if to be certain each brother feels he is her one and only, there is a firm ground rule. If one of them should enter the room while she is with another, the intruder must go into exile for a year.

Sorting all of this out, thinking about how nowhere in the West do we have such a mix of genres as this, where saintliness and sexuality coexist so comfortably and sometimes hilariously, I found myself remembering something my own teacher had never tired of telling us years before: that nobody who's trying to make progress in meditation should feel discouraged or embarrassed about having strong sexual desires, because the sex drive is our fuel for the journey. The desire for sexual union is really the desire for Union, misread because of our conditioning. Its intensity is the measure of what we'll one day be able to bring to meditation itself.

No, the point about Draupadi wasn't that she was desireless but that she was not mastered by her desires. She couldn't have repelled her assailants the way she did—the tradition is unequivocal on such questions—if so much as a flicker of lust had disturbed her consciousness. Her capacity for self-restraint, and the bounty it lets her bestow on others, is symbolized by her possession during the Pandavas' twelve-year exile of a copper cooking pot (a gift from a sympathetic deity) that produces food all day long for as many as she wishes to feed—but only until she has taken her own meal. Once she has eaten, the pot remains empty until the next day.

Enclosure

Obviously, the question of enclosure is central to Draupadi's story. She is dragged into a public space, and once she is out there, she is treated as if she had deliberately flouted custom, for nobody offers her any protection. But of course what is really significant about the enclosure from which she's been dragged is that it is the space set aside for women who are menstruating. And to know why *that* holds such meaning, we need to know something about the way menstruation is regarded in Indian culture.

Most of us long for seclusion during our periods, even if we've been conditioned to think it's a weakness to feel that way. Indian women, like women in many traditional cultures, have no illusions on this score. The time of menstrual flow is the time when they feel themselves to be most closely identified with the earth and with the Goddess that the earth embodies. It is a time to regather one's powers.

Hindus, I learned, recognize the sacred significance of menstruation in a variety of ways. Anthropologist Frederique Apffel-Marglin, who has been doing fieldwork in coastal Orissa since 1975, has brought some of these to Western attention. Drawing upon interviews with participants, she describes a four-day festival of the menses that takes place each year in that region.

The festival of the goddess Harachandi is emphatically not a celebration for women only but a time, rather, when everyone rests, including the earth itself and the farm animals. The festival takes place in a sacred grove on the top of a hill where no trees or plants have ever been cut, and nothing is cultivated.[3] One man from every family in the region stays in the grove throughout the festival. Women visit during the day but come back to the village at night. Men and women are separated during these four days, and the village resounds with the laughter of young girls and women swinging on swings specially hung for the occasion.

The grove *is* the goddess Harachandi, whose temple is here, but it also represents all menstrual women, for it is understood that during her period a woman sinks into a kind of primordial state. "Uncultivated," she is to rest in seclusion—isn't supposed to cut vegetables or even her nails, isn't to bathe or comb her hair or bind it up or adorn herself. A woman's period, Apffel-Marglin emphasizes, *is* her sacred grove.[4]

During a similar festival called Thesmophoria that took place in ancient Greece, women would take an herb that brought on their menses, so all would actually be menstruating. During Harachandi's festival this is not the case, but "this festival is almost like our menstruation," an Orissi woman explains. "We do not bleed but we follow the same rules as during our menses since we are of the same kind as Her. She is a woman, and we are all women. We are *amsha* (parts) of her."[5]

And indeed, their menfolk take that connection seriously. In the words of one male informant:

> We come here now because She is at her periods which is
> good for each and everyone. This means that She is ready,
> that She will give forth. She will give us good crops and
> cause many things in nature to grow. Women are reflections
> of the Mother and of the earth. The Mother, the earth and
> women are the same thing in different forms. . . . It is in-
> cumbent upon us that we should please the Goddess and
> women at this time.[6]

It would be hard to imagine a custom more remote from Western sensibilities. You can see how it works. The annual festival serves to instruct, impressing upon the minds of *everyone* that the general well-being really does require that women be given the space and seclusion they need each month to replenish themselves in body and spirit alike. Hanging over the whole business, of course, the ultimate cautionary tale, is the story of certain men who flouted custom, pulled a noblewoman out of her seclusion, and saw their whole civilization destroyed.

The people of Orissa, along the southeast coast of India, honor young girls who are entering puberty much as the

Navajos do. The four-day ritual begins with a ceremony that teaches each girl what her place will be, not only within her home and community, but in the whole cosmic order. The mother and father together spread a mat and place a red cloth on it for the girl to lie on. At the four corners they set pitchers full of water—traditional symbols of auspiciousness. A fifth is placed midway between two of the others. Together these symbolize the five elements. Nine kinds of seeds are spread in a circle around the mat. These are staples in the regional diet, but they also represent the nine planets. "The circle of seeds is at once the cultivating activity of humans, and the cosmos. . . . The girl is placed at the center of the world, for the coming of her menses has placed her there." Secluded from men (her girl friends can visit) and from the sun, she is in a figurative chrysalis, "transforming in solitude and darkness, her generating power gathering strength within her." [7] On the fifth day seven married women take her to the pond and bathe her. She is dressed in new clothing and her mother's gold ornaments and returns in a procession. The whole day long, family and friends visit and bring gifts. The girl takes an offering to the temple for Shiva, and in the evening everyone shares a gala feast.

"*The girl is at the center of creation.*" Over and over, throughout Apffel-Marglin's account, that phrase recurs. And once again we understand that rituals are rehearsals for the rest of life. "There as woman she will remain; her activities of bleeding, conceiving, gestating, observing the rules of menstruation, processing the grain from the fields, cooking, feeding, keeping the accounts and the wealth of the household . . . and a myriad other activities generate and regenerate their lived world." [8]

We can begin to fathom now why it is so chilling for Indian audiences to know that when Draupadi is dragged into the assembly hall, she is coming from the menstrual chamber.

Draupadi, at that moment, *is* the earth regenerating Herself. Her unbound hair and simple, shapeless garment, one scholar observes, are the forests, uncultivated. She is "in flux," and in the flow of her tears, her blood, her hair, and her garments are represented the rivers of India, the land that's said to be "river-mothered." For Ganga, Jumna, Narmada, Sarasvati, and Kaveri are goddesses as well as rivers.

The story has immense power, then, for anyone who believes in the deep connections it assumes among woman, the earth, and "the feminine face of God." But what kind of power does it hold, and what kind of meaning, for Western women? We need to take this question very seriously, particularly if we aren't just exploring another tradition out of a kind of cultural voyeurism, but in the hope of understanding our own culture better, and even making our own culture work better for us.

So I have to ask, Doesn't the rendering of the sacred feminine in India's epic and mythic tradition strike us as being perilously close to the glorification of woman as the "angel in the house"? Doesn't it amount to what some feminists would call an essentialist view of women? The imagery is beautiful and persuasive, but as soon as I pull back just a little I realize I'm feeling claustrophobic, too. Because I don't really wish I could have spent four days of every month of the past forty years in my bathrobe—though having the option when I did want to would certainly have been wonderful. When so very much importance is attached to biology, it always sets me thinking: there's got to be more to life than merely seeing that life gets perpetuated. (Earth mother or virgin goddess. Feed the world or find my bathrobe. . . .)

And I do like to think that if Draupadi were making out her wish list today—the one that got her so *thoroughly* wedded—she would throw in something about a basketball scholarship to

Stanford or admission to Princeton's graduate school in molecular biology.

It's important to realize that these stories and customs emerge out of very traditional agrarian cultures, and we do both them and ourselves a disservice when we read them too literally. Rituals, once again, are narratives, meant to help us structure our thinking and behavior outside the ritual space itself. At the most basic level, the story an Orissi or Navajo girl is told at puberty tells her that she matters and that her know-how, her generosity, her prudence—her artistry, for that matter—can enhance enormously the well-being of her whole community. Surely every young girl should be made to understand this about herself, however she chooses to dispense her own unique gifts. When it is said that all women are "parts of Her," can't that be read to suggest that we see the magnificent whole of Her only when every girl and every woman has realized her full potential?

In the hope, then, of arriving eventually at models of spiritual feminism and feminist spirituality that will actually work for contemporary Western women—composites, perhaps—I want to look a little more closely at a couple of the assumptions behind India's reverence for the Divine Mother. When we do, I think we arrive at certain more fundamental principles, and these can be even more useful to us than the very literal and admittedly beautiful applications we see in the Orissi rites. Can be, in fact, rather exciting to contemplate.

The Goddess in the Woman, the Goddess in the Goddess

Let's begin with the belief that underlies the Orissi festival of the menses and that is so fundamental to India's regard for the sacred feminine: "we are all parts of Her." It's difficult for Western women to associate ourselves with a feminine version of divinity—or has been until recently—because the sacred feminine has so little visibility in our culture. The Virgin Mary is about it—and that only if you're a Catholic—and her virginity gets such heavy play that her full womanhood can barely be felt.[9] So it's fascinating to see how many faces the Goddess wears in Indian tradition and how many versions of womanhood get validated there. For that matter, in the Mahabharata itself she is everywhere at once, though you have to be reasonably familiar with the major players in Hindu mythology to know it.

That India has goddesses is evident to anybody who has wandered into an Indian imports shop and seen the colorful posters that depict them. They all seem to have roughly the same gentle smile and the same great, dark eyes ("lotus eyes," which I think means they are shaped like lotus petals), and the same shapely figure. They. are differentiated only by their accoutrements. Lakshmi, goddess of wealth, is glamorous in her jewels; and Sarasvati, who presides over music and eloquence, holds a musical instrument called the *vina;* Durga, destroyer of buffalo demons, rides on the back of a lion or tiger. There are hundreds of other goddesses, many of them local or regional, but our initial impression—that these are really all the same woman, gotten up in different costumes—is actually correct. The one all-important fact about all female deities is that each is a particular form that the Great Goddess, Mahadevi,[10] has taken in response to a particular situation. Every one of them is the Mother in disguise, including, of course, Kali, whose protruding tongue and rolling, bloodshot eyes and necklace of skulls sends Western sensibilities reeling. I'd known about this spectacularly diverse troupe, certainly, but now I saw in them a deep cultural affirmation of the feminine principle itself—its vitality and its inexhaustible variety.

And Draupadi, I discovered, to my utter fascination, is every one of them. For at one point or another across the length of the

Mahabharata, Draupadi does something to evoke all of the major goddesses and manifestations of the Goddess. Subtle as these instances might seem to Western readers, they could not conceivably fail to register—subliminally at the very least—with individuals who had grown up hearing stories about Lakshmi and Saraswati, Durga and Kali. Once you begin keeping track, you have to wonder whether whole episodes might not have been created just to establish Draupadi's identity as the multi-formed Mahadevi. And then you have to start wondering why.

Some of the connections are established explicitly, some by innuendo. One of the alternative stories that explain why Draupadi is married-times-five, for example, tells us that it all started in the heavens, when the god of heavy weather (Indra) got in trouble for some cattle rustling and had to do penance by coming to earth as five warriors. To mitigate his/their hardship, the goddess Lakshmi would come along as his/their wife. The Pandavas were those warriors, and Draupadi was actually Lakshmi. Draupadi is also praised as the embodiment of Sri, the goddess of splendor and brightness. A friend from India recalls that when a young bride comes into the family, the older women will typically watch her for a time, looking for a partic-ular quality and, when they see it, nod with approval, saying, "She has *sri* in her face." The word is also used as an honorific, appended to the name of a man or woman of great spiritual at-tainment: Sri Ramakrishna, Sri Sarada Devi.

When Draupadi stuns the court with her legal expertise, she evokes Saraswati, goddess of eloquence. In her fury, she is Kali. And as one who had appealed to Shiva for a husband, perform-ing great austerities in the bargain, she brings to mind the long campaign Parvati had waged to win Shiva himself. Daughter of the Himalayas, Parvati is described as having to struggle contin-ually to tame the Great God's excesses (he is so fiercely ascetic, for example, that his very gaze can shrivel up Kama, god of desire). Parvati is herself no mean ascetic, but she is also a very human sort of goddess. She is Shiva's devoted disciple as well as his wife, but she tends to fall asleep sometimes when he is discoursing. She *really* wants babies, and he doesn't. . . .

The poet keeps dropping elaborate clues regarding Draupadi's real identity, and I suspect that picking up on the clues and nudging one another at their subtlety must have been half the fun for the Mahabharata's early audience. Even more interesting than those linking her to particular goddesses, though, are the evocations of the sacred feminine not so much as a particular deity but rather as a life force—like Maya, the veil of illusion that makes us believe the world of name and form is real, or Shakti, the cosmic power or energy that Shiva's consorts are believed to embody.

And here, once again, I found myself awakening to the right-now relevance of a very ancient way of looking at things. To understand Shakti—even a little bit—is to begin mediating the conflicted discussions of desire that arise when feminism and spirituality are even in the same room.

Shiva is one with Shakti, it is said, as fire is with the power to burn. In one traditional representation, Shiva is prone like a corpse, and Shakti dances on his chest. Within the human being, Shakti is envisioned as a serpent coiled up at the base of the spine. As long as it (or "she") remains there, animating only the lowest centers of consciousness—consumption, elimination, reproduction—the life force it represents is used up in pursuing physical satisfactions. When we are awakened, though—by contact with an illumined teacher, for example, or by one of those sudden impulses that make us ask of ordinary life, "Is this really *all*?"—and when we take up spiritual disciplines, Shakti itself is said to awaken with tremendous force. Extricating herself from purely creaturely drives, she begins to rise, eagerly, through the remaining four centers of consciousness, a journey that culminates in ecstatic union—with Shiva—at the crown of the head.

The awakening of Shakti is often associated with sensations of intense heat. It's the reason great yogis are able to walk about in the Himalayas bare chested. But many Western contemplatives, too, allude to the phenomenon: the English mystic Richard Rolle, for example, spoke of a "merry heat," and Teresa of Avila described a vision in which she felt herself transfixed by a fiery spear.

Paradoxically, then, Shakti is both the engine that keeps ordinary life going and at the same time the intense yearning for something far more fulfilling than ordinary life. It is Shakti that causes the world as we experience it, a world in which every conceivable life form exists in seeming separateness. And yet it is also Shakti that equips us to soar beyond that world.

Draupadi is traditionally and explicitly associated with this tremendous force. It is understood, and is dramatized in certain religious festivals,[11] that when she goes into ecstasy at the very moment she is being assaulted and the sari unfurls in a blaze of bright color, she is Shakti made visible. Her desires, to put it another way, are absolutely united.

The Mother, then, in all Her manifestations, is earth and the continuance of life. She is death, too, because death is part of life. She is movement and flow and action and change—the other half of the stillness and immobility of deep meditation. Can there be light if there is no darkness? Silence, if there is no such thing as sound? Can there be salvation outside of the world as we experience it? Hinduism says no, there cannot be. This world is *karma-bhumi,* the realm of karma, where all our acts have consequences that teach us. We have to make mistakes in order to arrive at truth. Must learn firsthand to distinguish what is real from what is not. It is the feminine principle that makes sure

rivers keep flowing, grain keeps growing, and babies keep getting born—because if they aren't, there will be no bodies for all
of us sages-in-the-making to inhabit. Indeed, there is a whole
genre of myths structured around a great sage who becomes so
absorbed in his meditation that the created world begins to get
insubstantial, and a goddess or even a heavenly dancing girl has
to come draw him back down to *un*reality. "Maya."

It is imperative to remember, though, that when we speak of
Shakti or Shiva it really is a principle we are talking about and
not a gender. Within every one of us Shiva and Shakti circle one
another in their perennial dance. As if to underscore this point,
there is one legend that reverses the usual account of Parvati's
marriage to Shiva by saying that *she* had gotten so carried away
with austerities and prayer that the gods decided they'd better
intervene and give *her* a husband: Shiva was deemed particularly
right for the role because he was able to make love for a thousand years at a stretch. (It's an extraordinary tradition. . . .) He
could be Shakti to her Shiva when it was called for, just as
Mahatma Gandhi could voluntarily set aside the privileged life of
a well-to-do Western-dressed lawyer and give himself over to alleviating the suffering of India's millions. "A man should remain
man," Gandhi said, "and yet should become woman; similarly a
woman should remain woman and yet become man."[12] For anybody who chose to notice, Gandhi successfully *delinked* maternality from gender altogether, liberating men and women alike.

CHAPTER 5

🌿 *Draupadi's Daughters*

My reentry into Indian spirituality by way of the epics turned into a kind of second honeymoon. In examining the work of Western feminist historians I'd come to see the limitations of history as it's usually written, come to see that construction of a truly usable past requires inclusion of all kinds of material—imaginative, for example, or visionary—that would fall outside the interests of traditional historians. Now I saw that the narrative wealth of the Ramayana and Mahabharata (and their myriad spin-offs) constitutes for Indian women a boundlessly usable past, one that is pure story,[1] "true" not in the sense that dynastic records preserved in clay tablets are true, but true to human experience—instantly recognizable. ("Yes, that is how first love feels." And "Yes, oh, yes, that is exactly how you grieve when you bury a son") *True,* it must be added, in the sense that spiritual teachings are true, for this is sacred literature, and over and over it shows us that everything that happens in life can result in a deeper connection with the sacred.

Both the Mahabharata and the Ramayana were composed over hundreds of years by oral poets, and that very method of composition means that no two tellings were ever identical and that the here-and-now concerns of the audience have always gotten worked into the poem as it was recited. Each has a core story that goes back as far as imagination can reach, but the elaborations have been going on forever, too, and even if these accretions aren't absorbed into the poem, they enter the popular imagination, preserved in vernacular plays, folk songs, or dramas that offer altered or alternative versions of the classic tales. Even today, when oral poets are no more, the stories are still being reconsidered, and new meanings are still being teased out. A wonderfully irreverent tone pervades, for it is understood that even the gods aren't . . . *God*.

Clearly, I saw, India's epics represent a living tradition. But how well does that tradition really support women today? Have contemporary Indian women benefited observably from the reverence for the sacred feminine that is at least a recurrent theme in the Mahabharata and the Ramayana? Can they, for example, "adorned with all dress and ornaments, and unaccompanied by men, move freely and fearlessly" in the roads and lanes of Bombay or Delhi or Calcutta?

It would be foolish to pretend they could. There are at least as many elements in modern Indian culture working against women as there are working on their behalf, not least among them the simple fact that India was a British colony for nearly three hundred years. But it would be just as foolish to imagine that the thousands of years Indians have spent honoring the Divine Mother have done nothing to shape the conditions of life for Indian girls and women today. India's is a wildly multiform culture, and reverence for the sacred feminine is only one strand. There are plenty of others of a very different color and weight. Women don't necessarily fare all that well there.

And yet . . .

Gloria Steinem spent her first two years out of college in India (not during the early sixties, when it had become fashionable, but in the late fifties, ten years before the Beatles' and Mia Farrow's arrival), and she is still sorting through the meaning of her time there. Her assessment rings true with those of many Western women I know:

> At the time I experienced India, I felt as if I were "at home" though I didn't understand why. . . . In spite of all the horrendous problems and everything we know about dowry murders and what happens to female babies, there is a female presence in that culture. There is a kind of gentleness and humor in the culture in spite of outbreaks of terrible violence. . . . I hesitate to try to explain it, because it sounds as if I'm sentimentalizing the culture, and I don't mean to. For some reason, I just felt at home there, especially with those who had been raised in a Gandhian ethic.[2]

"A female presence," indeed. In India, the polite form address for women and girls is "Devi," meaning "Goddess," or "Srimati," which means "Blessed Mother." Simple usages like this are meant to cultivate in everyone—men, women, children, government clerks, and tax collectors—the understanding that all women and all girls are parts of the goddess. They are *amsha*—not to be trifled with. ("Gloria Devi," "Srimati Steinem" . . . she probably got used to it after a while.)

Tremendously innovative and energetic work is going on in India today on behalf of women and girls. The women's movement in India has a character all its own, however; it is markedly different from that of Europe or the United States, and the difference has everything to do with the tradition from which it springs.

Environmentalist Vandana Shiva and professor and journalist Madhu Kishwar are two of the reasons why I would love to see Indian and Western feminists come into more extensive contact with one another. There are many more, though, and after I've introduced each of these women I'd like to begin to explore some of the remarkable ways in which traditional Indian spirituality is nourishing the contemporary women's movement in India.

The Shakti in Us: Vandana Shiva

While environmental scientist Vandana Shiva was carrying out a ten-year study on the impact of mining in the Garwhal region, located on the lower slopes of the Himalayas, she got to know many of the women who lived there and who understood what kind of environmental devastation the mines were causing. Illiterate peasant women, for the most part, they know certain things intimately—the value of forests, for example, to increase rainfall and hold water in place, and which trees are best at holding water—because for thousands of years each generation of women has taught the next one as they worked in the forests, side by side. "Embedded in nature," to use Dr. Shiva's phrase, they enjoy a connection with trees, rivers, mountains, livestock, and plants that is simultaneously their connection with divinity, and that connection is seen as absolutely reciprocal. Their protective, conservative agricultural practices are believed to align them with nature's own regenerative forces.

When some of these women decided to start a satyagraha in protest of the mining, they invited Dr. Shiva to join them. The site where the protesters had camped was a two-hour drive and a four-hour climb from her home, and she had a baby at the time, so she could go up only on weekends. One day some boys came to her office on motorbikes telling her the women were being attacked by hired thugs with irons and chains. She got there as soon as she could, expecting to find the women had returned to their village. None had left, though. Bandaged and bruised, they'd held their ground, undaunted. She spoke with one of them, a village elder who was seventy-eight years old.

"What keeps you going?" the younger woman asked. "I thought I was coming to console you and here you are still sitting in protest. . . ."

The two of them were walking near the campsite.

"Can you see these trees?" the old woman asked. "Every year we take fodder from them, every year they bounce back. And the grass on the banks of the stream, we walk upon it, it springs right back. The *shakti* . . . in the grass and the tree and the stream is the same as the *shakti* in us. And that *shakti* is what keeps me going."[3]

Vandana Shiva's passionate opposition to GATT (the General Agreement on Tariffs and Trade) has brought her to this country several times in recent years. Dr. Shiva, who heads up her own research foundation,[4] believes that global corporate greed is out to destroy the very principle of regeneration. Her brand of feminism, therefore, is inseparable from ecology. Characterizing the corporate approach as "reductionist agriculture and forestry" and as "crisis-mind" at work, she documents point by point the inconceivable violence it has unleashed in India—against nature, against women and children, against knowledge itself. She cannot say enough in praise of the subsistence farmers, mostly women, who are currently putting up heroic resistance to Western-based corporate assaults on India's forests, fields, and rivers. "It is in reclaiming life and recovering its sanctity," she maintains, "that women of our region search for their liberation and the liberation of their societies."

Madhu Kishwar's "Points of Strength"

Manushi: A Journal about Women and Society circulates throughout India but has a wide readership abroad as well. Its editor, Madhu Kishwar, who also teaches at Delhi University (where Gloria Steinem spent her first year in India), believes that "India's cultural traditions have tremendous potential within them to combat reactionary and anti-women ideas, if we can identify their points of strength and use them creatively."[5]

Manushi wades without hesitation into the most controversial issues: the embattled rights of widows to inherit property; the failure of Delhi courts to prosecute police officers charged with raping a ten-year-old girl; the proposed construction of a dam in the Himalayas that would turn the Ganges into a dead river; the work of an organization that helps South Asian women living in the United States who are encountering violence in their lives; the dubious impact beauty contests are having on Indian society (in 1994 the Miss Universe and the Miss World crowns were both won by young women from India).

But the journal always addresses women's issues in the full context of India's cultural and spiritual heritage. Its feminism is rooted in India's most deeply held beliefs regarding the power of the sacred feminine. You sense it in the indignant report of an Indian woman living in the United States whose American feminist associates had urged her to stop wearing her sari because "it is seen as backward and subservient." You catch it in Kishwar's own horror at the idea of damming the Ganges and sending her waters into reservoirs so immense the river cannot oxygenate herself. "Ganga is not just any river." Woman, the earth, Mahadevi—all are one, all sacred, all charged with the immense power to generate and regenerate life. In a recent interview, Kishwar was asked what kind of inspiration contemporary Hindu women are able to draw from traditional female goddesses. Her answer was, to my mind, something of a revelation.

> India is not like Greece, where the earlier gods and goddesses were destroyed by the new religion, Christianity. Here, goddess worship is a living tradition. . . . Most of these goddesses are not simple, divine creatures who descend from heaven. . . . They are described as women who rose in righteous anger and indignation when a man tried to tamper with them. *And it's that extraordinary sense of rage which raises them to their status of divinity.* . . . The moment a woman, for instance, acts in righteous indignation, acts out her rage, people say . . . "She has assumed the form of Chandi," which is to say, that every woman has . . . this aspect latent in her, that a woman is both gentle and nurturing, as well as capable of superhuman rage. . . ." (emphasis mine)[6]

Because Indian men know the stories of Kali and Durga—of Draupadi, for that matter—Kishwar adds, they are actually better able to deal with strong women than men are in many other parts of the world. "They see rage as an innate expression of womanhood. It's not unwomanly to be strong and ferocious. That's as much an expression of womanhood as is nurturance. . . . " India is very complex, she points out. Numerous women lead very restricted lives there. Yet, "you will simultaneously see the ease with which women can enter into male citadels, power citadels, and take charge, start ordering men around. . . ."

Just beneath the surface of everything that Vandana Shiva and Madhu Kishwar write and say flows the quiet understanding—it's like second nature to both of them—that in a mysterious, powerful way the Goddess, the earth, and every individual woman really are one. All one, and all the Mother. To those of us who've never imagined such a thing, the degree of confidence one might feel who really believed it seems almost unfathomable. Not only do we have nothing comparable in the West (the only available model of a triune reality being male on two counts and neuter on the third), many of us are actively threatened by the suggestion that we identify more closely with the natural world. We have good reason to feel this way, as I've already suggested (see Chapter Nine). As late as the seventeenth century one could still hear echoes of old assumptions, drawn from agricultural practices. Nature is a woman: woo her tenderly and she will bear fruit. But with the industrial and scientific revolutions, everything shifted. Nature is a woman: master her, use her, exploit her. Women would seem to have everything to gain from breaking all metaphoric links between themselves and the natural world.

But that's where we've got it all wrong, according to Vandana Shiva. Women need to feel degraded by the idea of living out closer connections with the natural world only if they believe that the natural world itself is really degraded, and to think that way is bad science—seriously outdated. We know now that nature is not mechanically repetitive and inert at all but rather infinitely complex, creative, and resourceful. Might it not be possible, then, to affirm some of the values that "cultural feminism" wants us to without raising the specter of essentialism? It would seem that this very spirit—of sacralizing the embodied as well as the disembodied—could be a powerful corrective to the sharp cleavage the West has long made, and that has been so damaging to women in particular, between Spirit and Flesh. Can women not be seekers of truth and sustainers of life simultaneously—and divine in both aspects?

This vision of things gives rise in turn to a version of spirituality that seems wonderfully well suited to "women, interrupted," because it suggests that maybe we're never really interrupted after all, that we're always doing what we're here to do. When your three-year-old breaks up your meditation, you groan and wonder when you'll be able to pick up the thread again, but here, now, are love and laughter and cheeks like flower petals that won't be here forever. Look again, *she* is Parvati. *He* is Krishna. And if for a moment you all but lose yourself in loving one of these small deities, chalk it up as . . . rehearsal.

It is the particular good fortune of Indian women that their spiritual tradition has articulated this ideal all along, refusing to compartmentalize spiritual practice, as if nothing in the day counted but meditation itself and as if nothing short of monastic withdrawal from life could bring one to God-consciousness. Alongside the pantheon of great monastic saints, India has its honor roll of householder saints as well, women and men who show us that no matter what is going on around oneself, or *inside* oneself, there is always something to do that will, in the long run, deepen meditation. Nothing esoteric, just simple, practical methods for maintaining your focus as you walk through the extraordinary turmoil of an ordinary day among ordinary folk.

My own teacher, of course, comes from that tradition, and as I think about this I remember, almost startled, feeling the significance as if for the first time, that his teacher was his mother's mother. And I look again at the one photograph we have of her. She is scowling into a bright sun and looks a bit fierce as a result. That isn't deceptive, he says, she *was* a little fierce. Her hair is white, parted in the middle and pulled back. She is barefoot, and she's tucked her sari up so that it falls well short of her ankles. She liked to move about freely and used to tease the young girls in the large joint family about their fashionably long saris, saying that thanks to them one almost never had to sweep the floors. In her right hand she holds a small brass waterpot. Leaning against her on the other side, looking back at the camera warily, is her granddaughter, Easwaran's cousin, who is about eleven in this picture.

Did his granny teach him how to meditate? I asked him that once and he said no, she didn't really teach so much in words as by the way she lived. "She taught me," he said very simply, "that devotion to God is no different from devotion to family. Only it doesn't stop with the family. It extends beyond every horizon."

The Warrior Caste: Found Wanting

Without having had the opportunity to visit India yet, I believe I know something of what that "female presence" might be that Gloria Steinem kept feeling. And I think she's right that it has something to do with humor. In essence it is this: that to the extent that India has never altogether stopped honoring the sacred feminine, it has also sustained a capacity to see through the lies that patriarchy tells itself about itself. That lie, in particular, that says, "We're here to protect you. You don't think we *like* living this way, do you? All these guns, all these troops—they're to see that nothing happens to you." I would like to turn now to

India's two great depictions of war and peace—mostly war—and touch upon some of the surprising ways in which they lend support to feminist perspectives.

The Mahabharata and the Ramayana are both dominated by accounts of stirring battles: heroic deeds, foul treachery, and weapons of fantastic power slipped into the melee by enthusiastically partisan deities (one of these weapons is a precursor of today's heat-seeking missiles). Any reader who's familiar with Western epics, particularly the *Iliad,* will recognize the territory. But at the same time one can discern within the epics and the stories that have developed around them a continuous thread of bemused skepticism toward the assumptions and mental states that bring great wars into being.

In the Mahabharata the boorishness of the Pandavas' enemies is recurringly the springboard for rich humor. There is a moment not long before the fateful dicing match, for example, when the fortunes of the Pandavas are high and they invite their cousin Duryodhana to a palace they've built to celebrate. The building is an architectural wonder, and Duryodhana is sick with envy. At one point he gasps at the beauty of an inlaid floor so perfectly crafted it gives the illusion of being a lily pond. He steps out upon it and plunges into water up to his knees. Moments later he looks through a doorway into a beautiful room, tries to enter it, and discovers only when he's nearly broken his nose that it is trompe l'oeil. Worse still—and there are some who say this moment is when the war really begins—he hears from behind him the tinkling laughter of the beautiful Draupadi.

Over and over the epic's bad guys are shown to be sufficiently greedy, impure, and violent to justify their eventual extermination, and we understand that Draupadi's husbands are contrastingly magnanimous, chaste, and peaceable. But if you look at what happened the day of the dicing match from a woman's point of view, as the epic encourages us to, you see that the Pandavas' behavior, too, is flawed in a very serious way. As members of the knightly caste, the kshatriya, their foremost obligation by any reasonable reckoning is to safeguard their queen, particularly when she has withdrawn into the seclusion of the menstrual chamber. Their failure to do what is right occurs because their attachment to honor among men, perhaps the core value of patriarchy, has deluded them.

Repeatedly the epics poke fun at the elaborate pretenses around patriarchy and the assumptions that make it sacrosanct. Playfulness is the hallmark of the good guys, a quality that is embodied to perfection not in any of the Pandavas themselves, however, but in the figure of Krishna, their best friend and mentor—not in Rama, for that matter, hero of the Ramayana, but in his friend the Monkey King, Hanuman. As valuable to human beings as a stable and militarily viable kingdom might be—and the epics certainly glorify such kingdoms and the kings who run them—certain other things are shown to be at least as important. If one of those kings takes himself just a little bit too seriously, some storyteller will come along and narrate the consequences in an illuminating postscript. This is what happened to the Ramayana, and only because it did is the epic genuinely usable for contemporary Indian feminists.

On the face of things, the Ramayana is a very different sort of narrative from the Mahabharata. It is spectacularly romantic, containing all the elements of the sort of novel that fed the imagination of Teresa of Avila and Delia Grinstead. A splendid king, a beautiful queen, and an evil interloper who steals her away; proud and devoted chastity on her part while her beloved struggles to retrieve her; a battle unto the death with the arrayed forces of evil, and, at last, victory. Reunited, the lovers ascend to the throne, and we fade to "happily ever after." It's a wonderful tale, full of magic and whimsy. A Monkey King assists the hero, and a Bear King joins in, and even hordes of chipmunks. Let's look at it more closely.

Like Draupadi, the heroine of the Ramayana was born of the earth. Sita turns up, quite literally, as a baby, in a plowed furrow. Like Draupadi, she is identified as an incarnation of the goddess of prosperity, Lakshmi. Rama, who wins her hand in an archery contest, is depicted as the embodiment of human perfection. When he is wrongfully banished from his throne and kingdom, Sita insists upon accompanying him into the wilderness. Kidnapped from there by a demon-king, she is held captive on an island stronghold until her husband rallies his forces and, after a protracted and ferocious battle, destroys her captor. In a ceremony called *agnipariksha,* she walks through fire to demonstrate that her chastity had remained unbroken while she was captive, and the two return to their kingdom. Rama resumes his reign, and all would seem to be well. Indeed, that is the end of the story in early versions, leaving one to conclude that a woman really needn't trouble herself to think far past hooking up with Mr. Right and that a man can go off to a fairly cataclysmic war and reenter civilian life afterward unchanged by his experience.

A sequel, however, the Uttara Ramayana, is well known throughout India, and once it became joined to the original story, as it is now in the popular imagination, the epic would never again come across like pure, unadulterated romance. It is as if the whole culture had gotten swept up for a time, as cultures do, in the mythology of Perfect Love and had to be reeled back in to sanity—to the deeper, more timeless wisdom that characterizes the earlier Mahabharata.

The corrective addition goes like this: After a time, certain of Rama's subjects let it be known that they really don't believe his queen had been chaste while she was gone. To his everlasting shame (and in a recent *Manushi* article on the Ramayana's reception by contemporary Indians Madhu Kishwar makes it clear that his reputation really was hurt by this act)[7] Rama acquiesces to their suspicions and sends Sita off to the forest, even though she is pregnant—in fact, close to full-term. Heartbroken, she gives birth in an ashram to Rama's twin sons. Years later, the two boys turn up at the palace during a ceremony celebrating Rama's kingship. As part of the festivities, the two sing their parents' story: Rama's adventures and Sita's sufferings. Remorseful, Rama asks Sita to rejoin him at the palace, on the condition that she prove her fidelity once more by walking through fire again ("It's not for me, you understand—it's for my people . . ."). This time, though, she flatly refuses. Instead, she calls upon the earth, her mother, to split open before her if she has been chaste. The earth does open, and when Sita steps in, it closes up behind her.

Rama is now alone. He has failed his flawless queen in a way that is unmistakably symmetric with the way Draupadi's husbands had failed her in the Mahabharata. For Sita is wrenched from her home just as she is about to give birth: in one of those moments, in other words, when a woman absolutely requires safe enclosure. Once again, a gracious and virtuous queen is cheated of the protection her culture would seem to guarantee, and not by a scoundrel at all, but by one who has been presented throughout the story that bears his name as "the very best of men." The *fact* that Rama is so extraordinarily fine and good and still could behave so appallingly when he is threatened by the loss of "honor among men" forces us, I think, to step back and look at the attitudes that swayed him. Quietly, but powerfully, the composers and recomposers of the Ramayana and Mahabharata have demonstrated something women know very well even while they try to persuade themselves otherwise—that the protection and security patriarchal structures offer us in exchange for fealty are only paper thin and that a woman's only real security lies in the strength of her own connection with the sacred.

Does such a conclusion signal the end of romance? Only, I think, of "romance as we know it." In the words of Mexican poet and essayist Octavio Paz, "The history of love is inseparable from the history of the freedom of women," [8] and that history is only just beginning.

To understand how very usable India's past is for her feminists, and how seamless is the join for them between feminism and spirituality, one has only to look back at various campaigns on women's behalf that have taken place there over the past century and see how regularly the projects are framed in terms of the stories we've been looking at.

When Gandhi died in 1948, a European woman who had come to India to work with him set up a center for the education and empowerment of hill women in Garwhal. She called it Lakshmi Ashram, because her goal was to show them "that they were not beasts of burden but goddesses of wealth, since they rear cattle and produce food, performing 98 per cent of all labour in farming and animal husbandry." [9] The movement that began there laid the foundations for the famous Chipko movement, a nonviolent protest conceived and led by women against the destruction of forests on the slopes of the Himalayas that lasted from the 1970s until 1981, when logging was finally banned from the Himalayas.

In 1989, in very much the same spirit but with an interesting twist, a massive farmers' organization launched a highly successful campaign called Lakshmi Mukti (literally "Set Lakshmi free") to empower women with land rights. The campaign leader went on tour throughout Maharashtra State asking that a portion of every family's land be transferred to the wife's name. By keeping their wives powerless and economically dependent, he maintained, the men of Maharashtra were treating them no better than Rama had treated Sita. Before huge crowds he outlined in moving detail the sacrifices Sita had made and her husband's failure to honor them. By transferring land to their wives, he maintained, they were paying back something of what Rama owed Sita, but more than that, if they were to be successful at resisting their *own* exploitation, he argued, they must first redress the wrongs committed against today's Sitas.

In other words, simply by *telling these men the story*—a story they already knew intimately—this activist was able to tap into a profound yet unspoken shame he knew they felt, and should feel, with regard to their treatment of the women in their own lives. Because the story of Sita and Rama had already shown them what was right—shown them dharma "by default"—they couldn't help but respond when the connections with their own life, and their own suffering, were spelled out for them. The strategy behind this campaign is quintessentially Gandhian.

Insofar as it has evolved into a vast complex of interlocking corporations, as hungry for new markets as it is for resources, the set of assumptions about self and others that we've thus far identified as patriarchy is recast now in a new and ominous form. Because these corporations are transnational in scope, they are unconstrained by the various codes of decency and justice that are written into national constitutions, and for this reason they appear to many of us to be almost invincible. But when Vandana Shiva takes them on, the odds seem to change. In effect, she is standing on a mountain—standing on the rock-solid knowledge that by dint of her very womanhood she is charged to take on exactly this sort of adversary. A Westerner who has worked with her remarks, "With Vandana it's never just tactics and strategy, it's never just science and law, it's always a larger spiritual vision, always a larger, more humane vision."

But that isn't all. "And most important, it's also the gift of laughter. Somewhere at the very center of her is this lovely laughter. It's a nice quality, and it's rare among activists."[10] Among most activists maybe, but not among the daughters of Draupadi.

It is fair to ask, I think, what good it does Western feminists to know about Indian feminists and their usable past. We certainly can't construct its equivalent for ourselves out of whole cloth, and the snippets we have on hand don't piece themselves into anything remotely comparable.

The good it does, I believe, is that it shakes up accepted versions of feminism, forcing us to recognize, for example, the extent to which Western feminism is still operating within male-centered and materialist paradigms. If we did nothing, upon seeing this, but start distancing ourselves from those paradigms, we'd be in a better position than we are now. It prompts us to think we might have an awful lot to gain from just *listening* to such women . . . hanging out with them, watching how they do things.

Look. All I know is that whenever I hear Vandana Shiva on public radio—her delivery so rushed, clipped, and throaty, her laughter so ready—and whenever I get a new issue of *Manushi* in the mail, I feel braver and more alive.

CHAPTER 6

The Girls' Movement: Feminism Reawakening

Kristen is twelve. So is everyone in the room, give or take a few months, except me and my friend Marian. Kristen is holding a ball of teal blue yarn in both hands and pulling a length of it free. "I want to be . . ." she announces, "a veterinarian. Not for, like, cows and *big* animals. Cats. And dogs." She looks around the circle and tosses the ball to Sarah but holds onto her end.

This is not "a sacred circle." We're in a public school classroom, and things don't get much more secular—a Michael Jordan poster hangs on the wall opposite me, and over to the left the Simpsons seem to be making a plea for recycling. But something is going on here that I've come to think is absolutely of a piece with the prayer circles at Saint Clare's convent.

"I want to be a medical technologist," says Sarah, visibly relishing the twin polysyllabics.

Lauren is waving her hand. Sarah pulls off some more slack, tosses the ball of yarn, and pulls her strand taut when Lauren catches it.

"I'm going to be an actress—movies, I think." The yarn arcs across the circle and drops into Alyssa's hands.

"I want . . ." Alyssa is tiny, with blunt-cut silky dark hair that drops in a diagonal curtain across her cheek. Big round glasses obscure her eyes. "I want to be a cosmetologist. My dad is a writer. He writes novels. He wants me to be something else, but I want to do makeup and hair design."

These are sixth graders; they are considerably less inhibited than the seventh graders I observed last week. They are a veritable circus compared with the high school sophomores I sat in with yesterday. Their web is building swiftly now, and there are lots of giggles as it has to be shored up here, reconstructed there. I've never seen so many braces.

"I want to do something for the planet," says Betsy.

"Yeah," Caitlin nods commiseratingly, "it needs some help, all right."

"I want to work with horses."

"I want a huge garden, with all kinds of plants, like . . . a botanist?" (They're already learning to end their assertions on a rising note, an early warning sign of female acculturation!)

"I want to be a brain surgeon."

At last all sixteen girls are connected to one another by a teal blue web of intricate design and many intersections. The web bobbles and tips as wave after wave of silliness ripples around its perimeter. My friend manages, with some effort, to get everyone's attention.

"This is only yarn," she says, "so I can just describe to you how this activity works when you use heavy twine and everybody is standing up. Sarah could actually lie down on it and we could lift her up—it would support her weight. Like a trampoline. And what you realize when you see this is that if you share your dreams—if you talk about them together, and you encourage each other and support each other, you can make them happen."

The web activity can be carried out in all kinds of ways. I particularly like seeing it used to talk about vocation, because something like 90 percent of today's high school seniors will work for at least twenty-five years, full-time, outside the home, and not many girls plan for that. Too many of them slip sideways, when they must, into "a job," and it rarely has much to do with what they might have dreamed of doing as girls. So it's good for them to spin out positive vocational imagery over and over again, at every grade level.

But plenty of other questions can be usefully posed with this exercise. Like, what the qualities are of a great friend. Or even what problems have come up in the schoolyard or classroom and what solutions suggest themselves. The lessons of the web are always the same, but always applicable:

> Confide in one another.
>
> Listen to one another.
>
> See how strong you are *together.*

How strong together . . . the perennial mantra of community. "I take refuge in the Buddha," goes the Buddhist vow. "I take refuge in Dharma (the Law)," and "I take refuge in the sangam." "Sangam" means the collective body of seekers—the brotherhood and the sisterhood.

Awkwardly sometimes, and self-consciously, but with enormous determination, a great many women like Marian are struggling today to begin repairing the broken connections between girls and women, girls and other girls, women and other women. The focal point of their efforts is the preadolescent girl. Over the past few years, for a variety of reasons, this girl has become my own focal point, too. An odd thing, at fifty-plus years old, to find myself feeling so unaccountably close in spirit to Kristen, Sarah, Caitlin, Alyssa . . . to feel in this wobbly blue web a sangam of sorts, fleeting but full of promise.

When I was first becoming aware of what is now called the Girls' Movement, and first feeling myself drawn to it, I'd have said without hesitation that this was feminist activism in its purest form—liberation politics at its liveliest and most recognizable, only focused now in a way that seemed to me full of new promise. The silencing and confinement that male-centered cultures impose on women, the demonizing of desire, and cancellation of self—most of this really only weighs in fully when a girl is at the threshold of adolescence. If we can figure out how to go and meet her there, I reasoned, along with many others, and get her across that threshold whole and safely, she stands a good chance of remaining whole and safe. And all we're really talking about is the full extension to everybody of the rights democracy has always promised: life, liberty, pursuit of happiness. Freedom of speech, freedom of assembly . . . nothing that isn't covered in the most basic high school civic classes.

Ultimately, though, I came to believe that a purely secular framework for this endeavor is just not adequate. To strengthen girls enough so that they can look patriarchy in the eye and keep walking, I feel certain we must be able to draw on something much deeper than our knowledge of constitutional law. In this and the following chapter, I'll try to explain why.

Turning a Girl into a Goddess

During the months that followed Polly Klaas's disappearance, many of us were uncomfortable with all the talk about how pretty she was—how perfectly she embodied the fairy-tale princess of European folklore. Would her loss have been any less tragic if she'd been duller of eye and complexion, pudgy, waifish, and indrawn—more like most of us had looked or felt at her age? What if, for that matter, she hadn't been white? Finally, though, I began to see that what was so compelling about Polly's photograph wasn't merely that she was pretty. What moved us so was not just the high, clear forehead, the smile that was at once shy and eager. It was that in her very alertness and clarity, one sensed that she was poised—*en pointe,* like a dancer—on the threshold between child and woman that so many other cultures openly recognize as sacred. Realizing this, it seemed more than appropriate now simply to consider with my full attention what it means to be a girl of that age in this culture.

In January 1994, a memorial service was held for Polly Klaas in Petaluma. The hundreds of people who could not crowd into Saint Vincent's Cathedral watched the service via closed-circuit television at several other churches around town. It was an extraordinary occasion for many reasons, but for me the moment that brought not just the evening, but the whole tragedy, into sharp focus was when a close friend of the girl's family spoke—a man who had known Polly since her birth. Recalling picnics and camping trips, school plays and impromptu clarinet recitals, he described the acute pain he was experiencing at knowing he would never see the lovely young woman she'd been about to become—and that he would never see her with children of her own. This was the first time I'd seen it that way—that the girl's life had been destroyed at the very moment when those who loved her were beginning to glimpse the woman she would have been.

The piece that Noelle Oxenhandler wrote for *The New Yorker* shortly after Polly Klaas's disappearance ends with an observation that undoubtedly startled some readers. Candidly, the author (who lives north of Petaluma) describes her irrational response to the omnipresence of Polly's image: "One afternoon as I stood beside a copying machine and watched her face pile higher and higher in the tray, I realized that in some deep, superstitious part of myself I believed that the sheer multiplicity of images must eventually reach critical mass and transform into her absolute and singular presence." To confront her belief was of course to see its folly, for weeks passed, and the girl did not materialize. Something else seemed to be taking place.

> A child, in her innocent and beloved particularness, was playing a game in her room one evening when she was stolen into another realm. And as those of us who remain here grow accustomed to her face, which everywhere denotes her absence, we cannot help participating in her transfiguration. Even as we refuse to give up hope for her return, we find ourselves going in and out of the bank, the post office, the bookstore, turning a girl into a goddess.[1]

And of course *if* the Orissi knew what they were doing, and if the Navajos and the ancient Celts were right, that was exactly what we should have been doing. Because a girl on the brink of womanhood *is* in a sense a goddess. More precisely, she is our window upon the Goddess.

There is an aspect of *kinaalda* of which I haven't spoken, and I want to now. While she is undergoing her initiation as a woman, a girl is understood to be inhabited by the Mother and therefore charged with sacred power and able to impart something of this power to others. After she has herself been molded and massaged, for example, the young children come to her, and she "stretches" them:

> She moves her hands upward from each child's waist to the tip of his or her head. The stretching is said to mimic the growth of a plant, from the sowing of a seed to its flowering at maturity. The girl lifts upward, bestowing the blessing of healthy growth on the children of the tribe.[2]

Family and friends bring blankets, tools, and keepsakes to her, because her very touch blesses ordinary objects. Most remarkably, she is believed to have healing powers. One of the most dramatic photographs I have seen of *kinaalda* is of a young girl, elaborately dressed in a beautiful beaded leather gown and heavy turquoise jewelry, standing before an elderly woman who is several inches shorter. The girl's face, painted with bright gold corn pollen, is grave and concentrated, and her hands are placed on each side of the woman's head. There is enormous tenderness in her manner, great force and authority. Looking on raptly from a few feet away are the men of her clan.[3]

How ironic it seemed, then, that winter evening, that the nearest approximation to a *kinaalda* I had ever witnessed was this memorial service over closed-circuit television: an inversion of *kinaalda,* of course, for the girl we'd gathered to honor was not there. Right there at the center of everything, where her radiant presence should have been, was an empty space and a silence.

Publicly, I didn't hear it said, and I never saw it in print. But privately, among ourselves, women were saying it over and over: what happened to Polly Klaas is the full and final extension of something that happens to virtually all young girls in this society. It is *on a continuum* with the intimidation, the premature sexualization, and the silencing that nearly all girls experience as they grow up. It is the logical endpoint of that continuum. The purpose of our saying this to one another was not to underscore the victimhood of women—not at all. It was to declare our wholehearted, vigorous repudiation of the entire continuum. No more. Not for us, not for our daughters.

The question came up often, and still does, as to why this particular tragedy stirred so many so deeply—why it galvanized our own community the way it did and why it captured the attention of the whole country. Local writer Noelle Oxenhandler provided one kind of answer when she contrasted the "bright world" where children chatter and play in their rooms and swing in playgrounds with the "dark world of unspeakable sorrows." She noted "how swiftly these two worlds connected, how easily the dark world made its claims." I think she is right, but I also think that what happened that winter happened in a specific, highly sensitized context—a matrix of awareness that was only just forming. For this particular child, pretty, yes, but also bright, creative, funny, and irreverent, embodied to perfection the "lost girl"[4] who was the focal point of a rapidly growing body of research that was reaching public awareness. I am quite certain that the passionate urgency of Petaluma's response derived in no small part from the concerns many of us were already feeling about *all* girls of Polly's age.

Losing Our Girls

Before the fall of 1993, the research that Carol Gilligan and her associates at Harvard had been carrying out for more than ten years on the psychological development of girls and women was certainly not in the mainstream of public awareness. Those of us who already had an interest in the subject were well aware of their findings, as we were of the related work of Jean Baker Miller and her associates at Wellesley's Stone Center and of Emily Hancock's *The Girl Within*. But the 1991 publication of *Shortchanging Girls: Shortchanging America,* by the American Association of University Women, followed in autumn 1993 by *Mother Daughter Revolution,* by Elizabeth Debold and colleagues, had made a signal difference. The loss of voice that girls are found to experience around puberty, the wall they come up against of negative cultural stereotypes, the drop in self-esteem and their subsequently plummeting math and science scores, had now become a matter of broad public concern.

In fact, I have a clipping from that period that brings it back vividly. My sister Wendy lives in Portland, Oregon, where she works for a foundation that supports math and science education (K through 12) with special focus on girls and minorities, and she happened to be in the Bay Area late that October. She had come to the UC Berkeley campus to observe a weekend conference for women engineers that she had put together and her foundation had underwritten. I went to meet her for breakfast at the hotel where she was staying, and as soon as we'd greeted each other she pushed the morning paper toward me, her eyes already swimming, too choked up to speak (we're a rather labile family—it comes from the paternal side). It was an interview with the authors of *Mother Daughter Revolution,* who were describing the anger and indignation felt by adolescent girls when they realize what kind of sacrifices their mothers have made to survive in a male-centered world and they wonder whether they will have to make them also. They feel betrayed, say the authors, and worse than that, "generation after generation, daughters translate betrayal by the culture into a betrayal by their mothers. *Ironically and tragically, mothers are blamed for the very betrayal that they themselves suffered."*

I'm sure that glimmerings of that perception had come to both of us before, but never all of a piece like this. I was as moved as Wendy was, and I think both of us felt enormously glad to be together, daughters of one cherished mother, while we were taking it in. We sat together for a couple of hours over cinnamon rolls and pots of Earl Grey tea, feeling our way back across family history, wincing at some of the places that were still raw, seeing a great many things in a light we hadn't before, and reflecting, finally, that, on the balance, we were just as glad to be mothers of sons, as both of us are. We knew we were missing a lot—we both admitted to catching ourselves watching little girls sometimes with acute longing—but really, in such a world, how can a mother begin to "get it right" for her daughter, given that she'd never gotten it right for herself to begin with?

The deeply troubling picture of American girlhood that was taking shape that fall would be confirmed and amplified the next year with the publication of *Failing at Fairness*, by Myra and David Sadker, *Reviving Ophelia*, by Mary Pipher, and *School Girls*, by Peggy Orenstein. Thanks to these writers and researchers, a growing number of us were coming to see with terrible clarity what it means to be a twelve-year-old girl in what Mary Pipher has called "a girl-poisoning culture."

I was familiar with many of these books because they were relevant to my efforts to understand the development of the women mystics I'd written about. But others had found their way onto our bookshelves because my husband had put them there. In his work with gifted fourth, fifth and sixth graders, he'd become increasingly aware, since the late 1980s, that he was losing many of his girl students sometime in the sixth grade. The imagery of sacred thresholds was painfully inapplicable to these girls. Phrases like "hitting a wall" or "going underground" or just "checking out" seemed much more to the point. Right around their twelfth birthday, girls who had loved everything they'd done in the class—cosmology, bridge building, ancient Egypt, tessellations—seemed to just turn off and shut down. By the spring of 1991, perfectly ready to assume it was a flaw in his own teaching style—that he just didn't "click" with sixth-grade girls—Tim had begun to think seriously about asking for a reassignment. That same year, though, he read about the AAUW research on the losses in self-esteem that girls suffer right around twelve years old and began to think there might be more to the problem than his own limitations. In the fall of 1992 he attended a conference on classroom gender equity that the organization hosted at Mills College (where he was one of only a half dozen males, and heartened to find himself made both welcome and comfortable). Soon afterward he began to develop a set of interventions—classroom procedures and activities that he hoped would make a difference for his girl students. And he joined the AAUW.

He had made, in other words, a real beginning, But when a girl the same age as his own students was kidnapped from her Petaluma home and murdered, that solid beginning wasn't nearly enough: the urgent needs of young girls—in particular, their betrayal by our educational institutions—became for the next several years the dominant theme of his professional life.

"Why Does the Boys' Baseball Field Have a Bathroom and Ours Doesn't?"

Three interventions formed the backbone of "Power and Promise of Girls," the program Tim launched with three other educators. In retrospect it is fascinating to me that he adopted the strategies he did. He was guided, to be sure, by the solid instincts of a veteran teacher, but he really discovered only as he went along how empowering these interventions were and only some time after that how much they corresponded with emerging feminist desiderata for girls.

Note, for that matter, how swiftly they bring to mind the four concerns we've been looking at all along—finding voice, strengthening the sense of self, supportive enclosure with other women and girls, and identification of desires—and also the ingredients for resisting patriarchy that were stirred together in the early Christian convents: recognition of a historic lineage of strong women, establishment of female community, and validation of one's own capacity to choose.

First, he set out to make his own classroom a more welcoming place for girls. He wanted them to be able to look up and see images of women who had transcended conventional definitions of woman and achieved great things. Sonoma County happens to be the home of the National Women's History Project, founded in 1979, which makes available a wide range of materials celebrating women's achievements. So before long his walls were bright with "Women Who Dared" posters; "Women of Science" calendars; reproductions of the work of Frida Kahlo, Georgia O'Keeffe, and Mary Cassatt; photographs of Sally Ride, Rachel Carson, and Janet Reno. Realizing that he'd been catering unconsciously to the boys' preferences in curriculum, he added more literary activities and scheduled a unit on opera. When he found out that the county's Commission on the Status of Women had a bureau of women presenters who would come to classrooms and talk about their work—including a computer engineer, a police officer, a building contractor—he jumped at the chance to shake up career stereotypes held by both girl and boy students.

Second, frustrated at how many of his lively nonstop talkers fell silent as their twelfth birthday approached, he introduced a six-week unit on public speaking that culminated in each child's giving a five-minute monologue in the guise of a particular historic figure. Napoleon was there and Neil Armstrong, but so were Amelia Earhart and Elizabeth Blackwell. "Amelia" was distressed at having left her flight jacket and scarf at home, but she rallied and delivered a mesmerizing talk that touched upon an idyllic tomboy childhood and parents who didn't mind at all. Tim filmed their performances with a borrowed video camera, and that was important. The kids watched themselves over and over, seeing themselves, I think, and hearing themselves, differently. . . .

Finally, acting on the hunch that girls needed time just to connect with other girls in a setting outside the classroom, Tim and his colleagues set up a weekly lunchtime gathering for girls. The format of "Power and Promise" was simple. For the first few weeks the girls ate their lunches while the adults took turns telling stories of women who had been, in one regard or another, courageous. After that, the girls themselves told stories about women in their own lives who'd been courageous—or times when they themselves had had to be. Seeing very quickly that even a grown-up sympathetic guy was still one guy too many, Tim reluctantly stopped attending.

The meetings evolved rapidly into a forum where anybody could bring her concerns or questions. Unfairness on the playgrounds would be a recurring theme:

"Why do the boys' baseball fields have a bathroom and ours doesn't?"

"How can we get the boys to let us play basketball at recess?"

Teachers who seemed to give preferential treatment to boys were another gripe:

"Why is it that when a bunch of boys are talking, it's fine, but if a teacher sees a bunch of us together she says, 'Why are you gossiping?'"

"Why do they say we're getting wild as soon as we do any little thing, like throwing grass or yelling?"

Girls' groups are as diverse as the individuals who start them up. One teacher, for example, has been experimenting with meetings that bring fourth, fifth, and sixth graders together. She's interested in seeing whether older girls can move into a mentoring relationship with younger ones, and also whether the brash aplomb of the younger girls might not reawaken the slipping confidence of the older ones. It seems to be working: members of her group who've gone into junior high school are coming back regularly now to help the sixth graders make the transition. Others are finding that racial tensions among girls can be eased when they meet together and talk about problems they share, like body image and difficult siblings. Some groups meet outside the school setting altogether: school "politics" can be daunting.

No scripts are floating about for the brave souls who undertake this work. Facilitators learn quickly that they will say things they wish they hadn't and will neglect to say things they should've—and that the meetings won't all be terrific. Three guidelines emerged early on in Power and Promise that are simple and crucial: respect, genuine listening, and confidentiality— "don't repeat things people say here outside this room." No one tries to talk the girls out of their perceptions, and they don't try to justify the unfair or condescending treatment girls experience. They do try to model effective problem solving continuously.

"Well, what can we do about this?" they ask. "What would you think about some of you going to your teacher together and telling her you think the boys are getting called on more than is fair?"

"Well, if you don't think she'll believe you, you can sit and keep track some class period and then show her. . . ."

And, "Actually, the law requires that girls have facilities for sports that are as good as the ones the boys have. Would you like to write a letter to the school board about getting a bathroom for the softball field?"

Respect, genuine listening, and confidentiality . . . if it sounds familiar, it probably should. In 1988, Carolyn Heilbrun urged women to resume the practice of consciousness-raising: "We must begin to tell the truth, in groups, to one another." The women who participated in the first CR groups, she says, learned "that, isolated in nuclear families, they suffered individual guilt, each supposing herself a monster when she did not fit the acceptable narrative of a female life." Just so, one might say of young girls today: "Isolated in middle school classrooms, they suffer individual guilt, each supposing herself a monster when she does not fit the acceptable narrative of a preteen girl student." By helping girls learn to look at the culture as if they were anthropologists, as Mary Pipher suggests, facilitators find they can help them realize they might not be the weird ones after all.

Faculty and parents sometimes express concern that Power and Promise discussions will degenerate into "boy bashing." The emphasis on courage, storytelling, and problem solving redirects that impulse effectively, but in fact, facilitators haven't found the girls to be particularly interested in putting the boys down. On the contrary, they've been moved by the girls' generosity—by their astuteness, for example, in seeing the sort of peer group pressures that can pick up the individual boy and hurtle him along past his better judgment and kinder impulses. They talk often about how come all the *hitting*—they'd really rather not be punched and poked and hammered so much—but basically, as one eleven-year-old said in one of the first Power and Promise meetings, "All we want is equal treatment. No more, no less."

Gradually, over the past couple of years, advocates for girls have stopped talking about their work in a piecemeal sort of way and have begun to see themselves as part of a grassroots movement, multiform and improvisational, but uniform in its dedication to seeing that girls have the opportunity to speak and be heard, to identify their needs and meet them, and to strengthen in every possible way their hold on "self." Everyone involved is working out of her own strengths and intuitions. Nobody is directing this movement from the top because there *is* no top. Just ordinary people with ordinary resources. The level of energy and commitment, however, is extraordinary and has to do with a very interesting process that takes place in the individuals who are drawn to this work.

CHAPTER 7

Our Daughters, Our Selves

When women are first introduced to the research on young girls and their fall from self-confidence, their first response is often to throw up walls of denial: "This is completely exaggerated." Or, as a George Bush appointee to the Department of Education insisted, "Our schools are islands of fairness!" But then, after continued exposure, a fissure opens. A buried memory stirs, and the walls give way. In a rush of recollected pain, women own their own silencing. They remember the bright, strong, vibrant girl they had been before the lights went out and feel for the first time overwhelming grief at her disappearance.

Grief at first, but then, in many cases, something more empowering. A profound determination to break the cycle of silencing.

When women go to the assistance of young girls who are colliding with this culture's expectations of women, they often make a discovery for which nothing has prepared them. They meet them*selves*—the parts of themselves they'd left behind, believing they had to, when *they* were eleven or twelve. In *The Girl Within*, Emily Hancock has written extensively and movingly about this encounter with "the spirited, playful, self-contained child, the independent, competent, purposeful girl that a woman carries with her in memory." When such an encounter takes place, it often turns out to be what we used to call a radicalizing experience, much like what happened when all kinds of women realized they did indeed believe Anita Hill. It is my strong hunch that many of the women who have gone through the process I've described above and have glimpsed the "lost girl" they once were are more inclined to think of themselves as feminists now, however much they might have dodged the label previously. If I'm correct in guessing that the twelve-year-old's loss of belief in herself is more widely experienced than out-and-out sexual harassment, this could prove to be an even more pivotal development in the history of the women's movement. In fact, there is little doubt in my mind that the Girls' Movement really does constitute the full reawakening of the women's movement, which has been so long in coming.

"Staying in connection, then, with women and girls," writes Carol Gilligan, "in teaching, in research, in therapy, in friendship, in motherhood, in the course of daily living—is profoundly revolutionary."[1] And everything we know about the history of patriarchy suggests that she is right, for patriarchy has sustained itself primarily by keeping us apart. The single most important strategy behind this revolution (and in our preoccupation with "finding voice" it would be easy to overlook it) is almost certainly the simple act of *listening,* carried to altogether new heights.

If I were to have to identify one time and place in recent years when I thought that feminism had reawakened and become once again truly radical—an occasion one could compare with Rosa Parks's refusal to change seats on a segregated bus in Birmingham, Alabama—it would be the moment in the spring of 1988 at the Laurel School in Cleveland, Ohio, when the team of psychological researchers led by Lyn Mikel Brown and Carol Gilligan voluntarily abandoned the protocols of a research project they had designed back at Harvard and moved instead—when they were almost two years into their research—to a method of interviewing their subjects that was truly open-ended and relational.

"We came to the school to learn from girls," Brown recalls. "Our work depended on girls' willingness to speak to us from their experience . . . yet we came with a research design that, by definition, presumed no relationship that we could call real relationship." The ironies were palpable. While the stated purpose of their research was "to understand more about girls' responses to a dominant culture that is out of tune with girls' voices,"[2] their method of inquiry replicated that culture to a T. As "neutral outsiders"—godlike observers, in other words, presumed to have no relationship to the girls themselves—they posed the same questions to all the girls, permitting the girls themselves to ask none in return and excluding them from any role in interpreting their answers. The girls themselves saw this instantly and responded in kind, creating their own counterculture—a kind of underground through which they informed one another about the questions being asked and the answers each of them had given.

Instead of continuing on, obedient to the standard practices in their field, the Harvard team decided to listen. The girls, they learned, had felt used by original interviewing procedures. They wanted to spend more time with their interviewers, ask questions about what they were finding, amplify their interpretations or disagree with them, and know what was being said about them outside the school. They wanted, in other words, to be truly subjects, treated with respect, *heard*.

When Brown and her associates complied, the results were breathtaking. "Our work gained a clarity we had not experienced before." Foregoing their research design, accepting in the process the likelihood that their work would be discounted by many of their colleagues, opening themselves up instead to "the messiness and unpredictability and vulnerability of ongoing relationship," they began to hear genuine voices uttering real truths. And in those ongoing relationships, to their astonishment, they began to learn about themselves: "We came to remember the forgetting of our girlhood by going back through the disconnections of adolescence."[3]

For these Harvard-trained researchers to have broken as they did with accepted scientific protocols was an act of great courage. It constituted a tacit critique of a scientific method that permits only one subject—the researcher herself—and reduces everyone she is studying to the status of an object. By adopting a participatory model instead, which they called their "listening guide," they helped reinvent social science along feminist lines. In so doing, they also brought into serious question the distinctions I outlined much earlier in this book between the positions that feminists and spiritual seekers are ordinarily *presumed* to take on issues like voice, enclosure, self, and desire.

In other words, what you see on the part of the Laurel School researchers is a willing adoption of silence and a concerted effort to set aside personal assumptions, projections, and desires for control so that the voice and full selfhood of others—the girls they were studying—could be heard and seen. Their motive appears to have been a mix of intellectual curiosity and the passion for empowering women-in-the-making that most of us would call feminism. How very interesting, then, that these exceedingly grounded and this-worldly researchers should have experienced what they did as a result: a powerfully enhanced sense of their *own* selfhood and fresh clarity on who *they* really are. Because, of course, this is exactly what mystics have always told us would happen—told us through whatever metaphor they could lay hands on—when we "get ourselves out of the way."

Altruism has always been a strong component of the women's movement, but when girls become the focal point of the movement, it really takes the lead. And it's in this regard that feminism is challenging patriarchy at a level never before addressed. Because it's one thing to protest various forms of injustice—wage inequities, glass ceilings, classroom bias—as slights against our humanity, and it's quite another to recognize that they all emanate from a particular set of assumptions about what actually constitutes humanity.

It is increasingly recognized today that sexism comes from exactly the same place in consciousness that racism does, and that is the belief that a sense of self is something you build and consolidate over time by defeating or disempowering other selves. I use the word *belief* intentionally, because something very like religious faith is involved here—the *faith* that I will be confident and secure, and, by extension, more fully a subject and "human," in proportion to the number of individuals I have defeated and disempowered—or know I could if I wanted to.

Knowing there are people I can beat at racquetball, others who don't make as much money as I do or who are six inches shorter . . . *helps*. And if entire categories of people can be understood to be by definition "other"—an entire gender, whole races or nations—that is all the better, because it provides a kind of baseline below which you can sink only by really working at it.

To name this theory of self, as feminist theorists have been doing, and trace out its effects and demonstrate what misery it breeds, is certainly a step in the right direction. But something even more significant is happening in and around the Girls' Movement.

When historian Margaret Miles talks about the immense power of "established public representations"—the sort of tacit agreements that can render whole classes of individuals invisible—she remarks that the alternative to relying on such representations would be to cultivate "a perspectivity that confers self all around," one that assumes, in other words, "that each person possesses a unique combination of integrity, intelligence, generosity, self-interest, belief, and experience."[4]

"Conferring self all around"—the phrase is wonderfully apt—is precisely what the Laurel School researchers decided to do. And in doing so, I realized, they aligned themselves with those who have opposed hierarchy and prejudice with particular vehemence from time immemorial: the sages and seers, for whom all of life is sacred and every living creature divine. "I was hungry," said Jesus, rebuking his followers, "and you fed me not. I was in prison, and you didn't visit me." When feminism follows its own inner logic most consistently, it finds itself in surprising company. . . .

For the past couple of decades, feminist psychologists have been drawing upon their work with women and girls to delineate a powerful new model for the development of self. The work of psychologist Dana Jack, for example, challenges the conventional equation of self-sufficient autonomy with maturity and proposes as an alternative model "the relational self," in which the developing individual's needs for intimacy and authenticity actually support each other. "Intimacy facilitates the developing authentic self and the developing self deepens the possibilities of intimacy." [5] Which is something one can observe in raising a child or even just being a good friend. In the safe place that a warm relationship provides, one can allow the more divergent parts of one's personality to emerge—including one's anger—and once those are acknowledged and assimilated, there's just "more of me there" to bring into that relationship and others. Conversely, of course, when I know that only a very narrow version of myself will find acceptance (the "nice and kind" parts, for example), I feel defeated before I even begin to unfold.

The model of *self-in-relation* is dynamic and reciprocal. It assumes a measure of ongoing healthy turbulence and continual fine-tuning. And it is utterly compatible with the very embodied, relational, and down-to-earth version of spirituality that is associated with reverence for the sacred feminine and its insistence that we are all "parts of Her."

Trust in the power of genuine listening has, of course, been central to feminism all along. The consciousness-raising movement of the early seventies was one channel through which this trust flowed into the contemporary women's movement. But there is another, not so widely recognized, and I think that when we do recognize it we begin to get a clearer sense of why feminism and spirituality have so much to say to each other these days.

Until recently, Gloria Steinem had said very little about her two years in India. Near the end of *Moving Beyond Words,* though, she tells a remarkable story about that period—most of which she spent wearing saris. Her first year she spent at Delhi University. During the second, she traveled around by train, supporting herself with bits of freelance writing. At one point she visited an ashram headed by Vinoba Bhave, a close associate of Gandhi's who walked around India for decades persuading landowners to give over some of their holdings to land trusts for the poor. At the time of Steinem's visit, violence and rioting had broken out in the area between castes, and teams of Bhave's followers were going out into the villages trying to calm things down. Inexperienced as she was, she was asked to accompany one team because they needed a woman. Otherwise the village women might not be persuaded to come out and talk. She accepted the invitation and walked from one village to the next for days, until her feet became so blistered she had to hitch a ride back to the ashram in an oxcart. The leader of her team was a man in his seventies who had given his life to this sort of work. Today, she recalls his advice vividly:

> If you want people to listen to you, you have to listen to them.
>
> If you hope people will change how they live, you have to know how they live.
>
> If you want people to see you, you have to sit down with them eye to eye.

"Only recently," says Steinem, "have I understood the resonance between what I have been doing and that long-ago and long-buried turning point." [6] I would be very surprised if more areas of resonance are not gradually recognized now between the contemporary women's movement and the work that Gandhi and his followers undertook in India. Let me explain why.

When parents or teachers talk with Tim about starting up a girls' group, they always express anxiety about their own competence. Tim sympathizes; he's certainly felt the same way. But he always tells them that no matter how successful or awkward they feel, "This work will change you." It will push them, he means, to depths in themselves that they may not have reached before.

Linda Christensen, for example—by way of illustrating this process—is a Portland, Oregon, high school teacher who has set out to help students "unlearn the myths that bind us" by critiquing fairy tales and films. Her experience resembles that of many individuals who set out with a limited objective and find that making inroads on one level draws them on in, inexorably, to the next level and the next.

Christensen begins her class by having her students read from Ariel Dorfman's *The Empire's Old Clothes: What the Lone Ranger, Babar and Other Innocent Heroes Do to Our Minds* and then keep track of their dialogue with Dorfman in a journal. Typical of their reactions, she observes, as they begin to peel back the veneer over societal injustice, is that of a high school sophomore named Justine, who was overwhelmed and discouraged at discovering how much of her self-image had been formed by others, particularly by television actresses and models. She almost wishes she were still ignorant—"and happy!"—except that she knows how much those media-induced fantasies are shaping her behavior and her thinking. "My dreams," she has come to see, "keep me from dealing with an unpleasant reality. . . ." [7]

Justine saw the dilemma she'd created for herself, and so did her teacher. Christensen recognized and accepted the responsibility she had not to leave students like Justine in the lurch. Once the process of questioning had begun, it couldn't and wouldn't remain inside the classroom. The "unpleasant reality" had to be addressed. "Turning off the cartoons didn't stop the sexism and racism. They couldn't escape, and now that they'd started analyzing cartoons, they couldn't stop analyzing the rest of the world."

Alongside the ongoing critique of things as they are, Christensen saw the need to initiate a more positive process: "to enlist students *in imagining a better world, characterized by relationships of mutual respect and equality.*" And merely imagining it wasn't enough. If critique was not permitted to evolve into action, the students could well fall prey to cynicism. Having come this far, the teachers really had to facilitate the next step. Christensen and her colleague decided now "to get the kids out of the classroom with their anger—to allow their writing and learning to become vehicles for change." The students were encouraged to think of audiences for their cartoon analysis, and they did. In a variety of ways—pamphlets for the PTA, articles for national publications—they addressed their peers and their parents. The writing, Christensen emphasizes, is far tighter and cleaner than normal because it's being written for a real audience. "As Tinkerbell inspects her tiny body in a mirror," wrote one girl, "only to find that her minute hips are simply too huge, she shows us how to turn a mirror into an enemy. . . ."

The achievement of teachers like Linda Christensen is real, and its good effects will not go away. But I suspect that Christensen herself would be the first to agree that the work is not complete. Just as its initial steps made the next ones imperative, so does the last phase reported in her article call out for still more. The students' articles are still critiques, after all. The one piece of a more positive world that they have—and this is a precious piece—is that now they have begun to see themselves as agents of change. But that sense is still fragile and limited. The need for adult allies and friends who have a positive vision of the *whole* of life and who are committed to realizing it, is absolutely vital.

Gandhi's first campaign to promote Indian freedom from British colonial rule ended badly. What had been intended as a nonviolent satyagraha turned ugly, and Gandhi refused to pursue it any further. Instead, he moved into the countryside and launched what he called a Constructive Programme. Village uplift was among its chief aims, as were prohibition, improvement in the status of women, abolition of foreign cloth, and an end to untouchability. He had come to see how meaningless political freedom would be for India if her people were still under the thrall of poverty, ignorance, and the ills that flow from both and if they exploited one another just as the British had all of them. He would free India from the ground up and from inside out, confident that once a significant number of Indians had achieved economic self-reliance and real self-respect, the British would have no choice but to depart: they would be superfluous, and they would know it.

But he never saw this work as fundamentally political or economic. India would rise up and claim her rightful place as an equal among modern nations, he believed, when she had first reclaimed her ancient spiritual tradition. When he came back to India in 1915, after 20 years in South Africa, his head was shaved and he wore the white cotton garments and carried the staff that symbolized for Indians the life of religious renunciation. Wordlessly, he was sending them a powerful message, and they got it. His sourcebook for revolution was not *Das Kapital* or the letters of Thomas Payne, but the Bhagavad Gita, and the way he described his relationship with India's most beloved scripture is telling:

The *Gita* has been a mother to me ever since I became first
acquainted with it. . . . One who rests his head on her
peace-giving lap never experiences disappointment. . . .
This spiritual mother gives her devotee fresh knowledge,
hope and power every moment of his life.[8]

Gandhi understood that India's problems went far beyond
political and economic oppression. Indian women and men had
lost confidence in themselves because they had internalized the
British government's view of them. It was like a form of hypno-
sis. Their sense of their own greatness as a people was like a tiny
ember, barely warm, buried in ashes.

By the same token, those who've been working with and on
behalf of young girls come gradually to understand how crush-
ingly public representations of girls weigh upon the girls themselves and continue to as they enter womanhood. The source of
these representations isn't a government, of course, or any particular institution, but rather the drive for unlimited corporate
profit, which has taken the commodification of girls to heights
undreamed of in our patriarchal past. The most direct means,
pornography, is only the beginning. Highly sexualized representations of young girls are featured in films and music videos and
are used to sell all kinds of products, but they also sell the notion
that this is what young girls are supposed to look like. Since almost nobody does look like that, insecurity abounds—fertile
ground for marketers of cosmetics, clothing, weight-loss programs, compact discs, soft drinks, and more. Girls are *needed* today, to a degree most of us haven't fully taken into account, for
the double role they play in corporate economics, as commodity,
on the one hand, and consumer, on the other. So a great deal of
energy is expended making sure this is how they see themselves.

When someone who has been working on behalf of girls begins to see all of this with some clarity—when she experiences firsthand how deep the resistance really is to the simple, reasonable reforms she's advocating, and from what surprising places it can suddenly lash out, so vicious it takes her breath away (or *his* breath—I've watched this happen to my husband, for example)—the levels of commitment involved in Gandhian satyagraha don't seem excessive at all. For that matter, the religious basis of Gandhian resistance no longer seems quaint or excessive, either.

Vandana Shiva tells us in devastating terms what the corporate eye sees when it looks at a river, a mountain, a field, or a forest—that the impersonal eye of global commerce sees only the potential to make a profit and make it this year, while the subsistence farmer sees an infinitely complex, balanced, and beautiful structure that is alive, sacred, and eternal: the body of the Mother. Just so, when we see a girl who is entering womanhood, we can imagine, as we are conditioned to, how she might look in an ad for Guess jeans—or we can exult with the Orissi: "Look! She's coming into her shakti!" This second option is rarely experienced firsthand. Novelist Ntozake Shange offers us a fictional glimpse in *Sassafras, Cypress & Indigo* the afternoon Indigo visits her good friend, Sister Mary Louise Murray.

Sister Mary Louise ("who must have been around roses too long. Her face glowed like petals with veins glowing, like the opals in her ears") is a deaconess in Indigo's family's church. As Indigo stands in her home talking, she feels a wave of intense emotion ("so mad she felt lightheaded; hot all over") and then realizes she has begun to bleed.

"Speak, child," Sister Mary Louise shouts, "raise your voice that the Lord May Know You as the Woman You Are," and she springs into action.

She gently took off Indigo's clothes, dropped them in a pail of cold water. She bathed Indigo in a hot tub filled with rose petals: white, red, and yellow floating around a new woman. She made Indigo a garland of flowers and motioned her to go into the backyard.

"There, in the garden, among God's other beauties, you should spend these first hours. . . . Take your blessing and let your blood flow among the roses. Squat like you will when you give birth. Smile like you will when God chooses to give you a woman's pleasure. Go now, like I say. Be not afraid of your nakedness."

Then Sister Mary shut the door. Indigo sat bleeding among the roses, fragrant and filled with grace.[9]

Here, puberty is presented as an awakening to a whole range of feelings and capacities, all at the same time: sexual desire and the capacity to give life and nurture it, but also, and unequivocally, *spiritual* power and *spiritual* hunger. Courage and joy. Sister Mary Louise invites her young friend to recognize all of these feelings in herself simultaneously and welcome them.

What is to me particularly interesting about the passage, moreover, is its explicitly religious language. Is there any way in the world Ntozake Shange could have conveyed the transformation of a girl into a woman with anything approaching the magnificence she does if she had not used words like *blessing, God,* and *grace?* If she had not called up that whole wretched biblical account of things explicitly and let Sister Mary Louise effectively rescind Eve's exile from the garden of Eden and revoke the curse God had laid on Eve and Adam by telling Indigo not to be afraid of her own nakedness? In any other version, the result would have been less powerful. In effect, Shange makes of Sister Mary Louise a kind of high priestess of a reinvented Western spirituality, reforging a connection between woman and the sacred feminine that four thousand years of patriarchy has striven to keep severed, and in doing that she gives us a tantalizing, heady glimpse of what life after patriarchy might actually feel like.

Of course it is also true that Sister Mary Louise is regarded in her community as more than slightly daft. And that's exactly the point. The two radically differing representations of the girl-child that I've delineated—one in tight designer jeans, the other awash in rose petals—exemplify radically differing attitudes toward life itself.

It appears to me now that corporate greed, the global and "transinstitutional" force that Vandana Shiva sees as the real enemy of women, the earth, and life in all its forms, is the ultimate expression of that belief in "self-by-conquest" I've just described. That belief, in other words, is the seed of one kind of culture—materialist culture—and we've been watching it unfold, watching it take up more and more room in our lives, for nearly five thousand years. Feminist theorist bell hooks states its central teaching in a few devastating words: "There is nothing in you that is of value; everything of value is outside you and must be acquired."[10] Its opposite number, the seed that's capable of producing another very different version of culture, is visible in the discovery of the Laurel School researchers that it is in "conferring self all around" that I experience a deeper, stronger sense of self. This other reading of human experience, and the possibilities it suggests, has been forced to the absolute margins of life—made to seem ridiculous. Well and good for Sister Mary Louise to respond as she does to Indigo's entry into womanhood—she's one of the neighborhood crazies. The girl's own mother reacts with the alarm you'd expect in a woman who knows very well the dangers a Southern town holds for an adolescent girl of color. ("Indigo, listen to me very seriously.")

The calculating gaze that a marketing consultant casts upon a young girl isn't really even sexist or misogynist. Nothing that specific. Rivers, forests, fields, children, animals—for the mind that has no category "sacred," let alone "sacred feminine," everything looks about the same. The bright fabric of life will be torn away like Draupadi's sari—casually, and greedily.

"Greed kills law," Draupadi teaches us. But she teaches us also that our protection from lawlessness and greed doesn't come from outside anyway. What saved Draupadi was her own understanding of what was at stake. She was, as the Orissi say, "part of Her," or as Sister Mary Louise says, "filled with grace," but just as important, she knew it.

Which is to say, I believe, that if a woman knows who she is, she cannot be drawn into an abusive relationship or manipulated by corporate media or prevented from playing the active role in politics that her country's laws entitle her to. She is quite simply immune to exploitation of any kind.

And to take it one step further, if a whole generation of girls could grow up knowing who they are, inoculated against sexism, their very presence would bring into question everything that has kept women at the margins of life, and from that nothing but good would come.

I have no daughters, but as I watch my son and his friends struggling across their own rough terrain, dealing with the very dubious scripts *they've* been handed, the conviction gets stronger and stronger that if this one thing happened, their lives would be incalculably the better, and while they're fastening surfboards to the roof of their cars or shooting baskets out back or puzzling over college admission forms, I breathe it out across them like a benediction: "May you always be surrounded by women who know who they are."

CHAPTER 8

Two Halves of One Reality

The blank space on the map of my life is blank no more. It's marked out with so many inviting trails and paths and avenues that I worry there might not be time to explore them all.

Much of this last three years I've imagined myself to be in "Julian time." Weeks on end would pass during which I felt so calm and well anchored in the quiet rhythms of my spiritual practice that it was hard to remember things had ever been otherwise. In one of her revelations Julian found herself walking about on the bottom of the sea and realizing, as she picked her way along through the seaweed and gravel, that "if a man or woman were there under the wide waters, if he could see God, as God is continually with man, he would be safe in soul and body, and come to no harm." And I read that as confirmation of something my own teacher has said—his stock answer, in fact, to moans of distress and reports of imminent disaster: Deepen your meditation. *Then* we'll talk. Because, of course, things generally do look very different when you've worked your way down past the first few layers of turbulence.

But for much of this same three years Draupadi was on my mind, too, and that has made for a much bumpier ride: Life crashing repeatedly through walls and disrupting hard-won meditative calm. No quiet anchorhold here, and scant little confidence in positive long-term outcomes.

In Julian's company, I seemed to have the time, space, and courage to open out the one place in my life where a certain amount of dissonance was making itself felt and to begin figuring it out. With Draupadi, everything was always *right now,* urgent and full of consequence. Reflecting at my leisure on Julian's struggle to reconcile the teachings she'd inherited with the truths she'd experienced, I began to understand better the two-way pull that I'd been experiencing, and this in turn helped me see that others were experiencing it, too, for every day I seemed to be meeting women who would start sentences and then trail off, unable, or unwilling, to finish them. And I thought I knew why. *Well and good,* said Draupadi. *Only the issue isn't just women who systematically keep their mouths shut, but little girls cut down before they ever get to be women.* Julian helped me feel my way back to how everything had gotten to be the way it was. Draupadi asked me what I was going to do about it.

Two voices in my head, two different kinds of assignment to be completed. Two halves, I saw at last, of one reality. I had long known I couldn't live without meditation, but now I knew that feminism was for me almost equally indispensable. "The beauty of feminism, for me," writes essayist Vivian Gornick, "was that it had made me prize hard truth over romance. It was the hard truth I was still after."[1] And so was I. The hard truths to which feminism had opened my eyes, my spiritual practice and perspectives would equip me to address. I've never labored under the notion that sexism is the one great evil in life, but it does seem to be the particular form of evil I'm called upon to address right now. I'm not sure how much choice one has in these matters.

I want to consider now what an active partnership between feminism and meditative spiritual practice might actually look like—and try to do. This in the most preliminary and exploratory sense, but guided by the hunch that the manner in which young girls make the transition into womanhood will be taken very, very seriously—because it affects everyone.

Kinaalda *on a Grand Scale*

The Karuk Indians are native to the Salmon River area seventy-five miles north of my home. A couple of summers ago a woman who is Karuk learned of a ten-day ceremony her people had been accustomed to performing for their girls at menarche. *Ihuk*, the Flower Dance, had not been carried out for 150 years, but one of the elders still knew something about it, and someone actually had a few old wax recordings, barely decipherable, of some of the songs sung at the ceremony. Aware that these were the fast-vanishing fragments of a culture that was her own culture and her young daughter's, this woman set out to learn everything she could about *Ihuk*. She knew that making the ceremonial dress alone, sewn with rows and rows of shells and beaded around the hem, would be an immense undertaking. But if she started immediately she might have everything ready for a Flower Dance she figured would need to take place in about two years. And so it was that in the summer of 1996 two "new-women" were welcomed into their circle of family and friends at the climax of a four-day reconstruction of *Ihuk*.

Ihuk resembles *kinaalda* in many regards, but there are differences, some of which reflect differences in the environment itself. Instead of grinding corn for a corncake, for instance, these girls ground acorns for soup, as their ancestors had. They fasted rather strenuously, and they were blindfolded for the entire time: when the blindfolds were at last removed, it was understood that the girls looked on the world now with a woman's eyes. Exacting tasks were carried out—not the least of which were the twice-daily dances themselves, performed without benefit of eyesight. At the very end the girls ran—just as Navajo girls run—with younger girls trailing along beside them. Once more they disappeared and emerged at last, surrounded by their mothers and other women—bathed, now, and magnificently dressed. Pale, but radiant.[2]

I think of Gandhi sometimes, looking at what three hundred years of British occupation had done to India, and I imagine him like someone down on his knees, trying to coax fire out of dying embers. The efforts women are exerting today to recapture a tradition of female strength and dignity place us sometimes in much the same position—worse, even, because, of course, most of us aren't even fortunate enough to have actual embers to work with. Nothing so substantial as a female initiation rite, for example, that's really your own, really your daughter's.

I'm not sure how genuinely useful I think it is to perform rituals and ceremonies that we borrow from other cultures. But I do think that even knowing about the ways different societies welcome their daughters into the adult community is of enormous benefit. Once you understand what the basic elements are of ceremonies like *Ihuk* and *kinaalda,* for example, you know what the people who designed those ceremonies think works to sustain a culture that honors women. And from one such culture to the next, those elements and the values they reflect are very consistent.

Sequestration, at regular intervals, in a female space . . . special songs and dances . . . the laying on of hands . . . adornment . . . athletic prowess . . . instruction in life skills . . . self-mastery . . . deferential support of menfolk . . . communion with divinity . . . opportunity to serve the community . . .

A girl who is granted all of this, *kinaalda* and its like imply, is the radiant center of a community that can regenerate itself—and that will want to. But the ceremony also implies that these modes of experience will be hers to enjoy for the rest of her life. And that if they aren't, something's wrong.

It's like a diagnostic checklist, and in light of how comparably bereft we are, we could do worse than adopt it for our own use, even just between friends:

"So, how are you doing? . . . Not so good? . . . When's the last time you got off someplace with your girlfriends? . . . Given a massage, or received one? . . . Worked in your garden? . . . Made a retreat? . . . Sang?"

"Sang?"

Yes, sang. All of the elements of *kinaalda* count. The Navajos knew what they were doing. *Kinaalda* teaches a girl in all kinds of ways that she and Changing Woman are one. She is massaged into Her likeness, she is painted with the corn pollen associated with Her fecundity, and she feeds her people much as the goddess Herself does. But the traditional songs, sung continuously, weave their own powerful spell. She knows she is "walking into beauty" because the songs tell her so.

The Congo Pygmies also knew what they were doing, according to anthropologist Colin Turnbull. Of *elima*, the Congo Pygmy initiation rite for girls, Turnbull wrote, "There are special *elima* songs which they sing to one another, the girls singing a light, cascading melody in intricate harmony, the men replying with a rich, vital chorus." At the climax of the ceremony, assembled with their mothers and grandmothers, the girls sing another set of songs: "songs whose words had no particular significance, but which in themselves were of the greatest significance, being songs sung only by adult women."[3]

What are our songs? What are the equivalent for women and girls of the gospel music that drove the Civil Rights Movement? In a 1991 interview with Bill Moyers, Bernice Johnson Reagon, founder-director of the choral group Sweet Honey in the Rock, talked about the place of gospel music in Black culture, and her remarks help us grasp what's actually going on with those "women-only" songs:

> When we sing, we *announce* our existence. . . . The songs are a way to get to the singing. . . . The singing is *running this sound through your body.* You cannot sing a song, and not change your condition. . . . This part of your being, the part of your being that is "tampered with" when you run this sound through your body is a part of you that *our* culture thinks should be developed and cultivated . . . that you should be familiar with, that you should be able to get to as often as possible, and that if you go through your life and don't meet up with this part of yourself, the culture has failed you.[4]

Of the song "This Little Light of Mine" in particular, she observed,

> A lot of old Black songs are "I" songs. . . . When you grow up in a culture where, as Black people, we really got strong messages about being visible. . . . people really had to go through a *barrier* to stick out. A song like "This Little Light

of Mine" *crashes* through that barrier: "*Everywhere* I go, I'm gonna let it shine!" . . . you are very clear that you are *sticking out.*

For women and girls who believe themselves to be invisible—a refrain that turns up regularly in women's writings—songs like this could be just the ticket. Songs about how good it feels to be strong, for instance, and swift—because athleticism in women has never been an embarrassment in cultures where womanhood itself is not an embarrassment.

> *I'm on my way running*
> *I'm on my way running*
> *Looking toward me is the edge of the world. . . .* [5]

Since 1972, when a federal law popularly known as Title IX went into effect, it has been mandatory, in all publicly funded educational settings, that girls have the same opportunities for athletic development and the same facilities for competing that boys have. The spectacular result is that on any given day now I can pick up the sports page of my local paper and see young women contending on a soccer field or basketball court—*girls* playing softball and breaking track records. I love knowing that many of these girls will be going to college on athletic scholarships, and I love even more knowing how protective their involvement in sports is: because it turns out that girls who participate in high school athletics are three times more likely to graduate from high school, 80 percent less likely to have an unwanted pregnancy, and 92 percent less likely to use drugs.[6]

Seeing that women and girls are encouraged to open out in all of the ways *kinaalda* emphasizes will be an ongoing priority for a feminism that is grounded in spirituality. We will support a *kinaalda* writ large—not a one-time-only ceremony, but a continuous campaign to enhance the lives of all girls and women *and thereby the whole human community.*

The beauty of this way of looking at things is that it doesn't pretend any of us can possibly do it all, or do it all at once. By focusing on the elements of *kinaalda,* each of us can identify in very concrete terms the places where we ourselves don't feel strong or adequate or supported and can address them. We can also identify the places where we have a lot to give.

Living Skills for a Global Culture

But the heart of *kinaalda,* and probably of all traditional feminine initiations—not merely the ceremony itself, but the time leading up to and following it—lies in the imparting of traditionally feminine skills: life-sustaining skills like spinning, weaving, knitting, pottery, cooking, healing, gardening, beekeeping, animal husbandry, and of course worship itself, the maintenance of an open line with the sacred. In sum, *How our people do things.* To have such skills *is* to enter the adult community. To be capable is to be powerful.

Years ago, a twelve-year-old friend asked me to teach her how to sew. We worked together for several months, and that Christmas she made her mother a beautiful flannel nightgown—white, with yellow roses and eyelet trim. Now that she is thirty-five and has children of her own, I know that the warmth of our relationship has much to do with the hours I spent that year teaching her seamstress tricks and an esoteric vocabulary to go with them: *facing, dart, placket, shank, bobbin, zipper foot. . . .*

The world girls are growing up into now, though, is enormously complex. Traditional nurturant skills aren't enough. Girls need to be equipped to make their way in the world outside the home as well. Yet the world's need for nurturance has never been greater. Perhaps the most exciting thing women can do for girls is to demonstrate the new forms it can take and the skills in which it is deployed. Like how to organize a food drive or a rent strike or a day care center for the elderly. How to protect a stand of old-growth redwoods, or a fragile wetland. How to set up a WEB page, for that matter, or a cooperative lending bank for women entrepreneurs, the way SEWA has done in India. How to get funding for a crisis hot line on your campus and then set it up and keep it going—as my friend Helen's niece just did when she discovered Berkeley didn't have one.

One could say that girls are no longer preparing themselves for life solely as homemakers; one could also say that a girl's sense of home may well extend much further, today, than the walls of her house or even the borders of her neighborhood. Changing Woman, "the first mother," looms behind every moment of *kinaalda*. Today, the passion to give and foster life that she represents takes many, many forms, and it has to. The authors of *Women's Ways of Knowing* describe the fifth and, for their purposes, final stage of feminine psychological development and hint at the extraordinary kinds of satisfaction it yields. They call this stage "constructivist":

> Constructivist women aspire to work that contributes to the empowerment and improvement in the quality of life of others. . . . They speak of integrating feeling and care into their work—"using my mind to help people" (in careers in human services, psychotherapy, education, child and women's advocacy, antipoverty legislation), "cradling the environment" (through social action and work in environmental protection

agencies and antinuclear movements), and "humanizing cities" (via city planning and community cooperatives).[7]

It seems to me entirely appropriate in working with young girls to hold this out as an ideal and as the quite natural culmination of women connecting with one another: a tremendous release into the stream of life of constructive, healing energies. In India they speak of *yajna,* which is literally "sacrifice," or "offering up," and they see *yajna* as the dynamic force that moves the entire cycle of life. Human beings come into their own, according to this view of things, when they habitually give and "offer up." We speak so much about "needs" when we think about young people, but the mystics never tire of reminding us that the human being's deepest need is to give.

It is important to bear in mind that in *kinaalda* a girl chooses her own sponsor. This "right to choose" alerts us to a vital aspect of this work. We are only as useful to these girls as we have been useful to ourselves. We must be *plausible.* If a girl is to accept my offer to escort her across a minefield, she has to believe I know where the mines are. Can I teach someone how to resist exploitation if I have never learned to be an effective resister myself? Where do *I* draw strength from, and courage? How good am *I* at establishing healthy, supportive relationships? It doesn't matter much what my own answers to those questions are; girls are astute observers, they'll draw their own conclusions.

This brings us to the most difficult questions that *kinaalda* and its analogues raise for contemporary women and girls. How do we replicate the timeless, implicit spirituality that shapes these beautiful ceremonies? Do we have to invent it? How do we find our way to spiritual forms and practices that will sustain us *as women* and connect us with other women and girls? How useful will they be if they don't come "alive" out of a living tradition, but where do we go to find a spiritual tradition that hasn't been contaminated with misogyny?

Spinning from a Broken Web

In the first place, many women *are* stepping outside their received traditions (if they've received one!) and borrowing what they need from elsewhere. Others are relocating altogether, and of course not merely because their womanhood feels unsupported where they are. We live in a time and place of unprecedented movement back and forth across religious borders. *New York Times Magazine* editor Stephen Dubner wrote recently about his own experience converting from Catholicism to Judaism, which was actually the faith of both his parents before *they* had converted to Catholicism prior to marriage.

> Ours is an era marked by the desire to define—or redefine—ourselves. We have been steadily remaking ourselves along ethnic, political, sexual, linguistic and cultural lines, carefully sewing new stripes into our personal flags and waving them with vigor. Now, more than ever, we are working on the religious stripe.[8]

For many of us, the very fact of proximity—that religious traditions other than our own are much more available to us than they were for our grandparents—makes it seem quite natural to incorporate observances and disciplines from other traditions. What is particularly impressive to me, though, is the capacity certain women have shown to find within their inherited tradition—a tradition that might in many ways be hostile to women—elements that allow them to remain there and feel nourished. I'm thinking of Catholic feminists, for example, unwilling to be edged out of the faith they love, who have declared themselves "defectors-in-place." Of Rita Gross, who has so effectively demonstrated the mutuality of Buddhism and feminism in her splendid book *Buddhism After Patriarchy.* Or of Rabbi Sue Ann Wasserman, who needed a ceremony to help her friend Laura Levitt after she had been raped and who adapted a traditional Jewish family ritual for that purpose. The manner in which their ceremony evolved seem to me extraordinarily representative both of the resourcefulness of today's women seekers and of the emerging conjunction of feminism and spirituality.

"When Laura was raped," Wasserman writes, "I wanted to find a way to support her as her friend. As a rabbi, I needed to find a way for Judaism to respond to her." [9]

The basis of the ceremony was *mikvah,* the age-old ritual of immersion and cleansing that orthodox Jewish women carry out each month twelve days after the onset of menstruation. The term *mikvah* refers both to the ritual itself and the vessel in which it takes place. Any naturally occurring confluence of waters can be a *mikvah:* a confluence of water, a reservoir, a pool, or a ritual bath. . . . In cities the *mikvah* must be built to meet traditional specifications: the water must be "natural," collected rainwater, typically, and it must actually flow.

Mikvah has wider meaning within Judaism, though, and Wasserman was tapping into this wider meaning deliberately. "*Mikvah* is also understood to be a source of hope and trust, another name for God. The *mikvah* ceremony refers to the ritual of immersion in such a place for purposes of ritual purification. . . ." (325 fn) The ritual has existed for centuries. She and her friend devised a liturgy to accompany it, though, that made the ritual specific to her friend's need, including in it excerpts from the poetry of other contemporary Jewish women. One passage, for example, says of *mikvah* that it "is not about 'uncleanliness,' but about human encounters with the power of the holy" (323).

In taking it upon themselves to carve out a larger place within their tradition for women, and particularly for women who have suffered sexual abuse, "a place for us and even our most painful experiences to be commemorated in Jewish community/ies," (322) women like Levitt and Wasserman are not only healing themselves, they are renewing and regenerating the tradition itself in exactly the way that the women of the Chipko movement are doing for Hinduism. They speak warmly of the restorative force of being able to come together "as a Jewish woman among other Jewish women I am close to," and what Levitt herself says about the healing process itself reminds one of the work of my local group Born of Woman and the experience of its members over time.

"For me," writes Levitt, "healing is not simply a return to some 'wholeness' in the past; it is an experience of growth and change. Healing is the careful rebuilding of a life in the present that does not deny what has happened." The *mikvah*, she explained, worked on many levels at once:

> (1) it was predominantly our foremothers' ritual. (2) It requires the whole body. (3) Its waters flow in and out—representing continuity and process. (4) Its waters symbolically flow from Eden, a place of wholeness. (5) The natural waters remind us of the constant intermingling presence of the Creator in our own lives. (6) Finally, water itself is cleansing, supportive, and life sustaining. . . . (322)

Working within a tradition that is not known for its support of women, these two found what they needed—pieced together

out of what they could find, making something strong and
beautiful. And almost everything in spirituality that I've identified as distinctly feminine is contained there in their ritual: connection with the natural world; the centrality of flow; dignity
granted the body itself; connectedness back through time with
other women; and a bearing witness to divinity that is imma-
nent as well as transcendent.

> Historically [says Levitt], the *mikvah* is a sacred space for
> Jewish women and our bodies. Through this ceremony, I
> was able to enter into that tradition. Sue Ann helped me re-
> constitute this place to attend to my own physical needs for
> healing. In a steamy room overlooking a pool of running
> water in a synagogue in Atlanta, we recited these words and
> I entered the water. In so doing, the violation of my Jewish
> female body was attended to. It was neither silenced nor
> ignored. (322)

Vandana Shiva speaks over and over of the immense creativity inherent in the feminine principle, Shakti, that India believes
lies at the heart of the natural world. Regeneration is not merely
reproduction at all, she maintains, it is profoundly innovative.
The insistence that is making itself felt within all the major religious traditions of the world *as feminism*—insistence on inclusiveness, on adaptability, on compassion, on the spirit of law as
opposed to its dead letter—is, I think, what Shakti looks like
within spirituality.

Before her immersion in the healing waters of *mikvah,* Laura
Levitt read a passage from a poem by Adrienne Rich. Writing
about violence against women—my reluctance to confront it,
and to name it, but the growing impossibility of *not* confronting
and naming it—I have had glimpses of the kind of balance I am
groping for, but never more perfectly imaged than in these lines:

Anger and tenderness: my selves.
And now I can believe they breathe in me
as angels, not polarities.
Anger and tenderness: the spider's genius
to spin and weave in the same action
from her own body, anywhere—
even from a broken web.[10]

The broken web is one of those images from out of the prophetic depths (Adrienne Rich does have the stature, I think, of
one of feminism's high priestesses). It is in our collective memory because it describes exactly what patriarchy did. Judaism cut
its baby teeth on the systematic destruction of the worship of
the Goddess. And yet in that very image, Rich suggests, we can
find hope. The web can never be permanently broken because
the spider spins it out of her very self: "from her own body, anywhere." One thinks of Spider Woman and her "continual, ritual
re-creation of cosmic and human harmony."[11] Renewal, regeneration, innovation, is *what women do.* In every religious tradition
and every institution and from *outside* all traditions and institutions, they are finding ways to do it—finding the seed, the foot-
ing they need to turn things around.

Alignment and Flow

For women to reestablish connection with the sacred so fully
that they are then able to recharge Western culture itself with a
renewed sense of the sacred feminine, I would suggest that two
things have to happen—have, indeed, already begun to happen.

The first is simply that women must be connected, or *recon-
nected, with one another* in a host of ways: it's like the wiring in a
house, or better still, it's like the way that water is supplied to the

Himalayan villages Helena Norberg-Hodge describes in *Ancient Futures: Learning from Ladakh*:

> Generations ago, channels were built, tapping the meltwater from above and bringing it down to the fields. The water is often channeled for several miles, across steep walls of rock and scree, stretching it as far as it will reach. An elaborate, well-maintained network of smaller channels weaves through each village.[12]

In each village, a man is appointed or elected who regulates irrigation, but

> Watching a mother and her two daughters watering, I saw them open small channels and, when the ground was saturated, block them with a spadeful of earth. They managed to spread the water remarkably evenly, knowing just where it would flow easily and where it would need encouragement: a spadeful dug out here, put back there; a rock shifted just enough to open a channel—all this with the most delicate sense of timing. From time to time they would lean on their spades and chat with their neighbors, keeping one eye on the water's progress.[13]

The *flow* of the life force and of spirit, too, has always passed through women—but if we aren't aligned, it can't. Vandana Shiva describes with great warmth the visit that women of the lower slopes of the Himalayas make into the local oak forests each spring to lop the trees for fodder. There is a real science governing when and how much these trees can be lopped. Properly done, lopping can increase the forest density and fodder productivity of the forest. "Groups of women, young and old, go together . . . and land expertise develops by participation." In a very real sense, Dr. Shiva observes, these expeditions are "informal forestry colleges

. . . small and decentered." They create and transfer knowledge of how living resources are maintained.[14] And, of course, they pre-date Oxford and Cambridge by thousands of years.

The historical lineage among women must be restored through exactly this kind of education, so that we see ourselves in continuity with our own grandmothers and the other women of our own ethnic or religious background.

Cross-cultural interconnections must be forged, too. Particularly crucial are the relationships between women in the developed and developing nations. The women of the third world have everything to do with us. If we recall what Gerda Lerner has taught us about the origins of patriarchy, we'll remember that one of the ways that women have been prevented from coming together *as* women and reclaiming what has been taken away from us has been to establish a system of perks that reward women for accepting their marginalization within their particular class: most notably, the right to exploit women *and* men who live one notch down the social ladder. If "right to exploit" sounds harsh, let's just say "the right to enjoy privileges and material satisfactions denied to others." Recognizing that an increasingly large "third world" exists within the borders of this country, it is fair to say that within the overall scheme of things, most American women do unconsciously exploit women of the third world simply by being members of a society that regularly and systematically profits on third world misery.

. . . Which is to suggest that it is time we began to examine ourselves closely and regularly (yes, just like a breast check) for signs of the presumed cultural and racial superiority that accumulate around economic domination. It is time we began to honor the daily heroism of third world women and to identify ways we may be making their lives even more difficult than they have to be.

One reason this challenge seems to me so important a
promising is that it is exactly what we are asking men to do. It
a form of divestment directly reflective of the voluntary letting
go of privilege some men are already trying to carry out and
that we've promised will reward them in all kinds of ways.
We can start modestly, by just reading a few books. *I, Rigoberta
Menchu: An Indian Woman in Guatemala,*[15] for example, or *The
Voice of Hope,*[16] a collection of interviews with the leader of the
Burmese resistance Aung San Suu Kyi, or anything by India's
Vandana Shiva. We can contribute money to organizations like
MADRE, which has carried out such generous and consistently
canny work on behalf of Latin American women and children
in particular. We can join the Women's International League for
Peace and Freedom. We can certainly align ourselves with whatever is going on in our area to perpetuate the spirit of the
Beijing Conference. But we musn't stop there. Women in this
country have access to information and power that we haven't
begun to use. We can refuse to vote for political candidates who
are insensitive to deteriorating conditions for women and children, and we can refuse to buy products made by manufacturers
that exploit workers overseas and undermine their constitutional governments.

Nothing we do "out there," though, will be of much use until
we strengthen the ties between older and younger women and
young girls here within our own culture, the connections that
Carol Gilligan sees as revolutionary. Grown women must find
ways to *be there* for young girls, available and encouraging and
inspiring by their own example. When a girl begins to menstruate, for example, she is entering a mystery. Womanhood really is

t—beautiful and potent—and we must help our girls feel ini-
ated—proud and joyful instead of stricken and vulnerable. Part
of the grand community of women. The single most important
thing women can do for girls, according to the authors of *Mother
Daughter Revolution,* is to provide a community of women they
can enter.

But beyond just being there, we must be capable of speaking
from real depths. To be truly and effectively open toward one
another, women must find their way into a genuine, active interior life. Through prayer and meditation practiced in disciplined,
systematic ways, women can steady themselves, *ground* themselves, and convey to young girls the sanctity of both the interior
and the exterior life—spirit, mind, *and* body. When women turn
inward through meditation and other disciplines, a new feeling
for what the word *sacred* means can come into their lives. When
it does, they don't even have to talk about it—it conveys itself
wordlessly to daughters, nieces, and students.

Catching Fire

In asking that feminism think of itself henceforth as a resistance
movement based in spirituality, I'm not saying anything about it
that couldn't be said as well about most of the effective political
reform movements seen in recent years. Religious commitment
has played a role in these movements that it has been difficult for
the left in this country to recognize. Liberals have for so long
seen religion as the antithesis of reason and the enemy of real
truth seeking that it's taken many of us decades to understand,
for example, how deeply rooted in spirituality the civil rights
movement of this country was.

Given the religious climate in the United States, the contemporary women's movement in America has had sound reasons for

adopting the thoroughly secular tone and perspective it did. The current machinations of the Religious Right make it feel dangerous even to use the words *politics* and *spirituality* on the same page. But surely it's way past time we stopped letting the Religious Right define and rope off spirituality from the rest of us. Organized religion does have a lockdown on some of the best music, art, poetry, and real estate in the world, and insofar as it preserves the memory of its saints faithfully and well, it has something more precious than all of these. But it has no monopoly on what Mechthild of Magdeburg called "the rippling tide of love, which flows secretly from God into the soul and draws it mightily back into its Source." Organized religion has been no great friend to women, but that must not discourage women from reaching out to reclaim the connection with the sacred that has so long been denied us. And if we restructure entire denominations in the process, well and good.

Feminism *catches fire* when it draws upon its inherent spirituality. When it does not, it is just one more form of politics, and politics has never fed our deepest hungers. What a Gandhi knew, a Mother Teresa, a Dorothy Day, is that when individuals are drawn to a selfless cause—the relief of human suffering, the dissolution of the barriers that separate us from one another—energy and creativity come into play that simply don't under any other circumstances. The Chipko movement, the Catholic Worker movement, the United Farm Workers, the liberation theology activists in Latin America, Vinobha Bhave's land reform movement—all were and are sustained by people who couldn't be discouraged by short-term setbacks because they believed themselves to be part of something larger, whose truth doesn't need outside validation.

The capacity to feel another's pain as your own, the nucleus of reform politics, is a spiritual quality. The capacity to endure whatever one must to address the sources of human suffering, for decades or a lifetime, arises out of the depths that Simone Weil reached in prayer, and Gandhi reached in meditation. Feminism must find its way into those depths.

Once we begin to recognize as meaningfully spiritual qualities that aren't necessarily associated with formal religion, it is possible to see that feminism all along has been far more closely conjoined with spirituality than historians would have had us think. Read Jane Addams or Olive Schreiner or Lucretia Mott. Read about contemporary Italian feminists, for that matter, whose patron saint is Teresa of Avila expressly *because* she was a teacher of meditation. Feminists regularly have had to set themselves up in opposition to exponents of institutionalized religion, and that fact has thrown too many of us off the scent for too long.

When facilitators of groups like Power and Promise sit with young girls and encourage them to name the injustices they experience in classrooms that give preferential treatment to boys, and when they help them find ways to resist—kindly but firmly—they are modeling, and teaching, something very like Gandhian satyagraha. The consciousness raising that goes on in girls' group is, for that matter, in direct continuity with the meetings held in Black churches all over the south at the very beginnings of the civil rights movement, where "speaking out" —voicing the injustices—constituted the first courageous steps toward demanding an end to institutionalized racism. But that struggle for freedom was rooted in a passionate gospel faith whose equally strong origins in African spirituality have only recently come to be recognized. It had to do, just as satyagraha did, with one's relationship with a divine order. By the same token, the Solidarity movement in Poland was led by a man, Lech Walesa, whose devotion to the Black Madonna of Czestochowa was known to all his followers. To the United Farm Workers, Cesar Chavez was not merely a political figure but a religiously inspired leader—a man, like Gandhi, of prayer and fasting.

American feminism does not presently have access to a common fund of spiritual resources or reference points, certainly none we could employ in a public classroom setting! We are religiously diverse, and many of us are at odds with institutionalized religion, for a multitude of good reasons. And yet many who are working with young girls feel a very real need for that other dimension—for ceremony, for quiet times that look a lot like prayer or meditation, and for time-hallowed stories and songs that convey the sanctity of life and womanhood—for that connection with the sacred, in short, that Gerda Lerner has indicated may be the single most important avenue women have toward full emancipation. Rebuilding that connection, for ourselves and our daughters, is to my mind the most complex challenge women face today.

Epilogue

Initially, this book was very personal and entirely local. Its focus kept expanding, and yet, at the very end, it seemed to circle back after all and become once again exceedingly local and personal.

I've spoken of the past three years in terms of spinning—of watching as certain strands of meaning took shape over time, and seeing those strands in turn begin to interweave into coherent and sometimes beautiful patterns. Several of these patterns I haven't mentioned, feeling the book's tapestry was getting complicated enough without them. But one declared itself very late in the game, and with its emergence I felt as if I saw the project whole at last.

I first met Suzanne Lipsett soon after I'd finished writing *Enduring Grace*, when she and my agent, Candice, hosted an event they called a Late Bloomers' party. Nearly fifty of us, mostly writers and mostly middle-aged, gathered on a sunny deck at

Stinson Beach and got acquainted over a potluck lunch. Though Suzanne lived in Petaluma, and in fact had dated my husband's roommate when they were all students and aspiring novelists at UC Berkeley, our paths hadn't crossed until now. She'd worked ever since college as a developmental editor and writing collaborator (her business card described her as a "book midwife") and then published three novels of her own after turning forty.

At some point during the Bloomers' party one of the guests raised the topic of breast cancer. Could we have a show of hands by women who had had it or were dealing with it now? Sure enough, of the forty-some women there, four raised their hands—which was the norm, it had recently been determined, for women living in the Bay Area—and Suzanne was one of the four. She'd first been diagnosed around the time her second novel came out, in 1987, and had already had one fierce recurrence in 1989. When I met her, a few years later, she was writing up a storm. She was a genius-level friend, I would soon discover, and an inspired conversationalist, so long as what you wanted to talk about wasn't cancer.

Cancer on the one hand, God on the other: Suzanne thought of herself as an atheist. I didn't, so much. Privately, I thought of her more as what Indians call a *jnani*—one of those individuals for whom the whole idea of belief is suspect, but whose passion for truth is easily as formidable as any avowedly religious seeker's. She would ask me sometimes about meditation, but when I explained what I did, and why I did it, she always scuttled away again at full speed, maintaining that her writing was her meditation, thank you. I never pursued the subject. We had plenty to talk about besides religion—our sons, our husbands, our friends, the books we were working on, Petaluma gossip, and the vagaries of the publishing world.

Suzanne's third and final bout with cancer began sometime early in 1995. Various treatments were tried, and some seemed to help for a little while, but by the summer of 1996, when it was clear that they were hurting her much more than they were helping, she and her husband, Tom, decided to suspend them. Around the first of August Tom called her friends and alerted us that she appeared to be slipping away. Candice cut short her vacation in Switzerland and flew back immediately; relatives and friends arrived from Washington, D.C., and Los Angeles, and dozens of friends in the area came around to see her and talk with her one last time.

Later, at Suzanne's memorial service, it would become apparent—grounds for shared laughter at a moment when laughter was needed—that at least four women all thought of themselves as having been her best friend. I knew that currently, at least, our mutual friend Candice had held that honor. The two had been on the phone together almost daily for years, sounding each other out on ideas for books, collaborating, arguing at regular intervals, and making up again like a pair of fourteen-year-olds. It was during one of those talks, sometime during the fall of 1994, that Candice mentioned a line from Julian of Norwich that she had read in someone's proposal. Mine, in fact, for this very book. The quotation was one that T. S. Eliot had used in *Four Quartets:* "All shall be well, and all manner of thing shall be well." They talked about it briefly and went on to other things.

A week later, Suzanne was writing a short story, and she couldn't quite get the ending she wanted. "Alice" was a lovely piece—a straightforward "day-in-the-life-of" that follows a Los Angeles social worker around from case to case while her mind keeps going back to her house and the teenaged daughter she'd left there that morning in a paroxysm of grief she knows is only partly over the death of Kurt Cobain. The story had resolved itself almost perfectly; the dark void that can open out between child and parent is miraculously closed, and in the last lines the mother lies down next to her daughter, who is sleeping peacefully now, reconciled to life after all—and to her mother—and as she curls in around her, relief and free-floating gratitude wash over her, and quite unaccountably, the words of a medieval English recluse pass through her mind. . . . "All shall be well, and all manner of thing shall be well."

Suzanne sent the story to her twenty or thirty best friends for Christmas, but she couldn't wait to call first and tell me how Julian's words had come to her just when she—excuse me, just when her *story*—had needed them.

But that was only the beginning.

Among the women who received "Alice" was Terri Garthwaite. Terri is a musician, singer, and songwriter of considerable gifts who had her own rock band in the sixties called The Joy of Cooking. For the past several years she has led a small choir—mostly women—that meets in her home and sings for a couple of hours every Sunday afternoon. Suzanne was a member, and so was Candice. When the group reconvened that year after a Christmas break, Terri passed out a new song she'd written, inspired by Suzanne's story and its resolution. "All will be well," it went, "and all will be well, and all manner of thing will be well." Just that, set to a simple, delicate tune. That first day, the choir sang it as a round for nearly an hour.

Again, Suzanne called right away to tell me. By this time, cancer had moved into her abdomen and had spread there. Her productivity those last months was phenomenal.

Our friendship deepened. We used to meet at Aram's, a Middle Eastern cafe in downtown Petaluma, and drink tea and talk. She was as adamantly resistant as ever to the idea of meditation—maybe even more so ("There's nothing like cancer to get you all New Agey," she'd grimace). But the truly night-marish spells she endured after particularly aggressive treatments persuaded her it wouldn't be a bad idea to have some kind of a mantra—something for the mind to hold on to *in extremis*. So we talked some about what constituted a mantra. I explained the tradition as best I could, that not just any word of phrase qualifies, that the great mantras are handed down through time and that the very fact that thousands—millions even—have used them is part of their potency. Suzanne wouldn't have any of the recognized mantras I proffered; most were way too theistic for her. She made several counteroffers, and I had to say I didn't think they quite met the criteria. We had the same conversation several times, me always coming away feeling vaguely shabby but determined not to yield on what could, after all, be a very important point. Mantras really had to come from someone who was God-conscious—they are charged with that person's direct experience of Self. What if she stuck herself with a dud?

Then I got a call.

"I've got it! My mantra! I know what it is now—I used it all last night. It's from Julian: "All will be well, and all will be well, and all manner of thing will be well. . . .""

Surely Julian of Norwich qualified as one who could give a mantra, and it was extraordinary for me to realize now how her haunting words had flowed through us all, from one woman to the other, like a river or like an electrical current. I knew that when they came to Suzanne in the middle of the night they must have brought something of Julian's own courage and trust, but also the loving support of her friends from the choir. And not just the words, but the music . . . And I remembered Bernice Johnson Reagon's words: "The singing is running this sound through your body. You cannot sing a song, and not change your condition."

The story took one final turn. Terri Garthwaite told us about it at Suzanne's memorial service. Just ten days before she died, when Suzanne was actually spending most of her days sleeping, she got a burst of energy—sat up in bed with her Rolodex and tortoise-shell glasses and started calling people. Terri was cooking dinner when her phone rang, but she set it all to one side when she heard Suzanne at the other end of the line, asking, "Could we sing?"

And sing they did—all of Suzanne's favorites. She kept perfect harmony with Terri as they sang, over and over, "All will be well, and all will be well, and all manner of thing will be well."

And of course we sang it together that afternoon in August in a room full of sunlight with the gentle sound of wind passing through tall trees outside. We sang Suzanne good-bye, and as we sang, I saw again that if we are merely *aligned,* if women can simply learn how to open out to one another, in trust and whole-hearted respect—and this is no small matter at all, because for thousands of years we've been trained assiduously to do everything *but* that—it really is like opening the locks on a canal. The waters of life can begin to flow unimpeded among us.

"In the end is my beginning," said T. S. Eliot—said it, in fact, right there in the *Four Quartets* where he'd also quoted Julian. Standing there singing "All will be well" and hoping I'd remember the tune later, glancing covertly about me and thinking what a sturdy and spirited gathering this was and how much Suzanne would have loved it, I knew that this moment had in a sense brought me all the way back to where I'd begun. Back to the image of another friend, struggling by candlelight—alone, and in silence—drawing Teresa to her, and Clare, and the two Catherines, by the sheer force of her need. "Let nothing disturb thee; let nothing affright thee."

It seemed now that struggles begun in silence—alone, in half-light—*can* bring us at last into brightness after all, and fine company.

This book had its genesis, it will be recalled, in two distinct instances of synchronicity. It ended with a third.

October first is my mother-in-law's birthday, and I usually remember that before I remember that it's also the eve of Gandhi's birthday. The past couple of years I've also remembered everything that happened on that afternoon and evening three years ago in Berkeley and Petaluma. In other words, it isn't a date that tends to slip past me unnoticed. Which explains why when someone gave me a package that day that had just arrived from India, I felt a small prickle even before I knew what it contained.

I hadn't ordered anything from India, so I opened the package in some puzzlement. It held four copies of a journal whose name I recognized. *Prabuddha Bharata* is published by the Ramakrishna Order, the monastic order formed by the followers of the revered Calcutta mystic and devotee of the Divine Mother, Sri Ramakrishna (its counterpart in this country is the Vedanta Society, founded by Swami Vivekananda). This issue included an article by one Carol Flinders, called "Spirituality and the Women's Movement."

Without my knowledge, let alone my editorial input, someone had transcribed the talk I'd given in Berkeley exactly three years earlier and had submitted it for publication in the journal. And here it was now, more or less as I'd delivered it—shot through, albeit with the kind of gaff that is bound to occur when a talk is transcribed without consulting the speaker (my favorite was the rendering of Catherine of Genoa's famous claim "My *me* is God!" as "My *knee* is God!"). It was disorienting in a way to read it now—a kind of rough preliminary draft of what would eventually become this book. One of the editors had written a brief introduction: "Very thoughtful and earnest . . . the talk is all the more stirring because of the way it draws inspiration from the ideal of soul-force behind Mahatma Gandhi's satyagraha."

I could hardly take in what had happened. My hesitant, rather inchoate, and tremulously delivered presentation had found its way halfway around the world to the members of a venerable Hindu monastic order, and, bless their hearts, they'd *gotten* it and included it in their journal and sent me copies. And these copies happened to arrive on the one day in three hundred and sixty-five that could not but raise the hair on the back of my neck and banish once and for all any last lingering traces of Presbyterian sobriety.

There had been times, as I'd struggled to reconcile my commitments to feminism and spirituality, when I'd felt myself beginning to drift rather perilously. My overheated intellect would encroach on meditation itself, and I was so chronically preoccupied that with respect to my community and the work I'd been accustomed to taking part in, I might as well have gone on one of those wild river expeditions to Borneo after all. Now that the struggles had subsided, I needed to slip quietly back into the ordinary rhythm of things and re-integrate myself into the community and life I loved. Would I be able to? Had I wandered too far afield? Thoughts born mostly of weariness, they persisted nonetheless. Hearing from the Ramakrishna monks was a great help. It felt like a kind of "welcome back," but it also suggested that perhaps I hadn't really strayed so very far. My last misgivings didn't really slip away, though, until a few weeks later, when my teacher read to us a passage from the *Upanishads*—one I know very well, that has to do with desire, and truth, and knowing who you are, and it was as though I were hearing it for the first time. . . .

Of the bond between teacher and student I have said very little. Years ago I might have tried to say more, but now the whole subject is for me wrapped in mystery and paradox. I do feel that I am joined to my own teacher from that place in myself that is least visible to anyone else, and least audible; and I believe that he in turn reaches toward me from the same sort of place. This might be some sort of a universal—"the deep calling unto the deep." It means that at any given moment, when thirty people are seated in the presence of a teacher, or two hundred, with hearts and minds as open as they can manage, thirty or two hundred distinct conversations are taking place. Distinct, and absolutely private. There were around forty-five of us in the room this particular afternoon, and I am all but positive that none of them heard what I did.

There probably isn't a line from the *Upanishads* that is more widely known than the assertion in the *Chandogya Upanishad* that we are all like strangers in a strange land, walking back and forth over buried treasure and never knowing it, the treasure being, of course, the core of human personality that, for want of a better term, translators generally call the Self. The passage that caught my attention now, though, precedes this haunting simile.

> The Self desires only what is real, thinks nothing but what is true. Here people do what they are told, becoming dependent on their country, or their piece of land, or the desires of

another, so their desires are not fulfilled and their works come to nothing, both in this world and in the next. Those who depart from this world without knowing who they are or what they truly desire have no freedom here or hereafter.

But those who leave here knowing who they are and what they truly desire have freedom everywhere, both in this world and in the next.

—FROM THE CHANDOGYA UPANISHAD,
TRANS. EKNATH EASWARAN

To do what one is told; to become dependent on the desires of another, so that her own desires are not fulfilled, and her own works come to nothing; to depart from this world without knowing who she is, or what she truly desires. . . . I had never heard, it struck me now, a more succinct and devastating summary of why women become feminists. That the passage was in fact a succinct and devastating summary of why women and men alike take to the spiritual life, composed by Indian sages living more than three thousand years ago, was, for just a moment, hard to grasp. But there it was. Not so much the reconciliation of feminism and spirituality as the strong suggestion that they were never really at odds in the first place.

No more than two rivers are, flowing swiftly toward the same sea.

"Those who leave here knowing who they are and what they truly desire have freedom everywhere, both in this world and in the next."

Acknowledgments

Some books just seem to write themselves.

I've heard people say that, anyway. Every one I've been involved with has been more like those children it takes a whole village to raise.

Gratefully, then, I acknowledge . . .

For seeing the possibilities in the first place, and editing the original proposal more times than I hope she ever lets on, my agent and good friend Candice Fuhrman.

For believing in the book and me, and acquiring it for HarperSanFrancisco, Tom Grady.

For presiding over the project with patience ("The deadline was *when?*"), grace, and discernment, and, again, for believing in it, my editor, Caroline Pincus.

For managing all the details, expertly and efficiently, Caroline's assistant, Sally Kim, and for covering my tracks brilliantly, my copy editor (once again, thank goodness!) Priscilla Stuckey.

For making HarperSanFrancisco a publisher with whom I've been proud to be associated, everyone who is currently in its employ, and a great many others, sorely missed, who used to be.

Closer to home . . .

For *being* home, and extended family, and spiritual companions, everyone associated with the Blue Mountain Center of Meditation. But in particular, for their warm encouragement with regard to this book, JoAnne Black, Helen Cornwall, Julia MacDonald, Laurel Robertson, and Gale Zimmerman . . . who also picked up the pieces of me after an exceedingly untimely automobile accident and with their skilled and tender caregiving made my recovery way more than bearable.

For supporting me always, my parents, Gib and Jeanne Ramage, my beautiful sisters, Wendy and Mary, and my brothers, John and Stephen.

Closest to home . . .

My husband, Tim, whose own work runs parallel to mine and intersects with it in a thousand places. Best of feminists, best of friends—co-creator and beloved companion.

And finally, our son, Ramesh, who has been subjected to far more frequent conversations about feminism—far longer ones, and far more impassioned—than he'd ever have chosen. Thanks, pal.

Notes

BOOK ONE

Chapter 1

1. *Julian of Norwich: Showings,* tr. by Edmund Colledge and James Walsh (New York: Paulist Press, 1978), 270.

Chapter 2

1. Quoted in Tim and Carol Flinders, *The Making of a Teacher* (Petaluma, CA: Nilgiri Press, 1989), 34.

Chapter 3

1. I received only a couple of letters critical of this passage. And it was interesting that over the next ten years Kerala itself came to be regarded as nearly unique among third world cultures. The "Kerala miracle" is lauded for its remarkably wise

and humane use of limited resources, but also for the status of women, who have a higher literacy rate than women any-where else in India, better health care, and full economic rights. One has to wonder whether there is not some strong connection between the high regard toward women evidenced in these policies and the existence of an essentially "maternal" economy.

Chapter 5

1. In their introduction to the critical edition of Julian's *Revelations,* her (male) editors congratulate her—with respect to the considerable learning they believe her to have accumulated—that she was not "a bluestocking."
2. Anne Taylor Fleming, *Motherhood Deferred: A Woman's Journey* (New York: G. P. Putnam's Sons, 1994), 76.
3. Elaine Hedges and Shelley Fisher Fishkin, eds., *Listening to Silences* (New York: Oxford Univ. Press, 1994), 170.
4. Ritamary Bradley, *Julian's Way: A Practical Commentary on Julian of Norwich* (London: HarperCollins, 1992), 17. Later the author maintains that "the attack is like a rape" and that "her experience epitomizes all the violence attempted on women in particular, whether on their body or spirit, or by their being reduced to powerlessness in the ecclesiastical and social order. The attacker is not a man but ugly, disembodied power, just as patriarchy is. It arouses feelings of revulsion" (166).
5. This caveat does not appear in the Long Text, leaving one to wonder whether: (a) women visionaries weren't attracting the same kind of negative attention they had been; or (b) she had by this time carved out a sufficiently secure and uncontroversial niche for herself (her contemporary Margery Kempe refers to her "as one who good counsel could give") that she no longer needed to shuffle and slide.
6. *The Collected Works of Teresa of Avila* (Washington, DC: Institute of Carmelite Studies, 1980), 314.

7. Luce Irigaray, *Sexes and Genealogies* (New York: Columbia Univ. Press, 1993), 21.

8. Ven. Thubten Chodron, *Spiritual Sisters* (Seattle: Dharma Friendship Foundation, 1996), 33.

9. Anne C. Klein, "Persons and Possibilities," *Buddhist Women on the Edge: Contemporary Perspectives from the Western Frontier* (Berkeley: North Atlantic Books, 1996), 42–43.

10. Catharine A. MacKinnon, *Toward a Feminist Theory of the State* (Cambridge: Harvard Univ. Press, 1989), 3.

11. Elizabeth Debold, Marie Wilson, Idelisse Malave, *Mother Daughter Revolution: From Good Girls to Great Women* (New York: Bantam Books, 1993), 212.

12. In fact, Mairs suffers from agoraphobia, which she connects with her fear of patriarchy, believing herself to offend it whenever she raises her voice in writing.

13. Alev Lytle Croutier, *Harem: The World Behind the Veil* (New York: Abbeville Press, 1989), 206, 17.

Chapter 6

1. See, in particular, *Listening to Silences*, ed. Elaine Hedges and Shelley Fisher Fishkin (New York: Oxford Univ. Press, 1994).

2. Carol Gilligan, *In a Different Voice* (Cambridge, MA: Harvard Univ. Press, 1993), xvi.

3. The phrase is used by Katherine Gill in a 1993 review of Gerda Lerner's *Creation of Feminist Consciousness, New York Times Book Review*, May 2, 1993, 12.

Chapter 7

1. Gloria Steinem, introduction to *Girls Speak Out: Finding Your True Self,* by Andrea Johnston (New York: Scholastic Press, 1997), xx.

2. Jean Baker Miller, "The Construction of Anger in Women and Men," in *Women's Growth in Connection,* ed. Judith V. Jordan et al. (New York: Guilford Press, 1991), 182.

3. Gerda Lerner, *The Creation of Patriarchy* (New York: Oxford Univ. Press, 1986), 217.

4. It's awkward to generalize with regard to a complex and still evolving body of understanding. To get a feeling for the "revisionist" view of gatherer-hunter cultures, see *The Forest People*, by Colin Turnbull (New York: Simon & Schuster, 1961); *People of the Lake: Mankind and Its Beginnings*, by Richard E. Leakey and Roger Lewin (Garden City, NY: Anchor Press/Doubleday, 1978); and *Toward an Anthropology of Women*, edited by Rayna R. Reiter (New York: Monthly Review Press, 1975).

5. Lerner, *Creation of Patriarchy*, 60.

6. Peggy Reeves Sanday, *Female Power and Male Dominance: On the Origins of Sexual Inequality* (Cambridge: Cambridge Univ. Press, 1981), 209–210. Cited by Bonnie S. Anderson and Judith P. Zinsser, in *A History of Their Own: Women in Europe from Prehistory to the Present* (New York: Harper & Row, 1988), Vol. 1, p. 14.

7. Lerner, *Creation of Patriarchy*, 52.

8. Lerner, *Creation of Patriarchy*, 211–12.

9. Lerner, *Creation of Patriarchy*, 211–12. In the enslavement of women, gender, class, and race are all involved, for the women in question were from "other" tribes. Women were henceforth "like slaves," but it was just as true that all slaves, and all who were perceived as of another race, were "like women." Lerner reaches a startling conclusion: "In its ultimate origins, 'difference' as a distinguishing mark between the conquered and the conquerors was based on the first clearly observable difference, that between the sexes. . . . The precedent of seeing women as an inferior group allows the transference of such a stigma onto any other group which is enslaveable."

10. bell hooks, *Sisters of the Yam* (Boston: South End Press, 1993), 114.

11. Catharine A. MacKinnon, *Feminism Unmodified* (Cambridge: Harvard Univ. Press, 1987), 172.

12. Lerner, *Creation of Patriarchy*, 134.
13. Lerner, *Creation of Patriarchy*, 140.
14. Lerner, *Creation of Patriarchy*, 139: "The division of women into 'respectable women,' who are protected by their men, and 'disreputable women,' who are out in the street unprotected by men and free to sell their services, has been the basic class division for women. It has marked off the limited privileges of upper-class women against the economic and sexual oppression of lower-class women and has divided women one from the other. Historically, it has impeded cross-class alliances among women and obstructed the formation of feminist consciousness."
15. Naomi Wolf, *Promiscuities: The Secret Struggle for Womanhood* (New York: Random House, 1997), 81.
16. It's intriguing, in this context, to think about our own time and place—about glass ceilings and the limited employment of women at the highest levels and the interesting fact that at the *very* highest levels now there are only a handful of career opportunities for *anybody:* this because where four record companies might have been doing business ten years ago, alongside ten magazines, three film studios, a dozen newspapers, and a publishing house, each with its own executive director, a single multimedia conglomerate stands in their place, with one individual at the helm. Women, these days, might actually head up a couple of the record companies, a few of the magazines, a film studio, a publishing house . . . but they are all still answerable to at least one male boss. They're in the chain of command now, only that chain extends further upward than it ever did before. Today, patriarchy concedes authority to women as willingly, and under exactly the same terms, as it did in the past. A woman is allowed to do anything, as long as there is still at least one power tier above her. Asked recently how long she thinks it will be before California elects a woman governor, political consultant Mary Hughes replied, "There's no question that the executive branch is the last

frontier. We've gotten women into the judiciary and onto the
Supreme Court. . . . There is a hesitance on the part of the
electorate to say: 'The last word, the last decision, the final
vote, we'll entrust to a woman.'" Quoted by Mark Simon,
"Helping Women Win Races," *San Francisco Chronicle*,
March 30, 1997.

17. Fatima Mernissi, *Beyond the Veil: Male-Female Dynamics in
Modern Muslim Society* (Bloomington and Indianapolis: Indi-
ana Univ. Press, 1987), 138.

18. Mernissi, *Beyond the Veil*, 31.

19. Lerner, *Creation of Patriarchy*, 10.

20. Lerner, *Creation of Patriarchy*, 211.

21. Lerner, *Creation of Patriarchy*, 218.

Chapter 8

1. Isabel Allende, *The House of the Spirits* (New York: Knopf,
1985), 60. I've learned recently that the Latin word *transitus*
refers to an apocryphal legend recounting the passage of the
Virgin Mary into heaven "body and soul." I believe the name
might be derived from that tradition. See Sally Cunneen, *In
Search of Mary: The Woman and the Symbol* (New York: Ballantine Books, 1996), 135. Ruthanne Lum McCunn's book is *A
Thousand Pieces of Gold: A Biographical Novel* (San Francisco:
Design Enterprises, 1981).

2. Edwidge Danticat, *Breath, Eyes, Memory* (New York: Soho
Press, 1994), 155.

3. Danticat, *Breath*, 155–56.

4. Alice Walker, *Warrior Marks: Female Genital Mutilation and
the Sexual Blinding of Women* (New York: Harcourt, Brace,
1993), 71.

5. Gerda Lerner, *The Creation of Feminist Consciousness: From the
Middle Ages to Eighteen-seventy* (New York: Oxford Univ. Press,
1993), 66.

6. Lerner, *Feminist Consciousness*, vii.

7. Lerner, *Feminist Consciousness*, 115.

8. Marcus Borg, *Jesus: A New Vision* (San Francisco: Harper & Row, 1987), 134.

9. Karen Jo Torjesen, *When Women Were Priests: Women's Leadership in the Early Church and the Scandal of Their Subordination in the Rise of Christianity* (San Francisco: HarperSanFrancisco, 1993), 127.

10. Margaret Miles, *Carnal Knowing: Female Nakedness and Religious Meaning in the Christian West* (Boston: Beacon Press, 1989), 55.

11. Quoted in Miles, *Carnal Knowing*, 55. Gregory's hesitation is understandable. The first-century Hellenistic Jewish philosopher Philo summed up late antiquity's view of woman as follows: "Progress is nothing else than the giving up of the female gender by changing into the male, because the female gender is material, passive, corporeal, and sense-perceptible, while the male is active, rational, incorporeal and more akin to mind and thought" (Miles, *Carnal Knowing*, 56).

12. Indeed, we know that Mechthild of Magdeburg had to defend herself on that score. "Master Heinrich! You are surprised at the masculine way in which this book is written? I wonder why that surprises you?" She proceeds to defend herself—to a Heinrich who could have been her confessor, Heinrich Halle, or her brother—pointing out that the apostles themselves had been weak at the outset but became strong and fearless once they'd received the Holy Ghost. See Mechthild of Magdeburg, *The Flowing Light of the Godhead* (London: Longmans, Green, 1953), 5.12. Indeed, the entire Beguine movement fell under criticism because its members' freedom from male supervision was deemed unnatural.

13. Croutier, *Harem*, 206.

Chapter 9

1. Mary B. Kelly, "Embroidery for the Goddess," *Threads*, June/July 1987, 25.

2. "The new image of nature as a female to be controlled and dissected through experiment legitimated the exploitation of natural resources." Carolyn Merchant, *The Death of Nature: Women, Ecology, and the Scientific Revolution* (San Francisco: Harper & Row, 1980), 189.

3. A friend has shown me how invisible representations of the Goddess can be to the uninitiated: the endpapers of an otherwise fine book on embroidery in Eastern Europe are embellished with a border design of upside-down goddesses.

4. Riane Eisler, *The Chalice and the Blade* (San Francisco, Harper & Row, 1988), 32.

5. Monique Wittig, *Les Guerillieres*, tr. David LeVay (New York: Avon, 1971), 89.

6. Eisler, 36.

7. Marion Zimmer Bradley, *The Mists of Avalon* (New York: Ballantine, 1982), acknowledgments iv.

8. Edwidge Danticat, *Breath, Eyes, Memory* (New York: Soho Press, 1994), 157.

9. Their names have to do with textiles: Indigo and Sassafras are both dyes. Cypress refers to gauze-like fabrics that originate in Crete. They also echo the biblical trio Shadrach, Meshach, and Abednego, whose faith allowed them to survive the fiery furnace of Nebuchadnezzar. One gets the impression Hilda Effania views the world outside her home as something of a fiery furnace.

10. Ntozake Shange, *Sassafras, Cypress & Indigo* (New York: St. Martin's Press, 1982), 3.

11. Tony Hillerman, *The Listening Woman* (San Francisco: HarperSanFrancisco, 1978), 150.

12. Virginia Beane Rutter, *Woman Changing Woman: Feminine Psychology Re-Conceived Through Myth and Experience* (San Francisco: HarperSanFrancisco, 1993), xvii, citing Bruce Lincoln's *Emerging from the Chrysalis: Studies in Women's Initiations* (Cambridge: Harvard Univ. Press, 1981), 101.

13. Rutter, *Woman Changing Woman*, 225–26.

14. Rutter, *Woman Changing Woman*, 3, xvii.

15. Rutter, *Woman Changing Woman*, 66–67.

16. Rutter, *Woman Changing Woman*, 39.

17. The phrase refers to the question Margaret Miles raises in her introduction to *Carnal Knowing*. She outlines the plot of the Gilgamesh epic and notes the role played in the hero's development by certain women, among them the mortal Siduri. Remarking the fact that "female subjectivity did not, until the nineteenth century, begin to receive the exploration accorded that of men," Miles asks, "where is the epic of Siduri?" One would miss the full thrust of her question, I think, who failed to notice that *Carnal Knowing* itself is dedicated "To my Granddaughter, Siduri." See Miles, *Carnal Knowing: Female Nakedness and Religious Meaning in the Christian West* (Boston: Beacon Press, 1989), 4.

Chapter 10

1. Anne Morrow Lindbergh, *Gift from the Sea* (New York: Pantheon, 1975), 23.

2. Elizabeth Coatsworth, *The White Room* (New York: Pantheon, 1958), 13.

3. Irigaray, *Sexes and Genealogies*, 66.

4. Riane Eisler, *The Chalice and the Blade* (San Francisco: Harper & Row, 1988), 36.

5. "The central project of humanity..." writes historian Margaret Miles, "formulated doctrinally as the incarnation of God in human flesh, is carnal knowing, embodied knowledge. It is experiential understanding that is aware and respectful of the particular and concrete conditions in which all learning occurs, whether that learning is named as socialization, religious orientation, or subjectification. In Christianity, however, the flesh has largely been scorned, the body marginalized, in the 'project' of a spiritual journey." See *Carnal Knowing: Female*

Nakedness and Religious Meaning in the Christian West (Boston: Beacon Press, 1989), 185.

6. Vivian Gornick, *Approaching Eye Level* (Boston: Beacon Press, 1996), 66.

BOOK TWO

Chapter 1

1. Mahatma Gandhi, *All Men Are Brothers* (Ahmedabad, Navajvam Publishing House, 1960), 77.

2. Susan Faludi, *Backlash: The Undeclared War Against Women* (New York: Anchor Books, 1991), 458–59.

3. I didn't have figures at my fingertips at the time, but here are some drawn from an editorial in *Fellowship,* the bimonthly journal of the Fellowship of Reconciliation: "The end of the Cold War failed to make a dent in the power of the military-industrial complex to dominate our federal budget. All the Congressional talk of cutting spending and balancing the budget exempts the Pentagon. Our current policy is to maintain preparedness to fight two wars. But Seymour Melman points out that those the US brands as 'rogue states'—North Korea, Iran, Iraq, Syria, Libya, and Cuba—have a combined military budget of only $9.64 billion; the US military budget is *twenty-seven* times that (*New York Times,* June 16, 1995). Our military budget is almost as much as the rest of the world combined and we have troops in seventy-five countries" (*Fellowship,* March/April 1996, 3).

4. This is from the "Santi Parva," a section of the Mahabharata in which the sage Bhisma discourses on "the sciences of the political state and of spirituality." It is cited by Swami Ranganathananda, a senior monk of the Ramakrishna Order, in a lecture called "Women in the Modern Age," delivered in Srinigar in September 1986. The lecture has been published by the Ramakrishna order.

or didn't count enough to have them aired." See Myron Benton, *The American Male* (New York: Coward-McCann, 1996), 13.

Chapter 3

1. Noelle Oxenhandler, "Polly's Face," *The New Yorker*, November 29, 1993.
2. There are in fact extraordinarily interesting interpretations of this myth that have to do with the autumn festival, Thesmophoria. See *The Feminist Companion to Mythology*, ed. Carolyne Larrington (London: HarperCollins, 1992).

Chapter 4

1. Huston Smith, *The World's Religions* (San Francisco: HarperSanFrancisco, 1991), 7–8.
2. *The Mahabharata*, tr. J.A.B. van Buitenen (Chicago: Univ. of Chicago Press, 1973), Vol. I, 369.
3. Today, the sacred groves set aside in various parts of India are treasured as preserves of genetic diversity, all the more priceless now that native plants are threatened by extinction because of the introduction of hybridized strains from the West. One does wonder how one might legitimately take samples of these native varieties away, but somehow one trusts the good sense of the Indian tradition to figure out how to rationalize doing so.
4. Frederique Apffel-Marglin, "The Sacred Grove," *Manushi*, May–June 1994, 29.
5. Apffel-Marglin, "The Sacred Grove," 29.
6. Apffel-Marglin, "The Sacred Grove," 28.
7. Apffel-Marglin, "The Sacred Grove," 31.
8. Apffel-Marglin, "The Sacred Grove," 31. The Sanskrit word *r'tu*, from which *ritual* comes, has as one of its central meanings "menstruation." Poet Judy Grahn suggests that menstruation rituals were the very first rituals human beings performed. For an amazing alternative reading of cultural his-

tory, I strongly recommend her book *Blood, Bread, and Roses: How Menstruation Created the World* (Boston: Beacon Press, 1992).

9. Certainly this situation is changing. See, for example, Sally Cunneen's fascinating *In Search of Mary: The Woman and the Symbol* (New York: Ballantine Books, 1996).

10. Scholarly Emily Kearns explains: "Goddesses appear as parts or emanations of one great Goddess . . . and the idea of a Goddess whose local, diversely named manifestations are fragments of a whole is given full mythical expression in the tradition that when Shiva, distraught at the death of [his first wife] Sati, picked up her body and began a wild, universe-threatening dance, Vishnu, in order to preserve the world, cut the corpse into pieces; the place where each piece fell became an important centre of Goddess worship." See *The Feminist Companion to Mythology*, ed. Carolyne Larrington (San Francisco: HarperSanFrancisco, 1992), 223.

11. Interested readers will want to look at Alf Hiltebeitel's two-volume study, *The Cult of Draupadi* (Chicago: Univ. of Chicago Press, 1988).

12. Cited by Vinay Lal, "The Mother in the 'Father of the Nation,'" *Manushi* (November–December 1995), 30.

Chapter 5

1. Space doesn't permit outlining the late A. K. Ramanujan's wonderful discussion of "women's tales" here, but anyone wishing to know more of the informal, vernacular end of India's narrative tradition will want to read his essay "Toward a Counter-System: Women's Tales," in *Gender, Genre, and Power in South Asian Expressive Traditions*, ed. Arjun Appadurai, Frank J. Korom, and Margaret A. Mills (Philadelphia: Univ. of Pennsylvania Press, 1991), 33–55.

2. Gloria Steinem, in *The Progressive*, a June 1995 interview by L. A. Winokur. She says in addition: "Both the political ethic

of right and left that I'd been exposed to in the U.S. essentially believe that the ends justify the means; both have historically tolerated and courted violence. And both were what I would call of a culturally masculine style which I never quite felt at ease with, though I pretended to so I would be accepted. I felt I always had to still this voice in me that kept saying, 'where are the women in all of this?'

"But Gandhian thought, of course, is really built on nonviolence, and on the idea that the means dictate the ends. And I believe that. So walking around the villages with this Gandhian group, I had this sudden feeling that, yes, this makes sense. This is the way real deep change happens. Little by little. Not from the top ..."

For a brief but illuminating description of Steinem's two years in India, see *Moving Beyond Words* (New York: Simon & Schuster, 1994), 263–67.

3. Taken from a recorded interview with Vandana Shiva broadcast on KPFA in April 1994.
4. The Research Foundation for Science, Technology, and Natural Resource Policy in Dehra Dun.
5. Madhu Kishwar and Ruth Vanita, *In Search of Answers: Indian Women's Voices from Manushi* (London: Zed Books, 1984), 47.
6. Downloaded from Manushi's Web site, http://www.arbornet.org/~manushi. A 1995 interview of Madhu Kishwar by Australian journalist Jennifer Severn.
7. Madhu Kishwar, "Yes to Sita, No to Ram!" *Manushi,* no. 98 (January–February 1997): 22ff.
8. Octavio Paz, *The Double Flame: Love and Eroticism* (New York: Harcourt Brace, 1995), 93.
9. Vandana Shiva, *Staying Alive* (London: Zed Books, 1988), 70.
10. Andrew Kimbrell, director of the International Center for Technology Assessment in Washington, D.C., quoted in Barbara Letterman, "Vandana Shiva Simply Wants to Change the World," *Ms.* (May/June 1997), 33.

Chapter 6

1. Oxenhandler, "Polly's Face," p. 94.
2. Virginia Beane Rutter, *Woman Changing Woman: Feminine Psychology Re-conceived Through Myth and Experience* (San Francisco: HarperSanFrancisco, 1993), 60.
3. *The Woman's Way*, by the editors of Time-Life Books (Alexandria, VA: Time-Life Books, 1995), 71.
4. The title of Jane O'Reilly's milestone article published in *Mirabella*, April 1994.

Chapter 7

1. Carol Gilligan, *In a Different Voice* (Cambridge: Harvard Univ. Press, 1993), xxiv.
2. Lyn Mikel Brown and Carol Gilligan, *Meeting at the Crossroads: Women's Psychology and Girls' Development* (Cambridge: Harvard Univ. Press, 1992), 9, 10.
3. Brown and Gilligan, *Meeting at the Crossroads,* 15, 16, 17.
4. Margaret Miles, *Carnal Knowing: Female Nakedness and Religious Meaning in the Christian West* (New York: Vintage Books, 1989), 11.
5. Dana Crowley Jack, *Silencing the Self: Women and Depression* (Cambridge, MA: Harvard Univ. Press, 1991), 48.
6. Gloria Steinem, *Moving Beyond Words* (New York: Touchstone Books, 1995), 266.
7. Linda Christensen, "Unlearning the Myths That Bind Us," *New Moon Network* (April/May 1996), 8.
8. Cited by Eknath Easwaran, *Gandhi the Man* (Petaluma, CA: Nilgiri Press, 1978), 106.
9. Ntozake Shange, *Sassafras, Cypress & Indigo* (New York: St. Martin's Press, 1982), 18–19.
10. bell hooks, "Contemplation and Transformation," *Buddhist Women on the Edge*, ed. Marianne Dresser (Berkeley: North Atlantic Books, 1996), 291.

Chapter 8

1. Vivian Gornick, *Approaching Eye Level*, 69. She also writes, two pages earlier, "I saw what visionary feminists had seen for two hundred years: that power over one's life comes only through the steady command of one's thought."

2. The story of the Flower Dance appeared in the Autumn 1996 issue of *Windchimes,* a young people's literary magazine published in Petaluma. The author, cousin of one of the initiates, is Oona Risling-Sholl.

3. Turnbull, *The Forest People,* 196–97.

4. Bernice Johnson Reagon, transcribed from a 1991 interview by Bill Moyers called "The Songs Are Free."

5. Traditional song for a young girl's puberty ceremony, Papago Tribe, cited by Annie Rogers, "Voice, Play and Courage," *Harvard Educational Review* 63, no. 3 (Fall 1993): 275.

6. Editorial in *The Press Democrat*, Santa Rosa, California, Tuesday, April 22, 1997, B4.

7. Mary Field Belenky et al., *Women's Ways of Knowing: The Development of Self, Voice, and Mind* (New York: Basic Books, 1986), 152.

8. Stephen Dubner, "Choosing My Religion," *New York Times Magazine,* March 31, 1996, 36.

9. *Four Centuries of Jewish Women's Spirituality* (Boston: Beacon Press, 1992), 322.

10. Adrienne Rich, *A Wild Patience Has Taken Me This Far: Poems 1978–1981* (New York: Norton, 1981), 9.

11. Larrington, ed., *The Feminist Companion to Mythology*, 346.

12. Helena Norberg-Hodge, *Ancient Futures: Learning from Ladakh* (San Francisco: Sierra Club Books, 1991), 11.

13. Norberg-Hodge, *Ancient Futures,* 21.

14. Vandana Shiva, *Staying Alive,* 66.

15. Elisabeth Burgos-DeBray, *I, Rigoberta Menchu: An Indian Woman in Guatemala* (New York: Verso, 1987).

16. Alan Clements, *The Voice of Hope* (New York: Seven Stories Press, 1997).

Index